OS/2 WARP
FOR
DUMMIES™

2ND EDITION

by Andy Rathbone

IDG BOOKS

IDG Books Worldwide, Inc.
An International Data Group Company

Foster City, CA ◆ Chicago, IL ◆ Indianapolis, IN ◆ Braintree, MA ◆ Dallas, TX

OS/2 Warp For Dummies™, 2nd Edition

Published by
IDG Books Worldwide, Inc.
An International Data Group Company
919 E. Hillsdale Blvd.
Suite 400
Foster City, CA 94404

Library of Congress Catalog Card No.: 94-73284

ISBN: 1-56884-205-8

Printed in the United States of America

10 9 8 7 6 5 4 3 2 1

2A/TQ/QR/ZV

Distributed in the United States by IDG Books Worldwide, Inc.

Distributed by Macmillan Canada for Canada; by Computer and Technical Books for the Caribbean Basin; by Contemporanea de Ediciones for Venezuela; by Distribuidora Cuspide for Argentina; by CITEC for Brazil; by Ediciones ZETA S.C.R. Ltda. for Peru; by Editorial Limusa SA for Mexico; by Transworld Publishers Limited in the United Kingdom and Europe; by Al-Maiman Publishers & Distributors for Saudi Arabia; by Simron Pty. Ltd. for South Africa; by IDG Communications (HK) Ltd. for Hong Kong; by Toppan Company Ltd. for Japan; by Addison Wesley Publishing Company for Korea; by Longman Singapore Publishers Ltd. for Singapore, Malaysia, Thailand, and Indonesia; by Unalis Corporation for Taiwan; by WS Computer Publishing Company, Inc. for the Philippines; by WoodsLane Pty. Ltd. for Australia; by WoodsLane Enterprises Ltd. for New Zealand.

For general information on IDG Books in the U.S., including information on discounts and premiums, contact IDG Books at 800-434-3422 or 415-655-3000.

For information on where to purchase IDG Books outside the U.S., contact IDG Books International at 415-655-3021 or fax 415-655-3295.

For information on translations, contact Marc Jeffrey Mikulich, Director, Foreign & Subsidiary Rights, at IDG Books Worldwide, 415-655-3018 or fax 415-655-3295.

For sales inquiries and special prices for bulk quantities, write to the address above or call IDG Books Worldwide at 415-655-3000.

For information on using IDG Books in the classroom, or for ordering examination copies, contact Jim Kelly at 800-434-2086.

is a registered trademark of International Data Group

About the Author

Andy Rathbone

An electronics engineer by trade, Andy Rathbone's father, Rhett, spent many hours showing his young son how to fiddle with shortwave radios, oscilloscopes, reel-to-reel tape recorders, and other gadgets.

Years later, Andy began playing with computers and camcorders, as well as working part-time at Radio Shack. When not playing computer games, Andy worked at several local newspapers, taking photographs and writing stories.

During the next few years, Andy combined his interests in writing and electronics by writing books about computers, as well as writing articles for magazines like *Supercomputing Review, ID Systems*, *DataPro,* and *Shareware.*

In 1992, Andy and *DOS For Dummies* author/legend Dan Gookin teamed up to write *PCs For Dummies*, which was a runner-up in the Computer Press Association's 1993 awards. Andy subsequently wrote *Windows For Dummies, MORE Windows For Dummies, OS/2 For Dummies, Upgrading & Fixing PCs For Dummies,* and *Multimedia & CD-ROMs For Dummies*.

Today, Andy writes for magazines like *PC World* and *CompuServe* and lives with his most-excellent wife, Tina, and their cat in San Diego, California. When not writing or making movies, Andy fiddles with his MIDI synthesizer and tries to keep the cat off both keyboards.

Welcome to the world of IDG Books Worldwide.

IDG Books Worldwide, Inc. is a subsidiary of International Data Group, the world's largest publisher of computer-related information and the leading global provider of information services on information technology. IDG was founded more than 25 years ago and now employs more than 7,000 people worldwide. IDG publishes more than 220 computer publications in 65 countries (see listing below). More than fifty million people read one or more IDG publications each month.

Launched in 1990, IDG Books Worldwide is today the #1 publisher of best-selling computer books in the United States. We are proud to have received 3 awards from the Computer Press Association in recognition of editorial excellence, and our best-selling *...For Dummies*™ series has more than 12 million copies in print with translations in 25 languages. IDG Books, through a recent joint venture with IDG's Hi-Tech Beijing, became the first U.S. publisher to publish a computer book in the People's Republic of China. In record time, IDG Books has become the first choice for millions of readers around the world who want to learn how to better manage their businesses.

Our mission is simple: Every IDG book is designed to bring extra value and skill-building instructions to the reader. Our books are written by experts who understand and care about our readers. The knowledge base of our editorial staff comes from years of experience in publishing, education, and journalism — experience which we use to produce books for the '90s. In short, we care about books, so we attract the best people. We devote special attention to details such as audience, interior design, use of icons, and illustrations. And because we use an efficient process of authoring, editing, and desktop publishing our books electronically, we can spend more time ensuring superior content and spend less time on the technicalities of making books.

You can count on our commitment to deliver high-quality books at competitive prices on topics consumers want to read about. At IDG, we value quality, and we have been delivering quality for more than 25 years. You'll find no better book on a subject than an IDG book.

John J. Kilcullen

John Kilcullen
President and CEO
IDG Books Worldwide, Inc.

IDG Books Worldwide, Inc. is a subsidiary of International Data Group, the world's largest publisher of computer-related information and the leading global provider of information services on information technology. International Data Group publishes over 220 computer publications in 65 countries. More than fifty million people read one or more International Data Group publications each month. The officers are Patrick J. McGovern, Founder and Board Chairman; Kelly Conlin, President; Jim Casella, Chief Operating Officer. International Data Group's publications include: **ARGENTINA'S** Computerworld Argentina, Infoworld Argentina; **AUSTRALIA'S** Computerworld Australia, Computer Living, Australian PC World, Australian Macworld, Network World, Mobile Business Australia, Publish!, Reseller, IDG Sources; **AUSTRIA'S** Computerwelt Oesterreich, PC Test; **BELGIUM'S** Data News (CW); **BOLIVIA'S** Computerworld; **BRAZIL'S** Computerworld, Connections, Game Power, Mundo Unix, PC World, Publish, Super Game; **BULGARIA'S** Computerworld Bulgaria, PC & Mac World Bulgaria, Network World Bulgaria; **CANADA'S** CIO Canada, Computerworld Canada, InfoCanada, Network World Canada, Reseller; **CHILE'S** Computerworld Chile, Informatica; **COLOMBIA'S** Computerworld Colombia, PC World; **COSTA RICA'S** PC World; **CZECH REPUBLIC'S** Computerworld, Elektronika, PC World; **DENMARK'S** Communications World, Computerworld Danmark, Computerworld Focus, Macintosh Produktkatalog, Macworld Danmark, PC World Danmark, PC Produktguide, Tech World, Windows World; **ECUADOR'S** PC World Ecuador; **EGYPT'S** Computerworld (CW) Middle East, PC World Middle East; **FINLAND'S** MikroPC, Tietoviikko, Tietoverkko; **FRANCE'S** Distributique, GOLDEN MAC, InfoPC, Le Guide du Monde Informatique, Le Monde Informatique, Telecoms & Reseaux; **GERMANY'S** Computerwoche, Computerwoche Focus, Computerwoche Extra, Electronic Entertainment, Gamepro, Information Management, Macwelt, Netzwelt, PC Welt, Publish, Publish; **GREECE'S** Publish & Macworld; **HONG KONG'S** Computerworld Hong Kong, PC World Hong Kong; **HUNGARY'S** Computerworld SZT, PC World; **INDIA'S** Computers & Communications; **INDONESIA'S** Info Komputer; **IRELAND'S** ComputerScope; **ISRAEL'S** Beyond Windows, Computerworld Israel, Multimedia, PC World Israel; **ITALY'S** Computerworld Italia, Lotus Magazine, Macworld Italia, Networking Italia, PC Shopping Italy, PC World Italia; **JAPAN'S** Computerworld Today, Information Systems World, Macworld Japan, Nikkei Personal Computing, SunWorld Japan, Windows World; **KENYA'S** East African Computer News; **KOREA'S** Computerworld Korea, Macworld Korea, PC World Korea; **LATIN AMERICA'S** GamePro; **MALAYSIA'S** Computerworld Malaysia, PC World Malaysia; **MEXICO'S** Compu Edicion, Compu Manufactura, Computacion/Punto de Venta, Computerworld Mexico, MacWorld, Mundo Unix, PC World, Windows; **THE NETHERLANDS'** Computer! Totaal, Computable (CW), LAN Magazine, Lotus Magazine, MacWorld; **NEW ZEALAND'S** Computer Buyer, Computerworld New Zealand, Network World, New Zealand PC World; **NIGERIA'S** PC World Africa; **NORWAY'S** Computerworld Norge, Lotusworld Norge, Macworld Norge, Maxi Data, Networld, PC World Ekspress, PC World Nettverk, PC World Norge, PC World's Produktguide, Publish& Multimedia World, Student Data, Unix World, Windowsworld; **PAKISTAN'S** PC World Pakistan; **PANAMA'S** PC World Panama; **PERU'S** Computerworld Peru, PC World; **PEOPLE'S REPUBLIC OF CHINA'S** China Computerworld, China Infoworld, China PC Info Magazine, Computer Fan, PC World China, Electronics International, Electronics Today/Multimedia World, Electronic Product World, China Network World, Software World Magazine, Telecom Product World; **PHILIPPINES'** Computerworld Philippines, PC Digest (PCW); **POLAND'S** Computerworld Poland, Computerworld Special Report, Networld, PC World/Komputer, Sunworld; **PORTUGAL'S** Cerebro/PC World, Correio Informatico/Computerworld, MacIn; **ROMANIA'S** Computerworld, PC World, Telecom Romania; **RUSSIA'S** Computerworld-Moscow, Mir - PK (PCW), Sety (Networks); **SINGAPORE'S** Computerworld Southeast Asia, PC World Singapore; **SLOVENIA'S** Monitor Magazine; **SOUTH AFRICA'S** Computer Mail (CIO), Computing S.A., Network World S.A., Software World; **SPAIN'S** Advanced Systems, Amiga World, Computerworld Espana, Communicaciones World, Macworld Espana, NeXTWORLD, Super Juegos Magazine (GamePro), PC World Espana, Publish; **SWEDEN'S** Attack, ComputerSweden, Corporate Computing, Macworld, Mikrodatorn, Natverk & Kommunikation, PC World, CAP & Design, DataIngenjoren, Maxi Data, Windows World; **SWITZERLAND'S** Computerworld Schweiz, Macworld Schweiz, PC Tip; **TAIWAN'S** Computerworld Taiwan, PC World Taiwan; **THAILAND'S** Thai Computerworld; **TURKEY'S** Computerworld Monitor, Macworld Turkiye, PC World Turkiye; **UKRAINE'S** Computerworld, Computers+Software Magazine; **UNITED KINGDOM'S** Computing / Computerworld, Connexion/Network World, Lotus Magazine, Macworld, Open Computing/Sunworld; **UNITED STATES'** Advanced Systems, AmigaWorld, Cable in the Classroom, CD Review, CIO, Computerworld, Computerworld Client/Server Journal, Digital Video, DOS World, Electronic Entertainment Magazine (E2), Federal Computer Week, Game Hits, GamePro, IDG Books, Infoworld, Laser Event, Macworld, Maximize, Multimedia World, Network World, PC Letter, PC World, Publish, SWATPro, Video Event; **URUGUAY'S** PC World Uruguay; **VENEZUELA'S** Computerworld Venezuela, PC World; **VIETNAM'S** PC World Vietnam.   01/03/95

Dedication

To my family and friends.

Acknowledgments

Thanks to Paul Cheatham, Christopher Clark, Kristin Cocks, Bill Hinkle, Jeremy Judson, Allan Katzen, Ray Marshall, Linda Magnuson, William McHugh, Pat Seiler, Irv Spalten, Matt Wagner, Becky Whitney, and Dave Wilson.

(The publisher would like to give special thanks to Patrick J. McGovern, without whom this book would not have been possible.)

Credits

**Executive Vice President,
Strategic Product Planning
and Research**
David Solomon

Editorial Director
Diane Graves Steele

Acquisitions Editor
Megg Bonar

Brand Manager
Judith A. Taylor

Editorial Managers
Tracy L. Barr
Sandra Blackthorn

Editorial Assistants
Tamara S. Castleman
Stacey Holden Prince
Kevin Spencer

Acquisitions Assistant
Suki Gear

Production Director
Beth Jenkins

Project Coordinator
Valery Bourke

Pre-Press Coordinators
Tony Augsburger
Steve Peake

Project Editors
Kristin A. Cocks
Jeremy Judson

Editors
Becky Whitney
Pat Seiler

Technical Reviewer
Ray Marshall

Production Staff
Paul Belcastro
Cameron Booker
Linda M. Boyer
Mary Breidenbach
J. Tyler Connor
Carla C. Radzikinas
Dwight Ramsey
Patricia R. Reynolds
Theresa Sánchez-Baker
Gina Scott

Proofreader
Henry Lazarek

Indexer
Liz Cunningham

Cover Design
Kavish + Kavish

Contents at a Glance

Cartoons at a Glance
By Rich Tennant

Page 264

Page 7

Page 198

Page 228

Page 152

Page 211

Page 163

Page 63

Page 279

Page 253

Table of Contents

Introduction

· ·

*M*ost computer nerds love playing with OS/2, especially the new version, called *Warp*. Their eyes widen lovingly at Warp words such as *HW_TIMER* and *DOS_FILES*. They punch buttons for hours, testing stuff just to see what happens. They put the words *power user* beneath their name on their business cards.

And you? You're no dummy, that's for sure. In fact, you're much too smart to waste time poking through your computer's innards. Who cares what makes it work? Leave the transmissions to the mechanics; you just want to move from Point A to Point B, park, and hope that you remembered to turn off your headlights.

That's where this book comes in. It doesn't bother trying to turn you into a OS/2 Warp expert, although you will pick up a few chunks of useful computing information along the way. You'll still be an OS/2 novice, but you'll know enough to work quickly, cleanly, and with a minimum of pain so that you can move on to the more pleasant things in life.

About This Book

Don't try to read this book at one sitting. (You probably don't need a warning like that. Yuck!) Instead, treat this book like a dictionary or an encyclopedia. When you are faced with a particularly malodorous bit of OS/2 ugliness, pick up the book and turn to the page with the information you need. Read the paragraph you need to get going, and say, "Ah! So that's what they're talking about." Then put down the book and move on.

Don't bother trying to memorize OS/2 buzzwords, such as *metafiles* and *dynamic link libraries*. Let the computer nerds wallow in their own vocabulary. If anything technical comes up in this book, a road sign warns you well in advance. (That way, you can either speed on past it or slow down and give it a quick once-over.)

You won't find any thick computer jargon in this book. Instead, you find subjects like these, discussed in plain old English:

> ✔ Installing OS/2 on your computer
>
> ✔ Finding a window "that was around here someplace . . ."
>
> ✔ Making DOS and Windows programs work right
>
> ✔ Dumping information from one window into another
>
> ✔ Copying work back and forth to a floppy disk
>
> ✔ Making your OS/2 desktop more comfortable

There's nothing to memorize. You don't even have to *learn* anything. Just turn to the right page, read the brief explanation, punch the right buttons, and get back to work. Unlike other books, this one enables you to step right over the technical gobbledygook and still get your work done.

How to Use This Book

Something about OS/2 will eventually leave you scratching your head. Look for that troublesome topic in this book's table of contents or in the index. You'll find the chapter, section title, or page number where your current head-scratcher is explained. Page through to that spot, read only what you have to do, close the book, and apply what you've read.

There's no learning involved. There's no remembering either, unless you don't want to grab the book the next time the same situation comes up.

Or if you're feeling strangely computer-tolerant, keep reading a little farther. You'll find a few completely voluntary extra details or some quick cross-references to check out. Don't feel pressured, though. You are never forced to wade through technical details that you simply don't have time for.

If you have to type something into your computer, you see easy-to-follow text like this:

```
C:\> TYPE THESE LETTERS
```

In this example, you type **TYPE THESE LETTERS** and then you press Enter on your keyboard. Typing a foreign language ("computerese") into a computer can be confusing, so a description of what you're supposed to type usually follows. Quick, digestible, and no heartburn.

If you're supposed to hold down two keys at the same time — the Alt key and the Ctrl key, for example — the instructions look like this: Alt+Ctrl. Just hold down the Alt key, press the Ctrl key, and let go of both of them.

Also, this book doesn't wimp out by saying, "For more information, consult your manual." Many parts of OS/2 aren't even listed in its manual. This book contains everything you need to know to begin using OS/2 and OS/2 programs. OS/2 can run DOS and Windows programs, however, as well as OS/2 programs. If you're especially interested in DOS and Windows, look for this book's best-selling grandfather, *DOS For Dummies,* in addition to *Windows For Dummies.* But this book still has enough information about DOS and Windows basics to start you down the path.

Please Don't Read This!

Computers are complicated, boring machines, full of whirling widgets and pointless puzzles. This book warns you in advance when you're nearing a chunk of technical gunk. Skip right past any section labeled "Technical Stuff." Chances are, it just gives more minute details about something you've already read about. If you're feeling particularly energetic, however, go ahead and sneak a peek. If you're lucky, none of your friends will notice.

And What About You?

I assume that you have OS/2 (or are considering buying it) and that you have a computer. Chances are, you *do something* with both OS/2 and your computer (whether you like it or not). The problem is not with you: You *know* what you want to do. The problem comes when you're persuading the dumb computer to do what you want it to do.

When problems arise, you usually bother the office computer guru or call up a technically minded neighbor. This book helps when they're not around. If you're just starting down the OS/2 path, you'll find full-disclosure, no-nonsense instructions for pulling OS/2 out of the box and installing it on your computer.

How This Book Is Organized

The information in this book has been well sifted. The book contains six parts, and each part is divided into several chapters. The chapters are divided into short sections, each covering a different point. The entire book is full of chunks; some-times you find your sought-after information in a small section chunk. At other times, you may want to read a chapter chunk. You may get lucky and find your solution in a brief one-paragraph tip. It depends on the particular task at hand.

Here's a look at the biggest chunks:

Part I: Bare-Bones OS/2 Stuff (Start Here)

This section starts out simply: It tells you what OS/2 is and what it's supposed to do. It talks about different parts of the computer and how OS/2 kicks them around. It explains all the OS/2 stuff that people think you already know. And best of all, it includes a hand-holding guide to installing OS/2 on your computer. Double yuck!

Part II: That Workplace Shell Thing

In this section, you find out how to force OS/2 to do something useful. You discover that you can write a simple letter without having to absorb all the *object-oriented* nonsense. You learn how to set up OS/2 according to *your* needs rather than the needs of IBM's marketing department.

Part III: OS/2 Applications (Those Free Programs)

Good news! OS/2 comes with bunches of free programs that aren't even listed on the box. You'll find word processors, chart makers, list makers, a spreadsheet, calendars, alarms, more list makers, a database, a fax program, and an Internet surfing program for sight-seeing down the information superhighway with a modem. This section separates these applications into the good, the bad, and the dorky so that you don't have to waste time fiddling with the *really* dumb stuff.

Part IV: Sticking with DOS and Windows Programs

OS/2 can run your favorite DOS and Windows programs, although you may need to whack it a few times. This section tells you exactly where to kick, how hard, and what shoes to wear.

Part V: Help!

Face it: If everything were working right, you wouldn't be wasting your time with a computer book. Phew! When something important in OS/2 is broken or bent or has ugly stains, turn to this section to find the fix.

Part VI: Tons of Tens

This section contains the now infamous lists of ten: ten common beginner mistakes, ten aggravating things about OS/2 (and how to fix them), ten helpful ways to set up the OS/2 desktop, ten dumb abbreviations OS/2 tosses your way — you get the idea.

Icons Used in This Book

Feel free to make your own notes in the margins; that's why they're there. But to help you find the important stuff (and stay away from the dumb technical stuff), I've added my own little pictures. Here's what those little icons mean:

Computer nerds can jump quickly to these sections without putting on their reading glasses; normal folks can conveniently avoid them.

Look here for little suggestions to simplify computing — stuff like "If you have a cat, buy a Pentium computer. Those computers run a little warmer, and cats like to sleep on the case."

If you're already a Windows user, keep an eye out for these icons. These sections show where OS/2 works either just like Windows or differently from Windows.

To understand how OS/2 and DOS live together, give these sections a look-see.

These little pictures serve as paper clips for the important stuff.

Most of the book tells you what to do. These paragraphs tell you what *not* to do.

Where to Go from Here

If OS/2 already beams from your computer's happy face, breathe a sigh of relief. If you have to install it yourself, brace yourself with two-by-fours and turn to Chapter 3. When OS/2 is installed, just set the book next to your computer within easy grabbing distance. OS/2 is a powerful operating system. When it gives you a powerful whack on the side of the head, use this book to fight back. Good luck!

Part I
Bare Bones OS/2 Stuff (Start Here)

"MY GOD, YOU'VE DONE IT! MILLIONS OF MICROSCOPIC SLINKY TOYS MOVING ACROSS CIRCUITS AT THE SPEED OF LIGHT FORMING THE FIRST SLINKY OPERATING SYSTEM!"

In this part ...

OS/2 has been around for more than seven years, so the computer nerds have had quite a head start. This part of the book is here to explain what you've missed.

You find out what the heck OS/2 is and why moisture appears on the foreheads of computer nerds when they speak of it. You find a handy reference to those computer things everybody thinks you already know, and you get a quick introduction to what all those little symbols on the OS/2 screen are supposed to do.

Finally, if you're unlucky enough to have to install OS/2 yourself, you learn how to put it on your computer. (Just setting the box on top of the monitor doesn't count, unfortunately.)

Chapter 1

Is OS/2 As Cool As They Say on TV?

*T*his chapter sums up a great deal of basic OS/2 stuff you've probably wondered about. It answers the questions everyone would love to ask the computer salespeople (the ones who are always so busy playing explosive computer games with names like Doom).

This chapter covers things you want to know before you buy OS/2; it also eases the confusion you may feel when you dump all the stuff out of the box for the first time (like why does the License Agreement pamphlet have 11 pages of fine print?).

What Is an Operating System?

An *operating system* is like a dashboard — a way to communicate with a piece of machinery. When you fiddle with the buttons and steering wheel on a dashboard, the car responds to your wishes: It moves to the right or left, for example.

All dashboards do basically the same thing, but they all look a little different. And some dashboards are easier to use than others are, as you discover when you drive an unfamiliar rental car. A computer's operating system is sort of like its dashboard. The operating system enables you to boss the computer around.

✔ OS/2, also heartily referred to as "OS/2 Warp Version 3," is an *operating system*. That means that it's a new way for you to boss your computer around.

✔ Buying OS/2 for your computer is like buying a new dashboard for your car. OS/2 sits between you and your computer's complicated internal processes. OS/2 is designed to make IBM-compatible computers a little easier to use.

✔ The big problem is yanking off the old dashboard and bolting on the new one. Instructions on how to perform that odious chore are in Chapter 3.

✔ Different brands of computers use different operating systems. In fact, OS/2 makes a computer screen look a great deal like a Macintosh. But don't get your hopes up: You still can't run Macintosh programs on a PC. IBM and Apple say that they're working together on the problem and should have it solved in about, oh, five years or so.

✔ MS-DOS is the operating system used by most IBM-compatible computers. OS/2 can replace MS-DOS, which is described in the very next section. Or if you don't quite trust OS/2, you can install it next to MS-DOS and let them run side by side. (That's called *dual boot*.)

What Is MS-DOS?

IBM released its first personal computer as a lark back in the early 1980s. Figuring that it would sell only a few computers to freak hobbyists, IBM didn't spend much time making the computers easy to use. IBM hired a small company named Microsoft to throw together a quick operating system, and the computers hit the stores.

As IBM predicted, the hobbyists snapped up the first few computers. But so did small-business owners, large-business owners, and thousands of people in between. The machines were an unqualified success.

Unfortunately, the computers were an unqualified failure in terms of ease of use. The operating system, dubbed *MS-DOS*, or just plain *DOS*, forced users to type robotic strings of code words into their computers. Howls of anguish filled the halls — except from the computer nerds, of course, who love to memorize such things as *MODE* commands and *NULL* outputs.

✔ Because MS-DOS is more than a decade old, it is yesteryear's technology, like those old six-wing airplanes you see crashing in historic movies at the aerospace museum. MS-DOS has trouble meeting the demands of today's technology.

✔ Computers have grown in both power and speed over the years, but DOS never really grew along with them. It couldn't change. If it did, it would no longer have been compatible with all the DOS software on the market, and nobody wants to buy a new operating system *and* new programs to go along with it.

✔ Because most of today's software still requires DOS in order to run, IBM stuck a version of MS-DOS into OS/2. So OS/2 can still run those old DOS programs.

✔ OS/2's version of DOS is pretty close to MS-DOS Version 5.0. It can trick DOS programs into thinking that they're running under other versions of MS-DOS, however. This sleight of hand is covered in Chapter 14.

✔ Because DOS makes you type specific commands to boss around your computer, DOS is considered a *command-line interface*. You type commands at the *DOS prompt,* shown in Figure 1-1. DOS gives you absolutely no clues about what you should enter at the DOS prompt.

✔ OS/2 comes with a command-line interface too. You don't earn any points for knowing that, however. (In fact, you'll probably never use the OS/2 command line.)

```
C:/>
```

Figure 1-1:
The
unfriendly
DOS uses
the
minimalist
approach.

Boring DOS details, already!

OS/2 can dish out more than 700K of conventional memory, which should be enough for the pickiest DOS program. Before OS/2, DOS computer users had to play interior decorator, by rearranging the TSRs and device drivers in their CONFIG.SYS and AUTOEXEC.BAT files and hoping to stumble across a memory combination that worked.

OS/2 simplifies DOS memory matters with a *DOS Settings menu*. Just click on the amount of memory you want to parcel out to each DOS program and then click OK. Quick and easy.

Actually, it's not that easy, because almost 50 different push-button settings enable you to customize your DOS session with frills you never even dreamed of. But that's why OS/2 is so popular among computer nerds: It makes fiddling with a computer's settings so easy.

What Is Windows?

Microsoft knew that MS-DOS was fading fast. People had grown used to remote-control tuners on their TVs. They didn't want to change channels manually. And they didn't want to have to type complicated instructions into their computers in order to get things done.

So Microsoft came up with Windows: a new, easier way to boss computers around. Windows put pictures, called *icons,* on the computer screen, as shown in Figure 1-2. People no longer had to type bizarre code words into their computers. They could simply point at the on-screen pictures — at a picture of a fountain pen, for example — and zap! — their word processor jumped to the screen.

Windows was a huge success. But a big problem remained: Windows didn't replace DOS; it ran on top of DOS. Windows just put easy-to-use buttons over the ugly DOS mechanics. DOS was still the workhorse that powered the PC. In fact, you needed to buy both DOS *and* Windows. And why shouldn't you, Microsoft reasoned. After all, by selling DOS and Windows, Microsoft makes twice as much money.

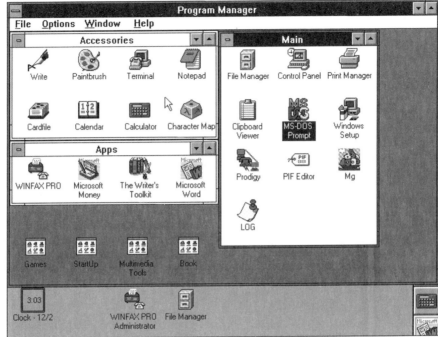

Figure 1-2:
To make the computer easier to use, Windows puts lots of buttons on the screen.

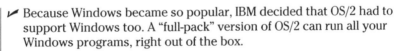

✔ Because Windows became so popular, IBM decided that OS/2 had to support Windows too. A "full-pack" version of OS/2 can run all your Windows programs, right out of the box.

✔ Many of the commands used to boss Windows around do the same thing in OS/2. In fact, if you're already familiar with Windows, you'll probably feel pretty much at home in OS/2.

✔ Pictures, called *graphics* in the computer world, require a powerful computer. That means that Windows requires a more powerful (meaning *expensive*) computer than DOS requires. And because OS/2 can run both DOS and Windows programs, it requires a more powerful computer than both Windows and DOS require.

✔ The "full-pack" version of OS/2 comes with a working subset of Microsoft Windows 3.1. Just about everything is the same as in Microsoft's version, except that IBM left out the Solitaire game. (OS/2 includes its own version of Solitaire, however, called Klondike.) With Warp, the Windows product is left *out* of the package; instead, Warp looks for and uses any copy of Windows it already finds living on your computer's hard drive. By not including Windows, IBM doesn't have to pay Microsoft, which significantly cuts Warp's retail price.

What Is OS/2 Warp Version 3.0?

OS/2 Warp Version 3.0, in addition to being a mouthful to say, is the latest generation of the OS/2 product. Like the versions before it, OS/2 Warp Version 3 brings an easy-to-use, push-button dashboard to your computer. Actually, IBM likes to call the dashboard a *desktop.* Indeed, if you squint, the OS/2 screen sort of looks like a desktop: You see several little folders lying around, along with a paper shredder in one corner. OS/2 calls these pictures *objects.*

This object stuff is sort of confusing, but here goes: When you work on a normal desktop, you move around objects: staplers, papers, and cans of soda. You work the same way in OS/2 with your *computerized objects.* To print a letter, for example, you move your *letter object* over to your *printer object.*

It's much easier than it sounds. And because OS/2 places such a weighty emphasis on the word *object,* OS/2 also sounds more boring than it is.

As Figure 1-3 shows, OS/2 Warp Version 3.0 looks much like Microsoft Windows. Like Windows programs, OS/2 programs don't take up the entire screen when they run; they run inside little *boxes* on the screen. So you can have several programs on the screen at the same time. Fun!

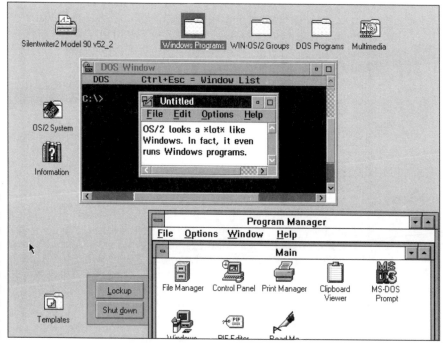

Figure 1-3: OS/2 puts buttons on the screen, just as Microsoft Windows does.

Technical legaloid stuff

Actually, Microsoft wrote not only DOS and Windows but also the first version of OS/2. IBM and Microsoft joined hands to release the first version of OS/2 in late 1987. Back then, OS/2 didn't have any fancy pictures (objects), and it needed a very powerful computer, so it never really caught on.

Even with OS/2 on the market, however, Microsoft kept working on its own project, Windows. When Microsoft released Windows 3.0 in 1990, people loved it. In fact, they bought more copies of Win-dows 3.0 in the first month than they bought of OS/2 in the preceding three years!

So Microsoft quickly dumped OS/2 into IBM's lap and began pushing Windows instead. Now OS/2, beginning with version 2.0, is IBM's own baby. And IBM and Microsoft aren't speaking to each other. Through some weird licensing agreements, however, they both have rights to use each other's programs for a while. That's how IBM managed to stick Windows and DOS support into OS/2 Warp Version 3.0.

Best of all, OS/2 can wear different faces. When you want to run a DOS program, just click a button to see a DOS screen. If you're ready to run Windows, push a different button, and Windows comes to the screen.

You can run DOS, Windows, and OS/2 programs simultaneously — in fact, all on the same screen. Depending on how you look at it, you may find that feature incredibly convenient or you may think that the screen is a little too cluttered.

- ✔ Because you use pictures to boss around the computer in both OS/2 and Windows, each of them is considered a *graphical user interface,* or *GUI* (pronounced "gooey," believe it or not).

- ✔ OS/2 is known as a *multitasking* operating system. Not only can you run several programs at the same time, but the programs also can all be *working* at the same time: You can format a floppy disk, download a file from CompuServe, and play a game of Radish Invaders with one hand while clutching a handful of Chee-tos with the other — all simultaneously.

Why Do They Call It Warp?

Before the latest release of OS/2, it was known simply by its version number — 2.0, 2.1, and 2.11. The latest release is OS/2 Warp Version 3.0. Why? Because it sounds flashy and cool. Mutter the word as you walk down the hall, and suddenly legions of "Star Trek" fans seep from the wallpaper.

Warp implies speed. It implies the future, and it implies technology. All these qualities are items IBM tried to incorporate into the image of the latest product.

- ✔ Warp doesn't come with a built-in copy of Windows. Instead, Warp searches for a copy of Windows on your hard drive. If it finds one, it sticks Windows on its menu and uses the Windows coding to run Windows programs.

- ✔ If Warp doesn't find a copy of Windows on your hard drive, you can't run any Windows programs (unless you buy a copy of Windows and install it while Warp is running, that is).

- ✔ If you don't have a copy of Windows — but still want to run Windows programs — buy the "full-pack" version of Warp. That version costs more, but it comes with Windows built-in, enabling you to run Windows programs.

Why Bother with OS/2?

Some people are getting fed up with DOS and are replacing it with OS/2. Why? The reason is that because OS/2 uses pictures rather than complicated code words, it's easier to use than DOS. And OS/2 is versatile: People can *still* type bizarre streams of computerese into OS/2 if they want.

But the real reason that people like OS/2 lies under its surface. IBM designed OS/2 to take better advantage of today's more powerful computers. Programs run faster and more efficiently.

- ✔ OS/2 offers a new way to save files. Under OS/2, you can save a file with the name Big Report on French Red Wine. In DOS, you're stuck with only eight characters, so you have to give your wine file a name like BGRPFRWN. OS/2's new file system is called *HPFS,* or *High Performance File System.*

- ✔ DOS makes you twiddle your thumbs when you are formatting a new box of floppy disks. OS/2 can format disks in the background at the same time you're running other programs.

- ✔ Running several programs at the same time is called *multitasking.* Both Windows and OS/2 can multitask. But because OS/2 was *designed* to multitask, it works better. If one program crashes in OS/2, the others keep on working. In Windows, if one program crashes, they all fall down.

- ✔ OS/2 can run DOS and Windows programs right out of the box. Buying one box of OS/2 can save you from buying two boxes: one of DOS and one of Windows. If you already have Windows installed on your machine — as it's preconfigured on most computers sold today — OS/2 Warp snatches the Windows code and uses it to run Windows programs more smoothly than ever.

✔ Although OS/2 is IBM's baby, OS/2 works on IBM-compatible computers that aren't made by IBM. OS/2 runs on not only IBM's PS/2 line of computers, for example, but also computers made by Dell, Compaq, Gateway, and smaller companies, like Leroy's Computer Shed.

✔ Not many programs have been written exclusively for OS/2. However, the number is growing every day. And because OS/2 can run both DOS and Windows programs, the lack of OS/2-specific programs isn't really a handicap.

32 bits of technical information

Just to give you enough jargon to spew at the water cooler, OS/2 is a *32-bit* operating system. That means that it can process programs much more quickly than the older 16-bit operating systems do. Not only that, but OS/2 is *multitasking*—capable of doing more than one thing at a time. And, get this, it's *preemptive* multitasking. This means that if one of your tasks crashes, only that single task dies — the other tasks keep working, churning away like zombies in *Night of the Living Dead.*

Here's one last word to stump your coworkers with: OS/2 is *multithreading.* A *thread* is the smallest component that a task, much like a business suit, can be broken into. By breaking tasks into smaller components, the entire operation can be completed much more quickly.

Chapter 2

Computer Stuff Everybody Thinks You Already Know

The ten-year-old kids down the street have been playing with computers for years. They're familiar with not only video modes such as VGA but also more arcane video modes, such as 8514/A.

But identifying and using pieces of a computer can be a problem for somebody who has never calibrated a joystick or tweaked a color monitor.

Luckily, this chapter explains some of the computer terms everybody thinks you already know.

Your AUTOEXEC.BAT and CONFIG.SYS Files

Down in the bare-bones 'n' gristle stew of your computer sit two important files: AUTOEXEC.BAT and CONFIG.SYS. Without these files, your computer is lost.

You see, computers are pretty dumb. When we wake up, we don't need anybody to remind us that we have to brush our teeth and go to work.

Computers, however, have to be reminded of their mission in life every time they're turned on. And the AUTOEXEC.BAT and CONFIG.SYS files are there to remind them. When the computer is first turned on, it reaches for its CONFIG.SYS file the way you reach for a morning cup of coffee. As the computer reads the information in the CONFIG.SYS file, it learns how it has been *configured:* what equipment it's connected to, how it should dish out its memory, and other information computers like to hear.

After the computer has found itself through its CONFIG.SYS file, it reads the second file, AUTOEXEC.BAT. There it finds its first set of *instructions* for the day. Some AUTOEXEC.BAT files contain commands — for example, the command to load a program such as Windows. Others display an appointment reminder, gently reminding you to pick up the dry cleaning.

The luckiest people have an AUTOEXEC.BAT file that runs a program to *pick up the dry cleaning.*

- ✔ Although both DOS and Windows are slavishly dependent on the AUTOEXEC.BAT file, OS/2 doesn't use one. It has outgrown it. But to make DOS and Windows feel at home, OS/2 graciously keeps one around anyway. In fact, both DOS and Windows read that file whenever you start them up under OS/2.

- ✔ OS/2 packs a *lot* of information into its CONFIG.SYS file. If you're accustomed to DOS, you're in for a shock: The OS/2 CONFIG.SYS file uses at least 60 lines of computer words. Yuck!

- ✔ Some DOS programs are so bold as to make changes to the AUTOEXEC.BAT file, usually when they're first installed. Other DOS programs force you to make changes to the AUTOEXEC.BAT file yourself. These merry little chores are covered in Chapter 14.

- ✔ Some DOS programs are even bolder: They automatically make changes to the CONFIG.SYS file. This audacity sometimes causes problems because OS/2 uses CONFIG.SYS, and OS/2 likes to control any changes to that file. This more troublesome area is also covered in Chapter 14.

A computer drinks in its CONFIG.SYS and AUTOEXEC.BAT files only when it first wakes up. If you change these files, the computer doesn't notice your handiwork until you *reboot* it. To make OS/2 reboot, use its Shut <u>d</u>own command, described at the tail end of Chapter 3. Then, when OS/2 starts back up, it finally notices the changes.

What Are Hardware and Software?

The parts of the computer you can touch lovingly or kick in frustration are called *hardware*. Hardware includes the monitor, the keyboard, floppy disks, and other tangible items, as shown in Figure 2-1. It even includes the stuff that's inside the computer's case. (Don't touch that stuff, though, at least not until you turn off the power.)

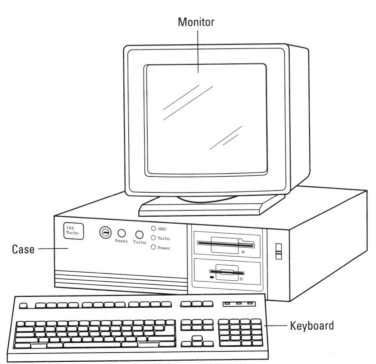

Monitor

Case

Figure 2-1:
Computer
hardware.

Keyboard

The parts of the computer you *can't* touch are called *software*. Software is the information stored on a floppy disk or on the hard drive. It's the information that tells the computer to do something: process your words, for example, or pick up your dry cleaning.

✔ Hardware often comes packaged with software. For example, a modem usually comes with software you can use to call up other modems.

✔ Some hardware comes with software called a *driver*. The driver works as a translator, enabling OS/2 to communicate with the hardware. For example, OS/2 needs a driver in order to put information on the computer's monitor. Don't consider these drivers to be *junk mail*. Chapter 19 tells you why you need them.

✔ OS/2 comes with drivers for some popular pieces of hardware; you have to pry other drivers out of the hardware manufacturer.

Some pieces of hardware don't work with OS/2 because there simply aren't any drivers: IBM didn't write one, and the hardware manufacturer didn't bother to write one, either. When you're shopping for new computer toys, such as video cards or compact disc drives, check to make sure that the toy will work under OS/2.

Monitors and Video Cards

Television has gone through only two major permutations: black-and-white, followed by color. Computer monitors are much more malleable. In fact, at least half a dozen different types of displays have come into and gone out of style.

The computer's display is dictated mostly by its *video card:* a chunk of hardware that sits inside the computer and gives you a place to plug in the monitor. As the newer video cards struggle to remain compatible with the older ones, they enable you to switch between different video *modes*.

Table 2-1 describes the video modes OS/2 can use. OS/2 is constantly being updated, however, with new drivers for new modes. Some drivers come from IBM, and others come from the video-card manufacturers.

Table 2-1		**OS/2 Video Modes**	
Mode	*Meaning*	*Resolution On-Screen Colors for OS/2*	*What OS/2 Thinks of It*
CGA	Color Graphics Adapter	640 × 200, 2	IBM's first attempt at color was aimed at Atari game players. It's awful. Don't bother.
EGA	Enhanced Graphics Adapter	640 × 350, 16	A giant step up from CGA, but still outdated.

Mode	Meaning	Resolution On-Screen Colors for OS/2	What OS/2 Thinks of It
VGA	Video Graphics Array	640 × 480, 16	Currently, it's the most supported mode under OS/2. VGA enables you to run all your programs simultaneously on the same screen.
8514/A	Display Adapter 8514/A	640 × 480, 256 1024 × 768, 256	An older IBM standard offering higher resolution, which means that you can fit more windows on a screen. Because OS/2 supports it, it's making a slight comeback.
XGA	Extended Graphics Array	1024 × 768, 256	IBM shunned other companies' video standards and released an expensive XGA card. Applications can run in high resolution.
SVGA	Super Video Graphics Array	640 × 480, 256 800 × 600, 256	Most video cards support SVGA, but there's no clearly defined SVGA standard.

✔ *Resolution* refers to the number of dots that make up the display. The more dots on the screen, the finer the grid and the finer the image. In a high-resolution mode, you can fit more information on the screen than you can in a low-resolution mode. The high-resolution mode makes everything smaller, though, so it can pack it all on the screen.

✔ The back of the OS/2 box shows Windows programs, DOS programs, and OS/2 programs running simultaneously in their own windows. The windows are *seamless:* You can see all the programs on the screen at one time. Some of the higher-resolution video modes *aren't* seamless. They make you switch to a Windows screen to run Windows programs and then back to an OS/2 screen to run OS/2 programs.

✔ To run seamless windows, you need a *seamless driver* for the video card. As OS/2 continues to mature, more video-card companies will offer seamless support for their cards. If your video card doesn't have seamless drivers, bug your video-card manufacturer to see what gives.

✔ OS/2 turns up its nose at those old Hercules and monochrome graphics cards. If your computer currently uses one of these cards, you have to buy a new graphics card when you buy OS/2.

✔ If you don't have a great deal of cash for splurging on your computer's video mode whims, take heart: Currently, the plain ol' VGA standard is the most compatible with OS/2. It's cheap, and it's the most common video card out there right now.

Playing with the Mouse

Like a first-grader coming home from a trip to the zoo, OS/2 demands a mouse. A mouse does basically the same thing as a keyboard: It feeds information to the computer. A mouse is simpler to use than a keyboard because it has only two keys: a left button and a right button.

When you slide a mouse around on a desk, you're sliding a corresponding arrow around on the computer screen. When the arrow points to something that looks interesting — a playing card, for example — push the mouse button. Shazzam! The playing-card program jumps to life.

✔ Actually, it gets a little more complicated than that. First, you don't just push the button, you push it twice in rapid succession. That's known as a *double-click*. Pushing and releasing the button only once is called a *click*.

✔ Also, unlike most programs, OS/2 uses *both* of the mouse's buttons. You use the *left* button to activate something you're pointing at: to start a program, for example. You use the *right* button to manipulate something on the screen — to pull up something's menu, for example, so that you can change its settings.

✔ This is too hard to remember, of course. So try clicking the left button first. If that doesn't do what you want, try the right button. Nothing bad will happen, and sometimes it really doesn't matter *which* button you click. You have to be a little more careful with double-clicks, however. (Although, at the worst, you'll just accidentally start the wrong program.)

✔ If you like to tinker, you can change these mouse-click rules. Under the System Setup folder (found in the OS/2 System folder), double-click the Mouse object. Then you can change the mouse to be left- or right-handed. You can also control how fast the arrow moves across the screen. Or you can even change the double-click and single-click rules. You can find out how to make these mouse adjustments in Chapter 9.

✔ To complicate matters, OS/2 refers to the left mouse button as *Button 1* and the right mouse button as *Button 2* (this book calls them the left and right mouse buttons). Also, some hard-core nerds refer to the left mouse button as *LMB* and the right mouse button as *RMB*. Pass the cheese-filled pretzels....

✔ When I simply say "click," I'm referring to the left mouse button. You have to use your right mouse button only when this book specifically says to.

The Key to Keyboards

Although the mouse is better at bossing OS/2 around, the keyboard works well in a pinch. In fact, sometimes the keyboard is quicker. OS/2 has several *shortcut* keys: key combinations you can press to bypass the steps of moving and clicking the mouse.

If you click a little picture (icon), for example, the picture changes color to show that you've *selected* it (which is also known as *highlighting* it). By pressing Enter, you can start the program represented by that icon.

Most shortcut keys involving windows use the Alt key. The Ctrl- and Shift-key combinations can do just about anything.

Table 2-2 is a handy chart of shortcut keys used in OS/2. You may not know what they all mean right now, but at least you know where to turn when you're ready to find out. (When you see keys with a plus sign [+] between them, hold down the first key while you press the second key.) If you don't want to wade through all these keys, you can find the most-used keys on the "Cheat Sheet" tear-out card at the front of this book.

Table 2-2	**OS/2 Shortcut Keys**
Key Combination	*What It Does*
Alt-key combinations	
Alt+Esc	Switches OS/2's attention to the next open window or open object on the desktop.
Alt+Tab	Selects a window.
Alt+Home	Toggles a DOS program between taking up the whole screen and running in a window.
Alt+Backspace	Whoops! Usually undoes the last thing you did.

(continued)

Table 2-2 *(continued)*

Key Combination	What It Does
Alt-key combinations	
Alt+F4	Closes the currently active window.
Alt+F6	Moves between an object and a Help window.
Alt+F9	*Minimizes* a window or hides it in the Minimized Window Viewer.
Alt+F10	*Maximizes* a window (makes it grow as large as it can).
Ctrl-key combinations	
Ctrl+Alt+Delete	This hard-to-reach combination completely resets the computer, in a process called *rebooting*. Use it only as a last resort if OS/2 has frozen on the screen.
Ctrl+Esc	Brings up a Window List window, listing every currently running program under OS/2. If the computer seems frozen, try pressing Ctrl+Esc and waiting 30 seconds or more. Eventually, OS/2 may wake from its stupor and display the Window List.
Ctrl+Insert	Copies the highlighted information to the OS/2 clipboard.
Ctrl+/	Selects everything possible from a list.
Ctrl+\	Deselects everything possible from a list.
Ctrl+S	Searches through Help for a word or phrase.
Ctrl+Right mouse button	Copies the object you're pointing at.
Shift-key combinations and miscellaneous shortcuts	
Shift+Esc	Calls up a window's menu (if there is one).
Shift+F8	Selects more than one object from a list.
Shift+F10	Makes an object's *pop-up* menu pop up.
Shift+Delete	Cuts the highlighted information from the window and places it in the OS/2 clipboard.
Shift+Insert	Pastes the information from the OS/2 clipboard to the cursor's current location.

Key Combination	What It Does
Shift-key combinations and miscellaneous shortcuts	
F1	Brings up helpful information to get you out of your current jam.
F2	Displays general help.
Home	Selects the first choice in a list.
End	Selects the last choice in a list.
F9	Displays help for key combinations.
F10	Moves to and from the menu bar.
F11	Displays the Help index.
Print Screen	Prints the contents of the window that contains the cursor. (This key is labeled PrtSc or PrintSc on some keyboards.)
Tab	Moves the cursor to the next logical place when you're filling out a form.

✔ OS/2 constantly fiddles with the Num Lock key, much to the annoyance of nimble-fingered accountants. It turns Num Lock off when you boot up OS/2. It turns Num Lock off when you switch to DOS. Head for Windows and you see the same thing: Num Lock is off. The fix? Either remember to turn Num Lock back on all the time or ask a computer nerd for a little program called NUMON that leaves the Num Lock key on all the time.

✔ Chapter 9 has instructions for changing the way the keyboard works. (But Chapter 9 doesn't have a fix for the Num Lock problem.)

If your mouse ever dies on you, you can shut down OS/2 by using just the keyboard. Press Alt+Shift+Tab, then Ctrl+\, and then Shift+F10. Then press D, followed by Enter. Instead of burying the rodent in the backyard, turn to Chapter 19 to find out how to revive dead mice.

What's Memory?

For years, DOS and Windows users have had to blunder through all sorts of memory problems. Programs have to load themselves into the computer's memory, which is known as *Random-Access Memory (RAM),* before they can appear on the screen.

In the world of DOS, however, programs crawl into little portions of conventional memory, extended memory, expanded memory, upper memory, or high memory. Or all of them. It's more complicated than buying a mutual fund for the first time.

In fact, the MS-DOS memory mess has driven many users to OS/2. OS/2 relies entirely on *extended* memory, the kind of memory that was summed up in megabyte-size chunks on your computer's invoice.

But OS/2 is not without problems. Because it relies on extended memory, it needs bulldozer loads of it. You need 4MB of memory just to see what OS/2 looks like. To run any OS/2 programs successfully, you need at least 6MB. And most OS/2 gurus nod their heads and agree that 8MB is a more realistic starting point.

- ✔ Although OS/2 programs aren't picky about memory, all the DOS memory problems resurface when you run DOS programs under OS/2. Luckily, OS/2 makes it easy to dish out memory for DOS programs. You just push some *DOS Settings* buttons to give DOS programs the kind of memory they're hungry for. (Those buttons are dutifully described in Chapter 14.)

- ✔ DOS and Windows memory managers, such as HIMEM.SYS, EMM386.EXE, QEMM, 386MAX, and a host of others, aren't necessary under OS/2, thank goodness. OS/2 handles all the memory-management stuff by itself.

- ✔ Like Windows, OS/2 can sometimes pretend that your computer has more RAM than you could afford: It creates *virtual memory* by staking out a big file on the hard drive. OS/2 then swaps information from memory to that file. By moving information back and forth, from memory to file, OS/2 can function as though your computer has more memory. Beware, though: This swap-file stuff works much more slowly than the real thing does.

- ✔ You need at least 6MB of RAM to even consider OS/2's cool new High Performance File System, or HPFS. (It's described in Chapter 3.)

Printers

Printers all do the same thing: move information from the computer's screen to a piece of paper, where it can travel through people's in-baskets. Although dozens of printer manufacturers have placed hundreds of types of printers on the market, something is kind of funny about them. Almost all of them behave like the three most popular types of printers: PostScript, Epson dot matrix, and Hewlett-Packard LaserJet.

Technical reserved-memory vulgarities

Some computers speed things up by reading information from their slow ROM chips and copying it to their faster RAM chips. Known as *ROM-to-RAM remapping, BIOS caching, Fast Video BIOS,* or (even worse) *twaddle,* these techniques all grab some of the computer's extended memory to speed up your computing.

If your computer has only 4MB of memory, however, you can run into problems: OS/2 needs all 4MB to get off the ground. If the computer reserves more than 128K of memory for its ROM-to-RAM shenanigans, OS/2 freezes up during the installation process.

The solution: Head for the computer's *Setup* or *CMOS* program. (Different computers call up that program in different ways; you usually have to press key combinations, such as Ctrl+Alt+Enter, at the DOS prompt.) From the Setup program, disable any *Fast BIOS* or *ROM-to-RAM* remapping options you see. Disabling them may free up enough RAM to enable you to install OS/2 on a 4MB system.

The simpler solution? Head back to the store and buy more RAM. And if OS/2 is giving you problems during installation, keep that stuff disabled, even if you have gobs of memory.

Even though OS/2's installation program lists a hundred or so printers in its *compatible printers list,* almost all of those printers use three drivers (the software that bosses them around).

Those three drivers can accommodate just about every printer on the market. So if you don't see your printer brand on OS/2's official list, don't worry. OS/2 thinks that only three types of printers are out there, anyway.

- On OS/2's list of printers, each printer's driver is listed in parentheses behind its brand name, like this: TI Omnilaser 2115 (PSCRIPT.DRV).

- *PostScript* refers mainly to expensive laser printers. PostScript is a special type of printer language for describing letters and graphics. OS/2 talks to these printers through the PSCRIPT.DRV driver.

- The Hewlett-Packard (often known simply as *HP*) LaserJet printer is copied by most mid-priced laser printers. OS/2 talks to these printers through the LASERJET.DRV driver.

- Almost all dot-matrix printers copy Epson's line of dot-matrix printers. OS/2 talks to these printers with the OMNI.DRV driver.

- IBM is the strange one here. IBM wrote OS/2, so it included a handful of drivers written specifically for its own brand of printers. Those drivers all begin with the letters *IBM.* Even so, some of IBM's printers copy Hewlett-Packard's stuff anyway.

- For information about installing a new printer, troop to Chapter 16.

- Almost every printer plugs in to something called *LPT1*. Rather than worry about what this means, just choose LPT1 whenever the computer asks where you've plugged in the printer. (On the oddball chance that you have a serial printer, however, choose COM1 or COM2.)

- Don't use a printer cable that's longer than six feet. The "print me" signals lose their chutzpah at that distance, especially the signals that come from the high-speed computers used with OS/2.

- Oh, some people don't have printers — they have *plotters* (an expensive type of printer that draws on the page with special pens). OS/2 talks to plotters with the PLOTTERS.DRV driver.

Just about everybody has tried to print something without first turning on the printer. OS/2 is very forgiving: It sends you a polite error message asking you to Abort, Retry, or Ignore. Choose Abort, turn on the printer, and print your work again. If you choose Retry or Ignore, the first few pages of your work may disappear.

Your Computer's Microprocessor (CPU)

You probably don't want to read this section because you see all the numbers in it. But that's the trouble with microprocessors. Until recently, they were all named after three-digit numbers. The bigger the number, the more powerful the microprocessor and the larger the total at the bottom of your computer's invoice.

A *microprocessor* is the computer's brain. It's also the computer's muscle because it pushes the programs around and makes them do tricks.

OS/2 insists that your computer use a 386 or higher microprocessor. You can use a 386, a 486, or a Pentium (which should have been called a 586, but Intel figured out that you can't trademark a number). OS/2 also can use 386 and 486 chips that have extra letters before or after the numbers, such as 386SX and 486SX. It doesn't run as fast on "SX" computers, though. And the letter *i* before the number — i386 and i486, for example — just means that the chips are made by Intel, the biggest chip manufacturer; they still work.

- Some folks call a microprocessor a *central processing unit,* or *CPU.* The more suave nerds just say, "What chip are you using these days?" as they reach for a glob of onion dip with their bare fingers.

✔ If you have a cat, buy a 486 or Pentium CPU. Those chips tend to run a little warmer, making your computer an irresistible spot for your feline's catnaps. (Make sure that the 486 has a *heat sink* attached or else it will be too hot for both the cat and the computer.)

OS/2 comes with a cool little program called Pulse. Pulse displays a fluctuating graph depicting how busy the CPU is at any given second. By keeping the Pulse graph in a corner of the screen, you can tell whether OS/2 has crashed (doesn't respond to anything you type) or is just breathing hard. (If the graph shows that the CPU is cranking away at 100 percent capacity, OS/2 may take a few seconds to get back to you.)

Disks and Disk Drives

Disk drives come in three basic types: floppy drives, hard drives, and CD-ROM drives. *Floppy drives* are those little slots in the front of the computer where you slide in floppy disks. *Hard drives* are hidden away inside the computer; that way, you don't have to worry about sticking the disk in upside down. Figure 2-2 shows the difference between a floppy drive and a hard drive. A CD-ROM drive is similar to the CD player in your stereo — the discs look identical. In fact, OS/2 can play Lynyrd Skynyrd CDs as well as computer CDs.

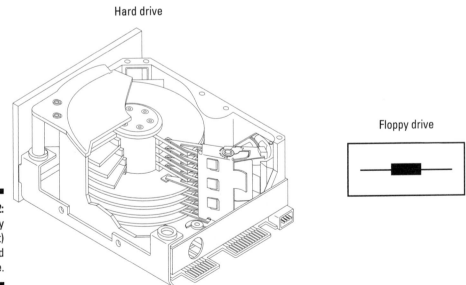

Hard drive

Floppy drive

Figure 2-2:
A floppy
drive (right)
and a hard
drive.

OS/2 insists that your computer have both a hard drive and a floppy drive. Not only that, OS/2 consumes at least 35MB of the hard drive just for itself. If you install all of OS/2 Warp Version 3.0 — including its Bonus Pack of bundled programs — OS/2 consumes 85MB of hard drive space. To leave room for programs, your computer's hard drive should be at least 100MB. The bigger, the better, and don't think that you're being silly for buying a 500MB hard drive, either.

OS/2 comes on either a CD — which is the easiest way to install it — or on high-density floppy disks. That means that your computer needs *high-capacity* floppy drives as well. You can't tell whether a drive is *high-* or *low-capacity* by looking at it, however, so dig out your computer's sales receipt. Table 2-3 shows how much information high- and low-capacity disks can store.

Table 2-3	Handy Floppy Disk Chart	
Storage Capacity	*Size*	*Identifying Characteristics*
Low (360K)	5¼ inches	Bendable; usually with a little reinforcing ring around the center hole.
High (1.2MB)	5¼ inches	Bendable; usually without the little reinforcing ring around the center hole. Sometimes it says *1.2MB* on the label.
Low (720K)	3½ inches	Rigid; hole in one corner with tiny, sliding cover.
High (1.44MB)	3½ inches	Rigid; hole in two corners with tiny, sliding cover in one. Usually says *HD* near metal part.

- ✔ OS/2 works with both high- and low-capacity disks of either size. When you install OS/2, however, you must use drive A, and that drive must be high density.

- ✔ The terms *hard disk* and *hard drive* both refer to the same thing: a large, spinning platter inside the computer that stores a great deal of information. Calling it a *fixed disk,* however, will win you a pocket protector at trade shows.

- ✔ You can find all you need to know about disks and disk drives in Chapter 8.

Chapter 3

Installing OS/2 on Your Computer without Crying

· ·

In This Chapter

▶ Getting ready to install OS/2

▶ Installing OS/2 by itself

▶ Installing OS/2 but keeping MS-DOS and Windows (Dual Boot)

▶ Installing OS/2 and keeping MS-DOS and Windows but keeping them separate (Boot Manager)

▶ Following the 13-step installation process

▶ Fiddling with FDISK

▶ Shutting down the computer

· ·

*H*ow would you feel if you had just bought a new car and the salesman handed you a box of parts and a wrench and said, "Here, you can put it together in the back room."?

You feel the same way when you first dump OS/2 out of the box. You see, you have to install OS/2 on your computer with your own hands. It's not as easy as installing a computer game or a word processor. If by some incredible good fortune OS/2 is already installed on your computer, count your blessings (and don't bother counting the 35 installation disks) and move swiftly to the next chapter.

Installing a new operating system is a considerable chore that forces you to wade through powerfully obtuse computer geekism at its worst. If you're in an office, get one of the office computer gurus to install OS/2 for you. They love challenges. If you're at home or in your own business, however, you probably have to take a stab at it yourself. Keep this book handy for the next several hours. It will serve as an air traffic controller does, talking down a passenger at the wheel of a pilotless 747.

Read the first sections and then follow the 13 installation steps, one by one, paying careful attention to the occasional Warning! messages along the way. . . . If you make a mistake, hey, at least you aren't at 30,000 feet. Just sigh, put down the keyboard, and make a computer geek's day by letting one of them show their OS/2 installation prowess. Phone your local geek, beg, stock up on Cheetos, and make sure that the vacuum cleaner bag isn't already full.

Preparing for the Head-Scratching Installation Decisions

First, the good news. IBM realized that one of the worst complaints about earlier versions of OS/2 was the number of physics degrees necessary to install the darn thing. To silence its critics, IBM wrote two installation routines for the latest release of the product — known as OS/2 Warp Version 3.

The Advanced Installation still requires a master's degree and should be used only by highly trained professionals. The Easy Installation, designed for the average user, is applicable to virtually every installation scenario.

Before you do anything, make sure that your computer has these muscles or else OS/2 won't budge:

- OS/2 needs *at least* a 386SX computer. (The program doesn't run at all on an XT or AT computer.) OS/2 runs much faster on a 386DX or 486 computer. (Stay away from those slower 486SX computers. Unless you already bought one. In that case, you can say, "Aw, what does this writer guy know, anyway?")

- IBM says that you need at least 4MB of RAM, but that's for bare-bones operation. To put some flesh and limbs on the skeleton, start with at least 8MB of RAM. You may need even more RAM later, depending on how many programs you try to run at the same time. If this memory stuff sounds confusing, head back to Chapter 2 for a short brushup.

- OS/2 lays claim to at least 35MB of hard disk space. If you install *all* of OS/2 Warp Version 3, OS/2 grabs 85MB of hard disk space. And that still doesn't include space for any other programs or data. To use OS/2, a computer should have at *least* 100MB of free hard drive space. Again, the larger the hard drive, the better.

- OS/2 works with VGA, SuperVGA, PS/2 Display Adapter, XGA, and 8514/A cards and monitors. The more expensive cards (VGA, 8514/A, and SVGA), of course, provide the most clarity and working area. The bigger the monitor, the better. You see, OS/2 mimics a desktop on the screen. The bigger the monitor, the bigger the desktop, and the more room you have to throw things around.

✔ OS/2 insists on being installed in a high-capacity disk drive. In addition, that high-capacity drive must be drive A. To be perfectly clear: You can't install OS/2 from drive B. If you bought the wrong-size disks for drive A, head back to your dealer. Or, if the OS/2 disks fit in drive B, check out the nearby "Technical mire box" for a numbingly nerdy solution.

✔ You need a mouse or a trackball to boss OS/2 around. You can try using the keyboard commands for a while, but the novelty wears off quickly.

✔ If you don't quite know what all these computer parts are, check out Chapter 2 for the rundown.

✔ Finally, you have to decide which way OS/2 will work best on your computer. You can install it in three different ways. The pros and cons of each are described in the next sections.

Technical mire box

OS/2 insists on being installed from a high-density floppy disk in drive A of the computer. Even if you buy the CD version, you must still boot your computer from an OS/2 floppy disk before being allowed to continue the installation.

If you want to install OS/2 from drive B, you can try using a sneaky trick. Turn off your computer, take off its case, and swap the cables that connect floppy drives A and B. (If you're lucky, the drives use connectors that are the same size. If you're not lucky, give up.)

Next, you have to tell your computer's Setup program that you've switched the drives. Reboot your machine and watch the screen. Some com-

puters notice your handiwork automatically and bring up the Setup program for you to confirm the changes. Others beep and tell you which keys to press to bring up the Setup screen. Others rudely make you dig through the manual for the Setup screen key combination.

After you inform the Setup program of the swap, save the changes and reboot your computer. The computer will recognize the former drive B as the new drive A, and everybody will be happy.

You can swap the cables back again after you install OS/2. Or you can just leave them swapped. Either way, this trick works in a pinch.

Deciding on an Operating System

Decisions, decisions. You have to decide which operating systems you want to keep on your computer before beginning to install OS/2. OS/2 Warp Version 3 can take up residence on your computer in two basic ways.

First, you can install OS/2 Warp as a stand-alone operating system, content to live on your computer by itself, running OS/2 and DOS programs without getting lonely. You don't have to have a *real* copy of DOS on your computer — OS/2 Warp Version 3 comes ready to run DOS programs. OS/2 Warp Version 3 can't, however, run Windows programs all by itself. No, for that luxury, you have to buy the "full" version of OS/2 Warp Version 3 — a slightly different version of OS/2 Warp that comes in a single box yet lets you run DOS, Windows, and OS/2 programs. (That's why it costs so much: You're essentially paying for a copy of OS/2 *and* Windows.)

The second option is to let OS/2 Warp share your computer with your existing copies of DOS and Windows. As it's being installed, OS/2 Warp Version 3 takes note of where Windows is living on your hard drive. Then, when you tell OS/2 to run one of your Windows programs, OS/2 borrows the copy of Windows from your hard drive, loads it, and uses it to run the Windows program. Frankly, this is the most popular installation option because most people already have copies of DOS and Windows installed on their hard drive.

Because this second installation option also lets OS/2 Warp share the hard drive with your current copy of DOS, you can easily switch between the two operating systems by using a trick called Dual Boot: To switch back to DOS for a while, double-click OS/2's little Dual Boot object or type the following line at the OS/2 prompt (it looks pretty much like a DOS command prompt):

```
C:\> BOOT /DOS
```

That is, type **BOOT**, a space, a forward slash (/), and **DOS**. OS/2 shuts down, the computer reboots, and the friendly face of DOS greets you. To head back to OS/2, type the following line at the DOS prompt while you're in your OS/2 directory:

```
C:\OS2\> BOOT /OS2
```

You use the same words and spaces as before, but you type **OS2** rather than **DOS**.

✔ When you type the BOOT command stuff, be sure that you type OS2 and not OS/2 (with a forward slash) or else the computer will pull its hair out in frustration.

✔ Under the Dual Boot option, you can switch to OS/2 or DOS on the fly, depending on your mood. Both OS/2 and DOS work with the same pool of data and programs that are already installed on the hard drive.

✔ The Dual Boot system enables you to get acquainted with OS/2 before you take the plunge and install OS/2 in all its glory. In fact, you can try all your DOS programs and computer toys under OS/2 to make sure that they all run OK. And when you're comfortable with OS/2, you can consider removing DOS altogether and going all the way with OS/2.

✔ Or, if OS/2 is acting up on some of your programs, use the Dual Boot to head over to your *real* DOS. While you're there, you can run your troublesome program. You can even run Windows and Windows programs.

Looking for the easy way out? Go with the Dual Boot option. In fact, OS/2 automatically installs the Dual Boot feature if you tell it to install itself the easy way.

The Technoid's Dream: Boot Manager

The rumor is true: There's a *third* option for installing OS/2 Warp Version 3. Some folks want a full taste of OS/2 before they ditch DOS completely. OS/2's *Boot Manager* option enables you to keep both DOS and OS/2 on the computer as bootable operating systems. You can still switch between the two operating systems at will. So what's the difference between Dual Boot and Boot Manager?

Well, the two operating systems live on completely separate areas of the hard drive. One doesn't know that the other exists. Every time you turn on your computer, you pick an operating system: OS/2 or DOS. The operating system of your choice comes up. In fact, both operating systems say that they're on drive C.

But those drive Cs are *different:* The programs and data on drive C under OS/2 aren't the same as the programs and data on drive C under DOS. Working under Boot Manager is similar to using two different computers, actually, each with a different operating system.

You can flip back and forth between DOS and OS/2 by rebooting your computer.

✔ Before you can install Boot Manager, you have to wade through a program called FDISK. It's a complicated program designed to make people chew their fingernails in horror. That's why OS/2 refers to the Boot Manager as the Advanced Installation in its opening menu.

✔ FDISK almost always requires you to reformat the hard drive. That means that you have to copy all the important information from the hard drive to floppy disks and then erase everything on the hard drive and start over.

✔ With the Boot Manager, you can install OS/2 in all its glory: You can take advantage of its special High Performance File System (HPFS), which enables you to use long filenames. Boot Manager is also a little faster with large hard drives, and it doesn't fragment disk space, if you care about that. And it's faster than its cousin, Dual Boot.

✔ Boot Manager keeps OS/2 and DOS completely separate. If you want both of them to share the same set of programs and data, you have to add a special *partition* to the hard drive. This partition, which appears on your computer as drive D, has to be formatted with the FAT system. If you're already throwing up your hands over these weird, new computer words, hey, stick with Dual Boot for a while.

What are HPFS and FAT, and why should I care?

Years ago, when computers first rose from the tar pits, programmers made some decisions about how they would store computerized information on disks. Computer disks couldn't hold much information back then, so the programmers worked up a simple little system, passed it out to the manufacturers, and passed around the beer pitcher.

Today, however, their *File Allocation Table* (dubbed *FAT*) method for storing information is out of date. It scatters information around the disk, *fragmenting* it and making the drive work harder to retrieve it. You have to work harder to retrieve information, too, because you can use no more than eight characters when you name your files.

OS/2 comes with the beefed-up, new *High Performance File System* (dubbed *HPFS*). HPFS enables you to use as many as 254 characters to name files. (Unfortunately, you can't use those long filenames when you store files on a floppy disk. Go figure.)

Because HPFS stores bits of related information close to each other, the hard drive can retrieve them faster. Also, HPFS makes it possible for OS/2 to stick extra descriptive information on files. These *extended attributes* (dubbed *EAs* by hip, young programmers) enable developers to embed stuff, such as objects, right on the files themselves. As a result, you (and your computer) have less to keep track of.

OS/2 can use files stored under either the FAT or HPFS storage method, but DOS is stuck with just the FAT method. If you install both OS/2 and DOS on a computer and want both of them to be able to access the same information easily, the information has to be stored in FAT format.

One last thing: Don't bother with HPFS unless you have at least 6MB of RAM. With less than 6MB, HPFS works even *worse* than FAT.

The Easy Installation Process

If you're reading this paragraph, you should have decided already which way you want OS/2 to live on your computer: all by itself; existing simultaneously with your current versions of DOS and Windows through the Dual Boot feature (the easiest way); or booting up separately from DOS through the Boot Manager (the most difficult way).

To install OS/2, follow the next 13 steps very carefully. Feel free to take notes and check off completed steps as you go. The installation process can take several hours, so seriously consider having a pizza delivered. If you're lucky, the delivery person will be a closet computer nerd who may be able to help you out of a jam.

Make a boot disk if you're the cautious type

When you first turn on your computer, it most likely *boots* from the hard drive. If something goes wrong while you're installing OS/2, however, your computer may not be able to boot from the hard drive anymore, and you'll be left staring at a numeric error message on the screen. If you make a *boot disk,* you can boot the computer from a floppy disk if something goes terribly wrong during the installation process. Here's the scoop:

1. **Place a new floppy disk (or one that contains destroyable information) in drive A.**

2. **At the C:\> prompt, type this line:**

    ```
    C:\> FORMAT A: /S
    ```

    That is, type **FORMAT** and a space, press A, and then type a colon, a space, and **/S**. Next, press Enter.

3. **Press Enter again.**

4. **After the computer formats the disk, it asks for a name. Type something, such as** BOOT, **and press Enter.**

5. **The computer asks breathlessly if you want to format another disk. Press N and then press Enter yet another time.**

6. **Next, type the following two lines, exactly as shown, one after the other, and press Enter at the end of each line. Wait for the drive's gears**

to stop whirring before you type the second line.

```
C:\> COPY C:\AUTOEXEC.BAT A:
C:\> COPY C:\CONFIG.SYS A:
```

Don't forget to type a space after you type **COPY** and before you type **A:**.

7. **When the little light on drive A goes out, remove the disk and keep it handy.**

Then, if anything goes wrong and your computer freezes up, stick this life-saving boot disk into drive A and press the computer's Reset button. The computer springs back to life. To restore order completely, type this command when you see A:\> sitting by itself:

```
A:\> COPY *.* C:\
```

That is, you type **COPY,** a space, an asterisk, a period, an asterisk, and a space. Next, press C and type a colon and a backslash (that key is on the same key as the question mark). Then remove the disk and push the computer's Reset button again. With any luck, you'll be back to normal. If not, howl unmercifully, admit defeat, and toss your computer to the nearest computer nerd you can find.

Most nerds will respect the fact that you tried so hard to make it work by yourself.

If you're choosing the easiest installation method — installing OS/2 Warp Version 3 and letting it coexist with the copy of Windows already living on your hard drive — dig out your Windows installation disks. OS/2 will ask for them, even though Windows is already installed.

1. **Back up the important files on your computer.**

   This step is the most important of all: Make sure that you've copied all the important information from your hard drive to floppy disks. Installing an operating system isn't like installing a simple computer program. The difference between the two installations is like the difference between merely changing a tire and replacing a car's entire chassis. If you're installing the Boot Manager, in fact, OS/2 will probably wipe the hard drive clean before it installs itself.

   A great deal can go wrong when you install OS/2; unfriendly terms leap out from behind trees and bite your ankles. The only way you can save yourself is by having important data saved to floppy disks.

   If you're the cautious sort, you can make a *boot disk,* as described in the nearby sidebar, "Make a boot disk if you're the cautious type." It can help bail you out if things go haywire. If you're foolhardy or impatient or if you already have a boot disk, hop along to Step 2.

2. **Boot the OS/2 Warp Installation Diskette.**

   Find the OS/2 Warp disk labeled Installation Diskette and push it into drive A. You don't want the disk labeled Diskette 1 — you want the one that specifically says *Installation Diskette.*

   When the disk is in drive A, exit from any programs you may be running on the screen. Then push your computer's Reset button. The computer churns and thrashes as it reads the information on the floppy disk and tries to decide what to do.

   Some computers today don't come with a Reset button. If your computer isn't blessed with one, do the next best thing: Hold down Ctrl+Alt+Delete simultaneously.

3. **When the program asks, remove the Installation Diskette, replace it with Diskette 1, and press Enter.**

   The poor computer makes more awkward thrashing noises as it reads information from the second disk. Eventually, a menu appears on the screen, as shown in Figure 3-1.

4. **Press Enter to choose the Easy Installation option.**

   Pressing Enter selects the Easy Installation; only grizzled technoids should bother playing with the other, more advanced option. The Easy Installation installs OS/2 by using the Dual Boot method, described earlier in this chapter. If you're installing OS/2 Warp, OS/2 ferrets out the version of

Figure 3-1:
Press Enter
to choose
the Easy
Installation
option; the
Advanced
Installation
option is for
grizzled
nerds who
enjoy
fiddling with
their
computers
for hours.

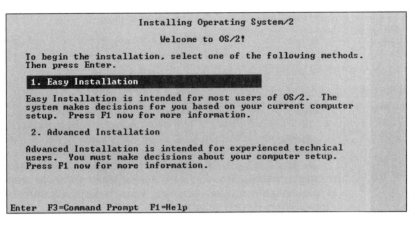

```
                    Installing Operating System/2

                         Welcome to OS/2!

To begin the installation, select one of the following methods.
Then press Enter.

   1. Easy Installation

Easy Installation is intended for most users of OS/2.  The
system makes decisions for you based on your current computer
setup.  Press F1 now for more information.

   2. Advanced Installation

Advanced Installation is intended for experienced technical
users.  You must make decisions about your computer setup.
Press F1 now for more information.


Enter   F3=Command Prompt   F1=Help
```

Windows on your hard drive and uses it to run Windows programs. If you're installing the OS/2 Warp "full pack," OS/2 uses its own, built-in version of Windows to run your Windows programs.

5. **Insert Diskettes 2 through 6 as OS/2 asks for them, pressing Enter after inserting each new disk. Or, if you're installing OS/2 from a CD, insert the CD when OS/2 asks for it.**

Remove the first floppy disk before inserting the second disk. They always fit better that way.

Throughout the installation procedure, OS/2 gives you chores to perform, such as "Insert Diskette 3 in Drive A." If you accidentally insert Diskette 4 by mistake, it's no big deal. OS/2 always checks to make sure that you've stuck in the correct disk. If it's the wrong one, OS/2 simply beeps. That's it. Nothing explodes. OS/2 doesn't remember the mishap. Just put the correct disk in, and kindly, old OS/2 resumes installing itself.

If you're installing from a compact disc, OS/2 begins copying files from the CD.

One last thing: Diskette 6 looks an awful lot like Diskette 9. If OS/2 doesn't like your Diskette 6, make sure that you're not feeding your computer Diskette 9 by mistake.

6. **When the program asks, reinsert the Installation Diskette, followed by Diskette 1. Finally, when OS/2 asks, remove Diskette 1 and press Enter.**

No, you're not stuck in some endless loop. OS/2 is just playing catch-up, grabbing off those two disks some stuff it missed during the first pass.

After OS/2 has copied its last bit of information from Diskette 1 — and you press Enter — OS/2 reboots your computer and you have your first taste of your computer's new operating system.

7. Verify that OS/2 correctly identified the parts of your computer, and then choose your printer and click OK.

As it installs itself, OS/2 takes a guess at the parts living inside your computer and then displays its guesses on the System Configuration screen, as shown in Figure 3-2. The screen lists such things as your brand of monitor, the country settings for your keyboard, your type of CD-ROM drive and sound card, and other things you don't really care about, as long as they work.

For the most part, the choices OS/2 comes up with will all work, but there's one big exception: OS/2 can't figure out what brand of printer is sitting on the end of your printer cable. So if you have a printer, click the Printer icon and stand back as a huge menu fills the screen (see Figure 3-3).

Press the up or down arrow to choose your printer from the list; when your particular printer's name is *highlighted* — covered with a dark bar — click the OK button.

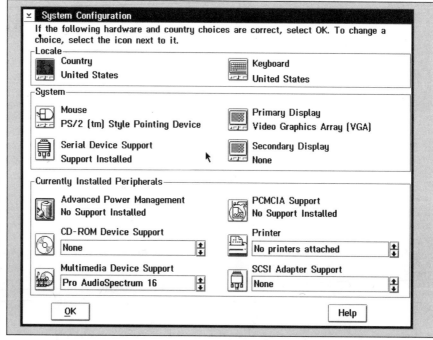

Figure 3-2: OS/2 takes a guess at the parts inside your computer and displays them on this screen.

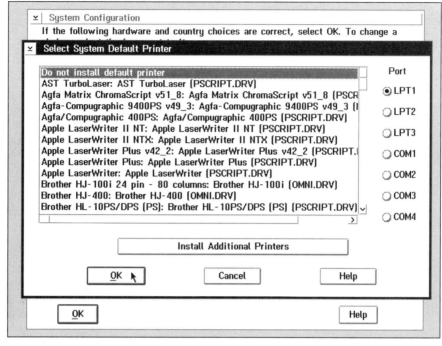

Figure 3-3:
Press the up
or down
arrow to
choose your
printer from
the list.

If you know for a fact that you have a *serial* printer, you have to choose among the COM1, COM2, COM3, and COM4 buttons along the right side of the menu. If you're not sure which type of printer you have, leave the LPT1 button selected. All but the most eccentric printers use the LPT1 setting.

Whenever OS/2 Warp presents you with an excruciatingly long list of names in a menu, fight back with the keyboard. To quickly move to the names of printers beginning with the letter *w,* for example, press the letter *w* on the keyboard. Presto! OS/2 quickly jumps to the Wang LCS15 FontPlus printer on the menu.

If OS/2 Warp didn't guess some of your computer's other parts correctly — the video card, for example — click that part's icon and choose the right part from the list, just like you did when you changed the printer.

Don't assume that OS/2 automatically installs your CD-ROM drive after you've highlighted the drive's name on the equipment list. No, if it's a *SCSI* CD-ROM drive, you also have to highlight the name of the SCSI adapter controlling the CD-ROM drive. For example, I had to highlight my Toshiba 3401 CD-ROM drive *and* the Future Domain 850 SCSI adapter before OS/2 would recognize the CD-ROM drive.

Finally, don't worry too much about choosing the wrong thing. If you've goofed up a setting, OS/2 lets you go back and fix it without having to reinsert all 35 disks. (Thank goodness, because OS/2 usually makes a few wrong guesses.)

8. **Insert Diskettes 7 through 13 as OS/2 asks for them, and press Enter after inserting each one.**

   After you've approved of OS/2's settings in step 7 — and clicked the OK button — OS/2 starts telling you to insert Diskettes 7 through 13. But if OS/ 2 skips a disk, don't fret. OS/2 might just be bypassing disks that don't contain stuff for your particular brand of computer.

9. **When OS/2 asks, insert the Printer Driver disks.**

   Just when you thought that you were done, OS/2 begins asking for a whole new set of disks. Luckily, OS/2 doesn't take long to grab its required printer goodies from its set of printer disks.

10. **Install your video card's special utility, if it has one. Otherwise, press Enter.**

    Huh? What's a "special utility"? Well, some video cards come with special utility programs that let them squirt lots of colors in high resolutions onto fancy monitors. These programs are different from video *drivers;* they're actual stand-alone programs. If your video card came with (or needs) one of these special programs, the disk would have come in the box with the computer or video card.

    Did your computer or card come with a special utility? Then find the floppy disk and click the Install Using Display Adapter Utility Program option.

    If you don't know whether your video card uses one of these programs — or you're sure that it *didn't* come with one — just press Enter or click the OK button. OS/2 lets you come back to this spot later if everything looks weird on the screen.

11. **When OS/2 asks, insert the requested Display Driver disks and press Enter.**

    OS/2 copies the files it thinks that it needs in order to work correctly with your computer's video card and monitor. It might ask for several of the four Display Driver disks before finishing up.

12. **If OS/2 Warp asks, insert your Windows disks.**

    Unlike OS/2 Version 2.1, OS/2 Warp Version 3.0 doesn't come with a copy of Windows built-in. Instead, it grabs the copy of Windows that's already living on your computer's hard drive.

    But here's the weird part: It also wants to grab some Windows files off your original Microsoft Windows disks. If you read the boring before-you-begin stuff at the beginning of this chapter, you already grabbed your Windows disks off your shelf. If you didn't read it, start searching for those Windows disks.

If your copy of Windows came on a CD, OS/2 grabs the files from there; put the CD in your CD-ROM drive and type the letter of your CD-ROM drive in the box on the screen. Otherwise, simply insert your Windows disks in your floppy drive in the strange order in which OS/2 asks for them. (And don't be surprised if it asks to see several of them twice.)

13. **Finally, when OS/2 says that it's finished installing itself, remove the remaining disk from the drive and click the OK button. Then, when you're instructed, reboot your computer.**

Your computer's hard disk whirs as OS/2 carefully records all its configuration details, and then it leaves a message on the screen saying that it's safe to turn off your computer or restart your computer by pressing Ctrl+Alt+Del.

If you're itching to start playing with OS/2, simultaneously hold down your Ctrl, Alt, and Del keys. Your screen darkens, and your computer reboots, coming back to life with OS/2 on the screen.

Or, if the installation experience has left you exhausted, turn off your computer and take a 24-hour breather.

Multimedia device settings malarkey

Multimedia devices are gizmos that turn your computer into an expensive TV set: sound cards, video-capture cards — even TV-set cards. These cards come with different settings you can change to keep them from arguing with each other. OS/2 installs these multimedia devices with their default settings — the same settings they had when they came out of the box.

If OS/2 finds a multimedia device in your computer, it tosses a Multimedia Device Settings box in your face. If you haven't changed any settings on your multimedia cards, simply click the box's OK button.

If you have changed any of these settings — complicated things such as interrupt levels, port addresses, and DMAs — you have to tell OS/2 about it by clicking the box's Selections button and telling OS/2 which interrupts, addresses, and DMAs you've chosen.

If you choose the wrong one, it's no big deal. The device doesn't work, of course, but OS/2 lets you return to this screen to try a different setting later down the road.

Multimedia device settings are complicated enough to fill an entire book — and they have: Check out one of my other books, *Multimedia & CD-ROMs For Dummies,* for more information about IRQs and DMAs.

You might be wise to take a breather. OS/2 often screws up when it's guessing your computer's exact components, so it generalizes: It comes to the screen displaying only 16 colors, for example, when your computer's capable of displaying 16 million colors. Or it might "forget" to install sound. Be prepared to do a little fine-tuning when OS/2 wakes back up after it's first installed.

Shutting Down OS/2

It probably took all day to install OS/2, so here's how to shut the thing down, turn off the computer, and do something a little more emotionally rewarding, such as tossing raisins at sparrows. Don't just turn off your computer. OS/2 doesn't like that. Instead, you have to warn OS/2 to brace itself for the shutdown.

1. **Look at all the objects, folders, and windows on the desktop. Now ignore them. You want to find an area in the background that's *not* covered up. Find a bare spot? Click it with the right mouse button.**

   A menu appears.

2. **Click the Shut down option with the left mouse button, and click the OK button when OS/2 asks whether you really want to close everything down.**

   OS/2 tells you to wait a few moments while it gets ready. Finally, it sends a message saying that it's OK to turn off your computer.

Always use the Shut down command before turning off your computer or rebooting. Interrupting OS/2 without warning can make some of your information go poof!

✔ You don't have to use the Shut down command unless you're turning off the computer or rebooting it because OS/2 told you to. If you keep your computer turned on 24 hours a day, you probably won't have to use the Shut down command.

✔ Before OS/2 shuts down, it checks to see whether you've forgotten to save any work in progress. You get a last chance to save your work before OS/2 starts to slumber.

✔ If you're using Dual Boot, switching to DOS is pretty close to shutting down OS/2. Make sure that you've saved everything before using Dual Boot to move back to DOS. OS/2 doesn't double-check to make sure that everything's been saved, and you can lose some important stuff.

Chapter 4
What *Are* All Those Little Pictures?

. . . .

In This Chapter

▶ The tutorial

▶ Your new electronic desktop

▶ Information

▶ OS/2 System

▶ Templates

▶ Printer

▶ Launch Pad

▶ DOS programs

▶ Windows programs

▶ Win-OS/2 groups

▶ Multimedia

▶ Just tell me how to start the card game (or any other program)

. . . .

*O*S/2 tosses little picture buttons in your face from the very beginning. The first part of the picture-button concept is fairly simple: To push a button, you point at the little picture with the mouse pointer and double-click it. Voilà! The button is pushed.

The hard part is figuring out just what those little picture buttons are supposed to do: The Shredder looks (and sounds) as though it will give you a Michael Jackson nose if you get too close. And sure, the Information object looks like a bookshelf, but what's the Template thing all about?

This chapter is a lightning-fast guide to what OS/2 dishes out when you first install it.

What's the Tutorial?

When OS/2 Warp first flies onto your monitor, it leaves a funny-looking poster on the screen, as shown in Figure 4-1.

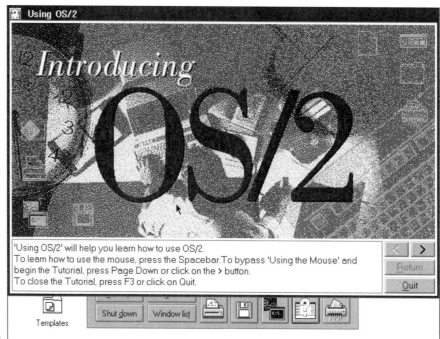

Figure 4-1:
OS/2 Warp's tutorial provides a decent introduction to the odd OS/2 Land of objects and applications.

If you've never played with OS/2, by all means give the tutorial a whirl. The tutorial might overwhelm you with information, but its little buttons let you skip over the boring stuff pretty easily. If you're accustomed to an Atari, Mac, or Amiga, you won't learn much. But if you're used to DOS, you may find all this *object* stuff a little scary. (It's much different from Windows, too, if you're driving in from that direction.)

- ✔ Don't know how to use a mouse? Then push the spacebar. The tutorial gallops into an explanation of clicking and double-clicking concepts. If you've used a mouse, click the button with the > symbol on it; that starts the *real* tutorial.

- ✔ If you're coming into OS/2 Land from Windows, click the <u>W</u>indows button in the bottom-left corner of the tutorial. OS/2 tosses a Windows tidbit at you, usually the Windows equivalent of what the OS/2 tutorial is demonstrating.

✔ Used OS/2 before? Then click the Expert button in the tutorial's bottom-left corner. It gives you a few advanced Warp tips to compare with older versions of OS/2.

✔ Click the Practice button, and OS/2 sets up a little area for you in which to practice the skill the tutorial has just explained. (That way, you can practice on fake stuff — not on your real checkbook files.)

Your New Electronic Desktop

OS/2 confused me at first, until I got a handle on the concept: Believe it or not, working with OS/2 is similar to working on a tiny desktop where you pick things up with salad tongs. Then you drop those things on top of other things in order to get your work done.

You see, OS/2 turns a computer into a tiny electronic *desktop*. Desktop accessories, such as reports, folders, printers, and whatnot, are represented by pictures known as *objects*.

In real life, you pick up some record-club junk mail from your desk and drop it in the wastebasket. On OS/2's desktop, you pick up the junk mail object and drop it on the *Shredder* object (a fancy, computer-geek name for trash can). In either case, you dispose of the junk mail.

Rather than choose salad tongs, computer designers chose a mouse. When you slide the mouse around on the desk, you slide an arrow around on the screen. When you point at something with the arrow and hold down the mouse's right button, you *grab* that item. After you grab it, you can drag it to someplace else on the desktop and drop it.

Because everybody is familiar with desktops, IBM figured that everybody would be immediately familiar with OS/2. And unless you start looking for a pencil sharpener, the concept works. Some people, in fact, say that OS/2's pretty pictures make computers easier to use.

Figure 4-2 shows how the desktop looks immediately after you install OS/2 and finish using the tutorial. (The desktop will look different after you start playing with OS/2, however, and begin moving things around.)

✔ IBM arranged the objects on the screen so that they look pretty when you first look at OS/2. They're not arranged very practically, however. You can find ways to tweak OS/2's desktop in Chapter 9 and in Chapter 21.

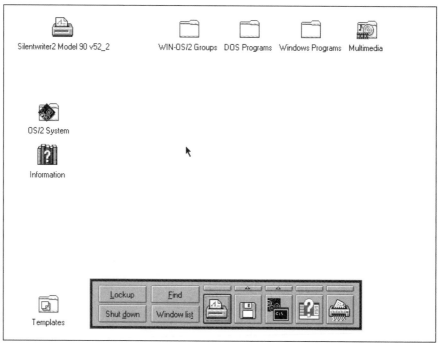

Figure 4-2:
OS/2's
desktop
looks like
this
immediately
after you've
installed
OS/2 and
finished the
tutorial.

✔ Windows calls its little pictures *icons,* but IBM calls the pictures in OS/2 *objects.* For more information about pictures, icons, and objects, flip to Chapter 5.

✔ An important part of an object is its title. The title for the laser printer object, for example, shown in the upper-left corner of Figure 4-2, specifically identifies the laser printer by its more scientific name, Silentwriter2 Model 90 v52_2.

✔ To change any object's title, click it while you hold down Alt. Edit the title by using the Backspace, Delete, or arrow keys and type new letters. If an exceptionally long title bumps into other titles on the desktop, break the title into two lines by moving the cursor to the title's middle and pressing Enter. Done editing the title? Then click anywhere on the desktop away from the object. The new title appears immediately. Figure 4-3 shows how to simplify the printer object's name to simply Printer.

What Do Those Little Information Books Mean?

Appearances can be deceiving in OS/2. For example, OS/2 lets you store programs and files in little *folders* on the screen. Yet the folders don't always look like folders. For example, the Information object — those books on the shelf — represent a folder, just like the other more realistic-looking folders on the screen. The Information object isn't a program, even though its icon might make it look like one. Nevertheless, you play with folders and programs in the same way: You double-click them.

Information

When you double-click the Information object, it opens up into a window on the screen, as shown in Figure 4-4.

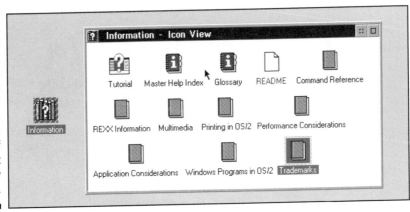

Double-clicking the Information object opens its folder, so to speak, so that you can see what's inside. Here you find OS/2's Tutorial program, in case you blew it off when you first installed OS/2. You also find an OS/2 Glossary for looking up funny OS/2 words, such as DBCS.

- To make an OS/2 object do something — to make a folder open up, for example, or start a program — double-click it with your left mouse button.

- The *Command Reference* and *REXX information*, both found in the Information folder, are designed primarily for computer nerds. These files provide help with OS/2's REXX programming language and command-line interface. They're about as much fun as drinking Coke with ChapStick-coated lips. (The Trademarks object is pretty boring too.)

- Some of the more helpful stuff lives in the little blue book objects titled Multimedia, Performance Considerations, Application Considerations, and Windows Programs in OS/2.

- When OS/2 tosses something really confusing in your face, double-click the Master Help Index; a helpful guidebook appears. To jump quickly to the subject you want to know more about, type that subject's first letter — the Master Help Index jumps to that page. Press P, for example, for subjects beginning with *p,* such as palettes and parameters. Or, if you're a mouse person, click the little letter tabs along the notebook's right edge. Or simply press PgUp and PgDn to flip notebook pages.

- You find the word *or* a lot in OS/2 because OS/2 offers you a plethora of ways to do a single task. Some people say that that's incredibly convenient. Others say that it's incredibly complicated. The key here is that you don't have to remember all the possible ways to do something. Just find one way that works for you and ignore the rest.

- Detailed help on OS/2's Help system is a few page flips away, in Chapter 17.

- The Master Help Index is only a portion of OS/2's complete Help system. Pressing the F1 function key, for example, brings up helpful information at any time. No need to mess with objects or clicking.

What's the OS/2 System Folder For?

The main guts of OS/2 hang out in the OS/2 System Folder. The OS/2 System object is a folder stamped with the OS/2 logo:

OS/2 System

When you double-click the OS/2 System object, the folder opens to reveal its contents: more folders, as you can see in Figure 4-5.

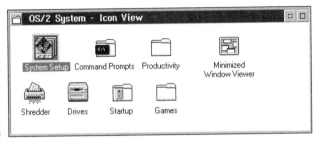

Figure 4-5:
Opening the OS/2 System folder brings yet another collection of folders.

Inside the OS/2 folder, you find most of the hard-core tools for OS/2. You come here to start Windows, start a DOS session, play games, change screen colors, copy files, and perform a bundle of other chores. The following folders are contained in the OS/2 System folder:

Productivity: OS/2 comes with a bunch of built-in programs, and they live in here: two text editors, an icon editor, a file finder, clipboard viewer, and a few others. Double-click this folder to see the programs IBM tossed in for free. They're covered in Chapter 11. Don't confuse these programs with the OS/2 Warp BonusPak, however; the BonusPak is a separate group of programs, and it's covered in Chapter 12.

Games: Surprisingly enough, for a bunch of dark-suited cigar chompers, the IBM bigwigs tossed in a decent assortment of games. If you like Solitaire in Windows, you'll feel at home with Klondike. OS/2's chess game offers the Latvian Gambit and, get this, network support. You can play against your coworkers in a window at the bottom of your screen! Finally, the Mahjongg game is a finely crafted time-waster. Flip to Chapter 11 for the rundown on OS/2 entertainment.

Command Prompts: Double-click over here if you tire of OS/2's little objects. Inside this folder, you find ways to start sessions in Windows or DOS. You can run a DOS program in a window if you like. The DOS command line (that C : \> thing) is here also. Or, if you're wearing a thick-enough flak jacket, you can head for an OS/2 command line. You can find this horrific command line stuff described in Chapter 13.

System Setup: Most of the nerdy stuff lives in this folder. The programs enable you to customize the way OS/2 looks and works. You can change its screen colors; switch the mouse buttons from right-handed to left-handed; change to a different country's currency symbols if you and your computer have moved; and perform other _under-the-hood_ operations. These messy chores are documented in Chapter 9. Bring some Handi-Wipes.

Startup: This folder is empty now, but it won't be empty after you figure out why it's there. The Startup folder is a launching pad for programs you want to run automatically when OS/2 starts up. I like a clock in the corner of my screen, for example, so I dragged the System Clock object from the System Setup folder to the Startup folder. Now the clock is waiting for me whenever I start OS/2. (Actually, I put a *shadow* of the System Clock object in the Startup folder. These mysterious shadows are covered in Chapter 5 and Chapter 6.

Drives: DOS and Windows users will feel relatively at ease with the Drives object. This folder brings up an object for each of your floppy and hard disk drives. Double-click a drive object to see the files on that drive. For more disk drive and file stuff, see Chapter 8.

Shredder: The Shredder provides a fancy way to delete something. Just drag the offending object over to the Shredder and leggo. The Shredder asks whether you're sure that you want to delete the object. Click the Delete button if you're sure. If you're not sure, click the "Oh my gosh, what could I have been thinking?!" button, which is also known as *Cancel*. The Shredder also lives on OS/2's Launch Pad, discussed later in this chapter. (In fact, the Launch Pad is a much easier way to reach the Shredder.)

Minimized Window Viewer: In OS/2, programs run in little boxes or windows anywhere on the desktop. By clicking in special places, you can maximize the windows (make them take up the entire screen) or minimize them (turn them into little icons). In Windows, icons line up along the bottom of the screen. In OS/2, however, minimized icons disappear. Click in this folder, and you see all your currently minimized icons waiting for you.

What's This Templates Stuff?

The Templates concept takes a little getting used to, especially if you're coming from the DOS world. The Templates object looks like this little folder:

Templates

The Templates folder contains a bunch of objects, including a program, a data file, an object file, and even such esoteric stuff as a mouse pointer object (as shown in Figure 4-6). When you need a specific object, you copy the template for that object and then customize it to meet your needs. This process sounds pretty obtuse, so here's an example.

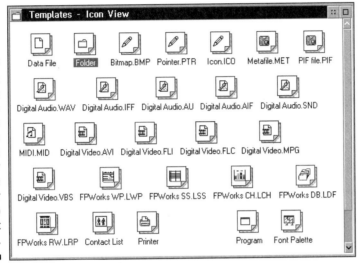

Figure 4-6: Templates are ready-made forms you can grab from the folder and stick on your desktop to represent new items.

To put a new folder on the desktop, double-click the Templates object so that the folder opens, as shown in Figure 4-6. Then drag a template marked *Folder* over to the desktop and let go. That's it; a new folder sits on the desktop, ready for you to fill with information.

Want to put a program in the new folder? Drag the Program template over to the new folder and leggo. The Program object opens to its settings page where you type the name of the program you want that object to represent.

Want to put a letter in the new folder? Drag a Data File template over to the new folder and leggo. Double-click the new Data File object, and a word processor appears, ready to help with the letter.

✔ Templates may be one of the most difficult areas of OS/2's desktop to grasp. Sure, the folder and program objects are relatively easy enough to grasp, but what's the Metafile for? Or the Scheme *palette?* Luckily, Templates are browbeaten in Chapter 5.

✔ You don't have to bother with templates if you don't want to. You can bypass them quickly and simply through an object's pop-up menus.

Printing with the Printer Object

Printing something in OS/2 is fairly easy, as long as the printer is turned on and plugged in. When you're done fiddling with an object — writing a letter or making a report — just drag the object over to the Printer object and leggo.

NEC Silentwriter2 Model 90

That's it. Shazzam! The printout appears in the real printer.

- ✔ Actually, the Printer object is more for image than for anything else. To print a file or document, just click its object with the right mouse button. Then press P or click <u>P</u>rint. That does the same thing as dragging it to the little Printer object.

- ✔ The Printer object comes in handy, however, when you want to change the printer's settings. Click the Printer object with the right mouse button and choose <u>S</u>ettings. From there, you can make the printer print in landscape mode, for example, or print on both sides of the paper (if you have one of those expensive printers). Check out Chapter 6 for more printing details.

- ✔ If you've forgotten how many things you've sent to the printer, double-click the Printer object. A Job Icon View box appears, listing the files waiting in line to be printed as soon as the first job finishes up. (This is known as a *queue,* by the way.)

- ✔ In some OS/2 programs, you print by selecting Print from a menu. In others, you save your work in object form and drag that object to the Printer.

The New Launch Pad

OS/2 Warp added a new goody from earlier versions of OS/2: the Launch Pad. As shown in Figure 4-7, the Launch Pad is a convenient collection of the most often used OS/2 goodies, all ready for action. All the Launch Pad's little programs can be found elsewhere, scattered throughout OS/2's collection of folders.

The Launch Pad not only brings them all together but also lets you arrange them the way you like. You can customize the Launch Pad to contain anything you want.

Figure 4-7:
The Launch
Pad brings
your most
frequently
used tools
together in
one handy
location.

When the Launch Pad is first installed, it consists of these buttons (marketing-minded Warp specialists refer to them as action buttons) and icons:

Lockup button: Want to protect your screen from prying eyes while you hit the water cooler? Click here to lock up your screen and keyboard. It unlocks only after you type your special password. (If you forget your password when you return, head for Chapter 19.

Shut down button: When you're finished using OS/2 and want to turn off your computer, don't! Instead, click the Shut down button first. OS/2 gracefully shuts itself down, saving all the important stuff, and then tells you when it's appropriate to flip your computer's Off switch.

Find button: Lost an object? (Or a file or favorite icon or program?) Click this button, type the name, and OS/2 searches for it by name. (Chapter 18 covers the Find command in more detail.)

Windows list button: Click here to see a list of every window that is open on your desktop.

Printer icon: Yep, this one does the same thing as the printer icon sitting in the upper-left corner of your screen. Drag something here, and OS/2 sends it to your printer.

Floppy disk icon: Click here, and OS/2 brings up a window showing the contents of the floppy in drive A.

Prompt icon: If you're ready to tackle the OS/2 command line — that [C:\] thing — click here.

Question Mark icon: Missed out on OS/2's detailed tutorial? Then click here, and OS/2 brings it back to the screen.

Shredder icon: Drag and drop any unwanted objects to the Shredder. Buzzzzzz. Piffle. Spurt. OS/2's Shredder grinds it to bits and deletes the object for good. (See Chapter 13 for undeleting any mistakenly shredded objects.)

✔ Never "dragged and dropped" anything? Point at the object and hold down your right mouse button. Then, without lifting the mouse button, point at the place where you want to drop the object — the Shredder, in this case. OS/2 "drops" the object onto the Shredder.

✔ The Launch Pad isn't as frivolous as it looks because of two tricks. First, it has secret drawers. See the little arrow above the floppy disk icon? Click it and yet another icon pops up: the disk drive. By clicking the little arrow to open the drawer, you can quickly access your hard drive.

✔ Best yet, the Launch Pad can be customized. Want to add the Mahjongg game to the Launch Pad? Then drag and drop it there. As you drag the Mahjongg icon over the Launch Pad, little black lines appear between the Launch Pad's existing icons or around the drawer arrows. When a line appears where you want the Mahjongg icon to appear, let go of your mouse button to drop the icon. OS/2 modifies the Launch Pad, and your icon appears where you dropped it.

✔ Want to add an icon to one of the ladders? Then click the little ladder arrow so that it opens. Then drag the icon to the ladder, dropping it when the little black line appears where you want the icon to live.

✔ To customize the Launch Pad even more — change colors, make it vertical rather than horizontal, and other neat tricks — click the right mouse button while pointing to an area of the Launch Pad not covered with buttons or icons. A little menu appears; click Settings, and OS/2 will offer you two pages of customizations.

DOS Programs, Windows Programs, and Win-OS/2 Groups

When OS/2 installs itself, it's kind enough to root through your hard drive, searching for any DOS or Windows programs. If it finds any it recognizes, it puts little buttons — objects — for them in special folders on the desktop.

You find your DOS programs in your DOS Programs folder, and the Windows programs in the Windows Programs folder.

And the Win-OS/2 Groups folder? That contains any Program Manager groups it found in your Windows program — you know, like the Accessories group that has Windows Paintbrush, Cardfile, Calculator, and other Windows programs.

✔ To start any of those programs, double-click the folder. The folder opens, showing its contents. See the program you want? Double-click its icon, and OS/2 will start running it.

✔ OS/2 doesn't grab all your DOS programs and put them in the DOS Programs folder. It grabs only the DOS programs that it recognizes. The good news is that, because OS/2 recognized the program, it knows exactly which settings that program needs in order to run right. You're assured that the program will run without too many problems.

✔ The bad news is that OS/2 recognizes only DOS programs that are on its special list. IBM's programmers created a list of popular DOS programs and included it for OS/2 to use as a reference. But if your favorite DOS program isn't on that list, you won't find it in the DOS Programs folder. You have to put it in there yourself, a chore tackled in Chapter 16.

Multimedia

OS/2 can play movies and sounds if your computer's equipped with the latest video and sound cards and if you know the right place to click. The Multimedia folder contains a bunch of sound and video toys, but you have to bother with only the ones listed in this section.

Volume Control: IBM's programmers are pretty proud of their Warp work, and they want everybody to hear about it. And when you first install Warp, everybody *will* hear about it: the volume control is set to Extremely Loud. Double-click the Volume Control object if Warp has suddenly turned your sound card into Pete Townshend's Marshall amp.

Sound: This is a shadow — a special copy — of the Sound object in the System Setup folder, so they both do the same thing: assign silly sounds to Warp activities. If you want to turn off the little "wooeep" sound that accompanies every open window, for example, head for this object. Or if you simply want to change the "wooeep" sound to a "beeoong" sound, you can do that here as well.

Movies, Sound Bites: These two folders contain packaged sounds and a movie, ready to be played back. Double-click the sound or movie you want to watch, and a box pops up, looking sorta like a tape recorder. Click the big, unmarked Play button; the tunes will begin, and the neighboring children will start to dance.

Digital Video, Digital Audio, Compact Disc: These three programs work the same way; they all play back multimedia, whether it's movies, sounds, or music from an audio CD. Each one uses little buttons that should be familiar to anybody with a VCR: play, fast-forward, rewind, and pause. These programs pop up when you double-click the files in the Movies and Sound Bites folders described in the preceding paragraph.

✔ None of OS/2's programs work any better than Windows' Media Player, although OS/2's players multitask better; the sound doesn't skip around as much when you move from program to program.

✔ OS/2 Warp's BonusPak includes two more multimedia programs: a Multimedia Viewer for seeing and hearing a variety of pictures and sounds, and Video In, a program for creating your own videos by using still pictures. They're both described in Chapter 12.

✔ Don't try to play sounds in Windows and OS/2 at the same time. It not only doesn't work but also results in bizarre error messages or, even worse, the complete lockup of your computer.

Just Tell Me How to Start the Card Game! (or Any Other Program)

Enough of this object stuff! How do you get to the Mahjongg game in OS/2? Luckily, the same steps open *any* program in OS/2:

1. **From the desktop, double-click the OS/2 System object (it has the OS/2 logo on it).**

   The folder opens, bringing more folders to the screen.

2. **Double-click the folder that says Games.**

   The folder opens, bringing several objects to the screen, as shown in Figure 4-8.

3. **Double-click the object titled Mahjongg Solitaire.**

   The Mahjongg game leaps to the screen, ready for action.

Figure 4-8:
Double-clicking on the Games folder displays several objects to choose from.

When you're ready to put away the Mahjongg tiles and return to the way things were, follow these steps:

1. **Double-click the little symbol in the game window's upper-left corner.**

   The Mahjongg game program closes and disappears.

2. **Double-click the little symbol in the Games' folder's upper-left corner.**

   That folder, too, closes and disappears.

3. **Double-click the little symbol in the OS/2 System folder's upper-left corner.**

   That folder, too, closes and disappears.

These steps work when you are navigating through any of the folders on the desktop. Just remember: Double-click the folder to open; double-click in the upper-left corner to close.

If you find yourself playing Mahjongg a lot, you may want to put a "shadow" of the Mahjongg game object on the desktop or Launch Pad for easy access. That's called customizing the desktop. Putting frequently used stuff on the desktop saves you from weaving your way through a trail of folders and then weaving back out of them. You find some customizing tricks in Chapter 9.

Part II
That Workplace Shell Thing

The 5th Wave By Rich Tennant

©RICHTENNANT

"TSK, TSK- ANOTHER FINE EMPLOYEE FALLS VICTIM TO THE SHREDDER OBJECT."

In this part ...

*T*his part of the book will collect the most thumb smudges. It holds instructions for all the knobs and buttons on OS/2's *electronic desktop*. Ah, the miracles of electronics. Just think: No more desk drawers full of bent paper clips and expired lunch-special coupons. No more pencils rolling off the edge and disappearing in the void between the back of the desk and the wall.

You haven't quite reached desktop nirvana, however. Remember how you had to practice for a while before you could stop your first electric pencil sharpener from grinding pencils into nubs? OS/2's electronic desktop requires a little getting used to as well.

In this part, you discover which button to prod, when to prod it, and how hard. You find out how to transfer the hand motion of opening and closing drawers into the electronic motion of opening and closing folders. You figure out how to open and shut those windows that pop up on your screen.

Finally, you figure out how to retrieve all those electronic folders when they disappear in the void beneath the piles of open windows on your desktop.

Chapter 5

What's All This Object Stuff?

*E*veryone is accustomed to seeing objects on their desktop: staplers, balled-up pieces of paper, trade-show coffee cups, and boring computer software reference manuals.

OS/2 tries to mimic most of the same desktop experience. The items on your new OS/2 electronic desktop aren't just *objects,* however: They're objects with special *computer nerd* significance. OS/2 considers the printer to be an object. So are those little folder things on the screen. So is the angry letter you wrote to the magazine subscription department last week.

Granted, the term *object* doesn't sound very new or exciting. The term is dreadfully boring, in fact, like cottage cheese or the Weather Channel.

But when you start playing with OS/2, you realize that objects aren't so bad. They can be kind of fun, actually. Just don't let your friends know that your latest reading has been a chapter called "What's All This Object Stuff?," and things will turn out all right.

What Are Those Little Pictures?

See all those little pictures on the OS/2 screen? Those little pictures are called *icons*. Programmers decorate their on-screen push buttons with icons to make it easier for you to figure out what the buttons are supposed to do. This icon of a notepad, for example, stands for an OS/2 program you can use to take notes:

Enhanced Editor

 Icons reached legendary status in Microsoft Windows. The little pictures were so popular, in fact, that Microsoft spent wads of money to add dozens of cute, new icons to the latest version of Windows. Windows users spend hours flipping through pages of icons until they find the one that's just right.

In OS/2 you can while away even more hours: It comes with an Icon Editor program. By calling up the Icon Editor, you can draw mustaches on OS/2's prepackaged icons or create your own icons from scratch. (Fun stuff — who needs serious computer work anymore?) The following icon is an example of what you can do with the Icon Editor:

Maitre d'
Report

✔ Windows uses icon files that end with the letters ICO, like UVULA.ICO. OS/2 does the same thing. But although the names are the same, the files themselves use slightly different formats: A Windows UVULA.ICO file isn't always compatible with an OS/2 UVULA.ICO file. That would be much too convenient for computer companies to even consider. So, try 'em — if they work, great. But be prepared for some disappointments.

✔ Even though Windows icons don't work as OS/2 icons, they do work as Windows icons in the version of Windows that comes with OS/2; don't throw away any Windows icons you may have collected over the years.

 ✔ To convert Windows icons to OS/2 icons, load up Windows and press Print Screen. The Windows screen is copied to the Clipboard. Paste that image into Windows Paintbrush and use the Cut or Copy tool to snip out the icon from the image. When the icon is on the Clipboard, call up OS/2's Icon Editor program and use the Paste command. It's a lot of work for a little icon, but, hey, it beats *real* work. For more Clipboard tips, head for Chapter 10. (And if the tip isn't working, you probably will have to make your Clipboard *public* — also described in Chapter 10.)

✔ To change an offensive (or just plain boring) icon in OS/2, click it with the right mouse button. A menu pops up. Click the arrow next to Open and choose Settings from the next menu. When the little pop-up notebook appears, click the General tab at the bottom right. Finally, click the Edit button. The Icon Editor pops up with the icon you want to edit inside, ready for you to change it around. You can find a description of the Icon Editor in Chapter 11 (in addition to tips for getting the old icon back if you mess up something fierce).

✔ To change an icon's title, hold down Alt and click the icon. If the title is too long, press Enter near the title's middle to break it into two lines. Done editing? Then click the desktop, away from the little title box, and OS/2 saves the changes.

✔ When you double-click an icon and its program, folder, or data file hops onto the screen, OS/2 draws little, diagonal lines, or *hash marks,* across the icon. The hash marks remind you that the icon is already open on the desktop somewhere so that you don't try to open it again. You can tell from the hash marks on the following icon that the Notepad program is open somewhere on the desktop:

Enhanced Editor

✔ When you double-click a program's icon in the Windows Program Manager, that program comes to the screen. But if you double-click that same icon again, Windows loads the same program again. You have two copies of the program running at one time, which often leads to confusion.

OS/2 doesn't work that way. If you double-click an object that is already open, OS/2 brings that open object to the top of the screen, as if to say, "Here it is! You don't have to open another one!" If you want a second copy of the program, however, head for the Window page under the object's Settings option. There you choose the Create New Window option. Whew! (Or you can turn to Chapter 9 for more details about customizing your desktop.)

✔ If you ever switch between OS/2's *video modes,* perhaps switching from VGA to SVGA, prepare for a little confusion: You have to rearrange all the icons on the desktop. Switching to a different resolution changes the size of the desktop, which increases or decreases the spacing between all the icons. You might have to move the icons closer together or farther apart to see them all.

✔ A quick way to arrange icons neatly is through a window's Arrange command. Click inside any disorderly window with the right mouse button and then click Arrange. OS/2 sweeps the icons into neat, orderly rows. Check out Chapter 9 to learn how to change the way OS/2 organizes these rows.

✔ *Icons* are the pictures on top of the little buttons. *Objects* are the things those buttons represent: the printer, the files, the programs, and the folders. Those object guys get their own section, coming up next.

Uh, What's an Object?

Computers can do bunches of things, from balancing your checkbook to fouling up your credit rating for years to come.

Yet OS/2 has narrowed the computing world to a mere four things. It calls each of those four things an *object*. By fiddling with these four types of objects, you boss the computer around. Here's the scoop:

Program object: Double-click a program object to start a program. The program that has been "hot-wired" to that particular icon push button roars into action. (OS/2 refers to computer programs as "applications.")

Data file object: When you write a letter with a program, you're creating the second type of object: a data file. If a file has some sort of data in it, OS/2 dubs it a data file object.

Device object: The computer's hard disk and floppy disks are considered device objects because you can touch them. Device objects represent tangible things. The printer is also a device object, as is the Shredder in the corner of the screen. (The Shredder is not touchable, however, so it's sort of an exception to the rule.)

Folder object: The last type of object listed here serves to keep all the other objects from getting lost in one, big pile. The folder object is just a container — a holding place — for organizing other objects so that they don't get lost.

That's it. By manipulating these four types of objects with the mouse — clicking them or sliding them around on the desktop — you perform all your computing chores under OS/2. These four types of objects all get their own section later in this chapter, so don't feel numb if you don't quite understand it all.

✔ OS/2 chose the admittedly bizarre *object* concept to make computing seem more *real*. You're no longer dealing with mysterious computer code words; you're working with common objects — recognizable office things, like the folders and letters normally found on a desktop.

✔ DOS users once had to remember the names of their programs and where those programs lived on the hard drive. Under OS/2, you can ignore those messy details. You merely grab the program icon from a folder or off the desktop and start working.

✔ OS/2 uses four types of objects, but you can't always distinguish between those four types of objects by simply looking at them. If you're lucky, a folder's icon looks like a folder, making it easy to identify. But OS/2's Information folder doesn't look anything like a folder: It's a collection of books. Yes, this can be confusing until you remember which icons do what.

✔ Immediately after you install OS/2, folders might take a long time to open, and programs might be slow to load. Don't worry; OS/2 eventually speeds up. It just needs some time to stretch itself out. Objects are at their slowest the first time they're used.

Why Does a Program Object Sound So Boring?

Programs are what make a computer do something worthwhile: calculate the mortgage or offer you a stress-relieving game to play immediately after it calculates the mortgage.

To start playing with a program in OS/2, you have to find that program's *program object:* the button that brings it to life. When you find the program object, double-click it. The program connected to that button leaps onto the screen, covering up any other programs that happen to be there. This behavior is natural for program objects.

The following icon represents the program object for OS/2's solitaire card game:

Solitaire - Klondike

✔ Another way to open a program in OS/2 is to click its object once to highlight it and then press Enter. That method takes a little longer, but, hey, it works.

✔ A program object isn't a *program;* it's just that program's *push button.* If you delete a program object, you don't do any major damage. It's just like knocking the third-floor button off an elevator panel. The button is gone, but the third floor is still there.

- ✔ You can find detailed instructions for putting your own programs on the desktop in Chapter 16.

- ✔ If you're a former DOS user, you'll recognize that *program objects* stand for files that end in EXE or COM.

Should I Date a Girl or Data File Object?

The whole point of a computer program is to create something. Some programs create an hour of entertainment; some create hours of frustration. Other programs create something tangible that can be saved, such as a letter or a schedule for upcoming soap operas. These tangible creations are stored in *data files*.

Data file objects perform much like program objects. Just double-click the data file object, and the data file not only hops to the screen but also appears within the program that created it.

The icon for a data file object usually looks like a dog-eared piece of paper, as you can see from the icon for the Fishing Report data file object:

Fishing Report

- ✔ A data file object may look like a piece of paper on the screen, but it can contain just about any kind of computerized information: a corporate report, a picture of the kids, a recording of the neighbor's barking dog, or a video of the trip to Disneyland (if you can afford the latest digital camera toys).

- ✔ Because you create most of your data file objects, you have to think up names for them when you are ready to store them. Here's where it gets tricky: If you're using OS/2's High Performance File System (HPFS), you can name a data file with as many as 256 characters. If you're using the age-old File Allocation Table (FAT) method, you can use no more than eight characters to name your work. This stuff is hammered out in Chapter 8. (If you chose the Easy Install option when you installed OS/2, you're probably using the FAT system.)

Don't know whether your drive is FAT or HPFS? Then click its icon with the right mouse button. (You can find icons for the drives in the Drives folder, which is in the OS/2 System folder.) Click Settings, and click the Details tab. The first line, File System Type, tells you whether the hard drive uses FAT or HPFS. Write that information on the "Cheat Sheet" tear-out card at the front of this book so that you never have to go through those steps again.

Program objects are just buttons that stand for programs. Data file objects, however, stand for the real ball of wax. If you delete a data file object — by dropping it on the Shredder, for example — you delete the actual data file.

Are Folder Objects Legal- or Standard-Size?

When a desk gets too crowded, things start falling off the edges. At that point, people either hire a secretary or buy a filing cabinet. OS/2 takes the filing cabinet route. In fact, that's where the third type of object comes in: a *folder object.* A folder object usually (but not always) looks like a folder:

Folder

Folder objects are less complicated than program objects and data file objects. They're merely containers. When you double-click a folder, a window showing the folder's contents opens on the screen. Folders usually contain a combination of program objects, data file objects, and, to keep things divvied up, even more folder objects.

By nesting folders inside other folders, you can organize your stuff as fastidiously (or as sloppily) as you like. For example, you can just toss everything into a single folder named JUNK. Or you can toss several other organizing folders into that JUNK folder: JUNK TO BE DELETED; JUNK TO FILE AWAY LATER; A FRIEND'S JUNK; and so on. (You can even keep an ELMER'S JUNK folder tucked away in your A FRIEND'S JUNK folder.)

✔ DOS users will recognize folders as *directories.* Folders and directories are really the same thing. And a folder stashed within another folder is a *subdirectory.* If you're not a DOS user, however, just pretend that they're folders. That subdirectory stuff gets kind of complicated after a while anyway.

✔ Folders can be deleted in the same way other objects can be deleted. Either drag them over to the Shredder and let go or click them once with the right mouse button and then click Delete from the menu.

What! My whole desktop is a folder?

That's right — OS/2 considers the desktop work area to be a mammoth folder. It opens when you start OS/2 and spreads across the desktop. It closes only when you shut down OS/2 with the Shut down command.

And because the desktop's a folder, it's really a subdirectory too. If you dare to head for the OS/2 command line and type DIR, you see the subdirectory's name: Desktop. That's the name of the desktop folder.

All those other folders on the desktop are really just subdirectories of the Desktop directory.

✔ If you delete a folder, you also delete everything stored in the folder: program objects, data files, and even other folders. Remove all the valuables from a folder before you delete it.

✔ Folder object icons usually look like a folder, but not always. For example, the Information icon stands for a folder object. When you double-click it, you see all the other objects stored inside.

✔ Take a deep breath because this one is kind of startling: The entire OS/2 desktop — that big, gray screen full of icons and objects — is really just a folder. And when you think about it, it really is just a big container filled with other objects. It's similar to using a fast-food bag as a place mat while you eat in the car: The french-fry objects come out of the fast-food bag folder and sit on top of it for easy access. Same with your desktop: It's a huge open folder, letting you play with everything inside.

Why Do Device Objects Sound So Sneaky?

OS/2 had to make it easy for people to talk to their computer's parts. So OS/2 introduced the *device object* to stand for the parts of a computer that bother to listen to their users. A printer, for example, listens for you to tell it what to print. A disk drive listens for you to tell it what to do with the floppy disk you've stuck in its mouth. OS/2 enables you to talk to these parts — the printer and the disk drive — through their device objects. The icons for the Drive A and Shredder device objects look like this:

Drive A   Shredder

By themselves, device objects don't do much. Their mission is to wait until you drag other objects over to them. To print a data file, for example, you drag that file's object over to the printer and let go. Want to delete that file? Drag it to the Shredder. Copy it to a floppy disk in drive A? Just drag it over to the Drive A object. Load a file into a program? Just drag it over to that program's object and let go.

To drag an object, point at it with the mouse. Then hold down the right mouse button and slide the mouse across the desk. The object drags along as the mouse moves. When you have positioned the object over its destination, let go of the mouse button to *drop* the object.

✔ To see what a device object is currently up to, double-click it. Double-clicking the Printer object, for example, enables you to see all the files currently waiting to be printed (as soon as the printer finishes printing its current file). Double-clicking the Drive A object enables you to see what's stored on a floppy disk in that drive. And when you double-click the Shredder, you can change its icon to something even more fearsome: You can add canines, for example.

✔ Device objects resemble program objects in that they're really just push buttons. If you drag the printer object over to the Shredder and let go, you're not really deleting the printer, no matter how mad at it you may be. You're just deleting the button you use to print things. (To figure out how to put the Printer object back after an accidental deletion, head for Chapter 16.)

What's That Thing That Pops out of an Object's Head?

To fiddle with your VCR's settings, heaven forbid, you usually have to flip down a little plate that hides the knobs. Fiddling with the settings for objects is similar: You have to pop up their secret hidden menu. Just click with the right mouse button the object whose settings you want to change, and its menu shoots out from the top of its head, as shown in Figure 5-1.

Figure 5-1:
Click any
object with
the right
mouse
button to
see the
object's
menu.

Tired of dragging objects to the Shredder? Just pop up an object's menu and click Delete. That does the same thing.

↝ You can copy an object by using the Copy command from its object menu. That's not as easy as dragging it, however. (It's not as much fun, either.)

↝ Head for Chapter 6 if you're rarin' to hear more about an object's menu options and special settings.

Do Shadows Disappear from Laptops in Bright Light?

One thing about the OS/2 desktop looks a little strange: Some of the titles are black, and some are blue. Don't start reaching for the monitor's contrast controls, however. The objects with blue titles are called *shadows,* and they're a sneaky OS/2 trick for spreading objects around. It sounds scary and complicated, but it's pretty simple, actually. Picture this: Creating a shadow of an object is merely creating a push button that can reach out and grab that object.

Suppose that you want to keep your address book handy. Normally, the address book is kept in a single folder. To look up the pizza-delivery guy's number, you have to root through several folders before you see the address book object.

To make the phone number easier to access, you can put a copy of the address book on the desktop. You can find your pepperoni faster, in fact, by putting a copy of the address book in all your folders.

But that can bring some problems: First, if the pizza restaurant changes its phone number, you have to find all the address book objects and update each one individually. What a colossal pain! Also, every time you make a copy of the address book, you take up a little more space on your hard drive.

The solution? Place a shadow of the address book into all the other folders. The shadow looks and feels just like the real address book, but with two big differences:

First, a shadow is just a button linked to the original address book object. It doesn't take up any space on your hard drive. And if you delete the shadow, you delete just a button. The original address book stays tucked away safely on the hard drive.

Second, if you open a shadow and change the file — update the address book with a new phone number, for example — you change the original address book. Not only that, but all the other shadows of that object are updated instantly.

- ✔ You already have several shadows on the desktop. Those objects on the Launch Pad — that island of icons floating near the bottom of your screen — are actually shadows of real objects that live in folders. For example, the original Shredder object lives in the Drives folder (under the System Setup icon).

- ✔ To find any shadow's original object, click it with the right mouse button. Then click the arrow next to Original and choose Locate. The folder containing the original object jumps to the screen. (Give it a shot with Shredder in the Launch Pad, if you don't believe me.)

- ✔ You can create a folder on your desktop called FAVORITE STUFF and stick a shadow of all your favorite objects in it. That way, they're easily accessible, and you don't have to wade through a bunch of folders to get to all of them.

- ✔ When you're ready to create a shadow, hold down Ctrl+Shift while you drag the object. A line appears, showing the link between the original object and the shadow you're creating. Let go of the mouse button to drop the shadow into place.

- ✔ If you delete an object, you also delete any of its shadows. If you delete the original address book from its folder, for example, all the shadows you created of that address book are also deleted.

- ✔ Because shadows are just push buttons, you can delete them whenever you like. The original isn't affected.

A Quick Tour through Templateland

The term *object template* will ring forever in the Worst-Sounding Computer Term hall of fame. The person at IBM who thought it up not only wears a pocket protector but also has a plastic protractor hanging from a belt loop.

But if you can get over your initial aversion to the name, the concept is not that bad. Here's how the OS/2 object template stuff works. You decide to write a letter to Kraft after you see the unsettling words *cellulose powder* listed in the ingredients of their grated Parmesan cheese. You have to create some data, so you're ready for the services of a data file object:

1. **Double-click the Templates folder and drag the data file object any-where on your desktop, as shown in Figure 5-2.**

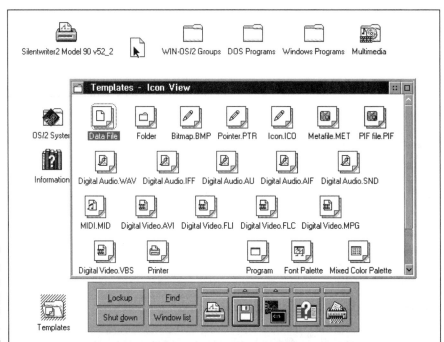

Figure 5-2:
A data file object being dragged to the desktop.

The Templates folder contains a variety of objects — all the objects you'll ever need. Its supply is inexhaustible too. You can peel off as many as you want and drop them on the desktop or into other folders.

You use the OS/2 desktop just like you use a real desktop: You pile stuff on it and work with that stuff.

2. Double-click the data file object you've dragged onto the desktop.

OS/2's System Editor leaps to the screen, ready to process your words as you type the letter, as shown in Figure 5-3. Type the letter asking about the quality level of Kraft's cellulose powder.

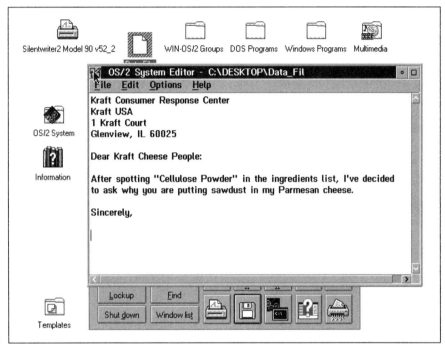

Kraft Consumer Response Center
Kraft USA
1 Kraft Court
Glenview, IL 60025

Dear Kraft Cheese People:

After spotting "Cellulose Powder" in the ingredients list, I've decided to ask why you are putting sawdust in my Parmesan cheese.

Sincerely,

Figure 5-3: Double-click the new data file object and begin typing the letter.

3. When you finish typing the letter, double-click the upper-left corner of the System Editor window to close the program. Click the Save button, click the Type button, and, finally, choose Plain Text. (It is just a letter, you know, so you can ignore the Save As command file option.)

To close any window or program in OS/2, you double-click in its upper-left corner.

Your data file is now saved; you can see it sitting on the desktop. But it's still called *Data File.*

4. Press Alt and click the title.

A box appears, enabling you to change the words.

5. **Press the Delete key to delete the words** *Data File* **and then type** KRAFT LETTER. **Done? Then click any place away from the box, and OS/2 saves the title.**

(Or if your numeric keypad has an Enter key, you can press that to save your new title.)

You've saved your first letter under OS/2.

6. **To print the letter, drag it over to the printer and let go.**

In a moment, the letter will fly out of your printer. Meanwhile, though, your letter looks out of place sitting on the desktop; it would be more organized inside a folder.

7. **Drag a folder from the Templates folder and drop it anywhere on the desktop. Then close the Templates folder; you won't be needing it.**

8. **Change the folder's name to Letters Folder, just like you changed the name of the Data File object to Kraft Letter.**

9. **Next drag the Kraft Letter object over to the Letters Folder and let go, as shown in Figure 5-4. The Kraft Letter disappears. Double-click the Letters Folder, and you see the Kraft Letter sitting neatly inside it.**

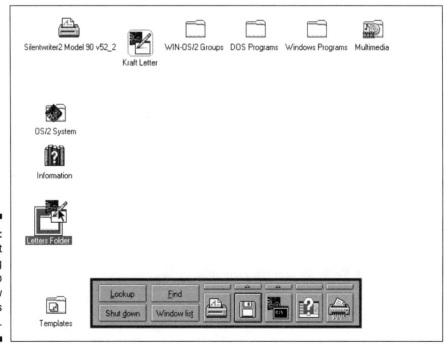

Figure 5-4:
The Kraft Letter being dragged into the new Letters Folder.

That's it! You've written a letter, printed it, and filed it away under OS/2, and all in fewer than ten steps.

✔ Templates sound complicated, but they're really quite simple. Think of them as a stack of form letters for any possible occasion. You just grab the one you need and begin working with it.

✔ Whenever you grab a template, you're grabbing a copy. The original template stays put in the folder.

✔ All the actions just described — things such as dragging or deleting objects — are described in the next chapter.

✔ You can create your own templates. You can create a template for letters that contain your letterhead, for example, and keep it in the Templates folder. Or you can keep it in any other folder, for that matter.

✔ You can find instructions for making a template in Chapter 6 in the section, "How to Adjust an Object's Settings."

Chapter 6

Doing Stuff with Objects

· ·

In This Chapter

▶ Opening a folder or starting a program

▶ Selecting objects or folders

▶ Dragging and dropping

▶ Copying, moving, or making a shadow

▶ Seeing what's on a disk

▶ Printing

▶ Deleting and undeleting

▶ Changing an object's name

▶ Editing an icon

▶ Adjusting an object's settings

· ·

Some people are mechanical whizzes. They can program a VCR not only to record "Saturday Night Live" while they're asleep but also to stop recording it if the show is a rerun.

Other people have a little more trouble, especially when they're figuring out things like OS/2 for the first time. After all, at least the VCR's buttons are called *buttons* — not objects.

This chapter has the information you need to put OS/2 to work immediately. Just skim to the heading for the task you need, read the quick instructions, and force OS/2 to start making things happen. In fact, one guy hooked up OS/2 to his X-10 CP290 Home Control Interface so that he could control lamps and appliances from his computer: Little on-screen slider controls enable him to dim light switches with a mouse.

That guy has his VCR set up not only to skip the reruns but also to begin recording automatically if a cable channel begins broadcasting the one "Gilligan's Island" episode he hasn't taped yet.

Making an Object Do Something

To make an object do something, point at it with the mouse, as shown in Figure 6-1. Then press and release the left mouse button twice in rapid succession. (Highly paid computer linguists have dubbed this action a *double-click*).

Figure 6-1:
To open a
folder or
program,
double-click
its icon.

OS/2 System

✔ If you double-click a folder, it opens, and you can see what's inside.

✔ If you double-click a program, it loads, ready to do your bidding.

✔ If you double-click a device, the printer or Drive A object, for example, you can change its settings or see what task it's working on.

✔ If you double-click a data file, the program you used to create that file loads, bringing the data file to the screen at the same time.

Getting an Object's Attention

To select anything in OS/2, point at it with the mouse. Then press and release the left mouse button. (CompuNerds refer to this computer activity as a *click*.)

✔ Clicking an object is like yelling out in a crowd — OS/2 immediately shifts its attention to that object. When OS/2 pays attention to an object, the object usually becomes *highlighted,* a fancy term meaning that it turns darker than normal. Check out Figure 6-2 to see the difference between an object that has been clicked and one that hasn't been clicked.

✔ If you see an open window or object partially covered by other windows or objects, for example, just click the part you can see. OS/2 shifts its attention to that object, bringing it to the forefront. The window's title bar — that strip across its top — becomes highlighted, telling you that it has OS/2's attention.

✔ You have to select objects when you want to copy or move them — to place them inside different folders, for example, or to copy them to a floppy disk.

Figure 6-2:
You can tell
that the
object on
the left has
been clicked
because it is
highlighted.
The object
on the right
hasn't been
clicked.

Grabbing Bunches of Objects or Folders

Sometimes you want to select two or more objects at the same time. But each time you click the second object, OS/2 highlights that one and ignores the first one you selected. To make OS/2 select several objects at the same time, you can try several tricks.

First click the first object you want, but keep holding down the left mouse button. Next slide the mouse pointer carefully over the screen, pointing at all the objects you're after. As the mouse pointer slides over each new object, that object becomes highlighted along with the others.

As an alternative, you can hold down the Ctrl key while you click all the objects you're after. Each object is highlighted, ready for more action.

The third way to highlight a group of objects is more fun. It's called the *rubber band.* Point at an area adjacent to the objects you're after and hold down the left mouse button. As you move the mouse, an expanding *square* fills the screen. All the objects inside that square are selected. Let go when you've highlighted the ones you want. They are all ready for more action — to be copied to disk, for example, or deleted. Figure 6-3 shows three objects that have been high-lighted by using a *rubber band.*

✔ Despite its cool name, the *rubber band* is always square. Because it doesn't stretch in different directions, the objects you grab have to be adjacent to each other.

✔ If you want to grab a few objects here and there, you're better off with the first method: holding down the left mouse button on the first desired object and then sliding the pointer over all the others.

Figure 6-3:
A rubber band is used to select three objects.

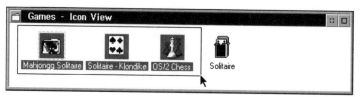

> ✔ If you want to select all the objects in a folder, using the menu may be the fastest way. Click the folder with the right mouse button, and choose S̲elect and then Select a̲ll from the pop-up menu. All the objects in that folder become highlighted.

The *Select a̲ll* shortcut key works the same way in OS/2 as it does in Windows. Hold down Ctrl and press the forward slash key (the / thing that shares the question-mark key). To deselect everything you've selected, hold down Ctrl and press the backslash key (the \ thing that's usually near the Backspace key).

Doing the Drag-and-Drop

OS/2 works much like a cat and a dead mouse: *Drag-and-drop* is an integral part of its life. With OS/2, however, the *mouse* gets to do the dragging.

You drag objects in order to print them, copy them, delete them, or perform a host of other chores. This section tells you how it works.

First select the object or objects you want to move around. (Selecting an object is covered in the two sections immediately preceding this one.)

Then point at the selected object (or objects) with the mouse and hold down the right mouse button. Wherever you move the mouse, those objects follow. You're dragging them around on the screen.

When the object (or objects) hovers over the correct destination (the Shredder, for example), let go of the mouse button. OS/2 handles the rest, performing whatever function is linked to the object's destination.

In Figure 6-4, a bunch of objects are being dragged to the Shredder.

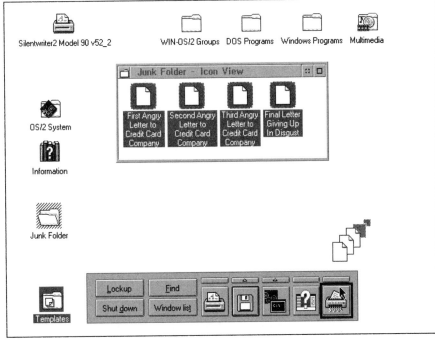

Figure 6-4:
Highlighted files are dragged and dropped on the Shredder to be deleted.

When a *dragged* object is properly positioned over its destination — the Shredder, for example — a little square appears around the destination, as shown in Figure 6-5. That square is the go-ahead signal to drop the object. If your pointer turns into a bar, as shown in Figure 6-6, though, OS/2 is telling you "No, you can't do that." Some objects, like templates, can't be deleted.

Figure 6-5:
The little, square box around the Shredder means that everything is positioned properly. Let go of the mouse button to delete the object.

Figure 6-6:
The little bar symbol over the Drive A shadow means that OS/2 won't let you drop that object there.

Drive A

- Before you can drag and drop, you have to be able to see the thing onto which you want to drop the object. If another folder covers the Shredder, for example, you can't drop anything on it. It's like trying to use the fax machine if Jeff left his jacket draped over it.

- Dragging and dropping is the easiest way to accomplish things in OS/2. It may seem a little weird at first, but it's much easier than what DOS users have had to struggle through for years. Just ask one of 'em.

- You can drag a single object or several objects. OS/2 drags whatever objects you've selected (those highlighted ones).

- Sometimes OS/2 wigs out and refuses to let you drop an object somewhere. For example, you can't drop the Shredder onto the Drive A object. If you try, you see a special "Hey, you can't do that!" symbol, as shown in Figure 6-6.

- If you start to drag an object somewhere and then change your mind, press Esc. Or drop it back on itself. When you see that "Can't drop that here" bar symbol, just ignore it. You cancel the *drag* operation and restore order.

- For more "cat and dead mouse" action, head to Chapter 11 to see the cat that comes with OS/2.

Copying, Moving, and Shadowing

To copy, move, or make a shadow of something, use the drag-and-drop method described in the preceding section. It's quick, easy, and, if you can believe it, kind of fun sometimes. No DOS commands to fiddle with. Just a little finger action with the mouse, and whoosh! Those files start rolling.

For example, Figure 6-7 shows some files being copied from a Desktop folder to the floppy drive in drive A: Just drag the data file objects to the Drive A object, found in the Drives folder (which is in the OS/2 System folder, if you haven't searched for it there yet). Or, to make things easier, you can also drag the files to the floppy drive icon in the Launch Pad.

Unfortunately, you have to remember a few things in order to tell OS/2 whether you're copying or moving:

✔ To move an object from one place to another *on the same drive,* simply drag it there while holding down the right mouse button. No tricks necessary.

✔ To copy an object from one place to another *on the same drive,* hold down Ctrl while you drag it there with the right mouse button.

✔ To move an object from one place to another *on a floppy disk,* hold down Shift while you drag it there.

✔ To copy an object from one place to another *on a floppy disk,* simply drag it there. No special tricks necessary.

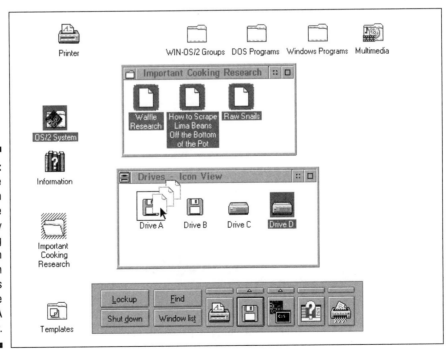

Figure 6-7: To copy the Green Bean Recipes file to a floppy disk, drag the Green Bean Recipes object to the Drive A folder.

✔ To create a shadow of an object, hold down Ctrl+Shift while you drag the object, no matter what drive it's on. Shadows are so cool that they are covered in their own section in Chapter 5.

✔ Yes, this stuff's hard to remember, and these pages are hard to find. That's why it's listed on the handy "Cheat Sheet" tear-out card at the front of this book.

✔ When you are copying or moving something to a floppy disk, OS/2 may take a few moments before it shows the object's icon in the floppy disk's folder. Don't be surprised if you don't see the results of your work immediately.

✔ You can find much more information about floppy disks and disk drives in Chapter 8.

Seeing Stuff on a Disk

The computer stores information in organized chunks called *files*. OS/2 can store great gobs of files on the hard disk or a more modest number of files on a floppy disk.

To prove that files can live on those little, plastic floppy disks, place a disk in drive A and double-click the Drive A icon on the Launch Pad that floats near the bottom of your desktop. A window pops up, showing the disk's contents. The window looks similar to the window in Figure 6-8.

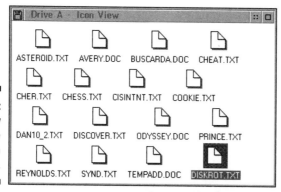

Figure 6-8:
This window shows the files in drive A.

To see what's on the hard drive, head for the Drives folder in the OS/2 System folder. When you double-click the Drives folder, it opens to show you an object for each of your disk drives. In fact, you see the *original* Drive A object. The Drive A object in the Launch Pad is just a *shadow*.

Double-click the Drive C icon to see what's stored on that hard drive. It appears in *Tree view* mode, which looks a little different from the traditional *Icon view*. Disks and disk drives get their own chapter (Chapter 8, if you want to scoot over there right now).

✔ For some reason, a floppy disk's contents don't always show up — especially when a disk contains a great deal of files. To make sure that you're seeing everything, click the right mouse button on a blank area inside the window and choose <u>A</u>rrange from the pop-up menu. Any previously hidden icons make themselves visible.

✔ Need to see what's on drive B? The object for that drive (if you have one) lives in the same place as the object for drive C. It's in the Drives folder, which is found in the OS/2 System folder.

✔ To see information about a file (files are also called *objects*) on any disk drive, click it once with the right mouse button. A menu shoots out of its head. Click <u>S</u>ettings, and an entire *notebook* pops to the screen, filled with information about that file.

Printing Something

To print something, drag it over to the printer icon and leggo. That's it!

✔ You don't have to hold down Ctrl while you drag stuff to the printer. Just a simple drag does the trick.

✔ If the printer isn't turned on, OS/2 displays a weird message on the screen, similar to the one in Figure 6-9. When you see that message, you have to click the <u>A</u>bort button, turn on the printer, and drag the object over to the printer a second time.

Figure 6-9:
OS/2
displays this
weird
message if
you forget to
turn on the
printer.

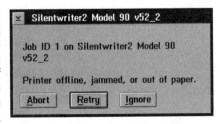

Getting Rid of Stuff

To delete an offensive, out-of-date, or otherwise undesired object, just drag it over to the Shredder icon and let go. The Shredder is that weird icon on the right end of the Launch Pad. (You'll also find the Shredder in the OS/2 System folder, if your Launch Pad is missing.)

> ✔ The Shredder puts a weird box on the screen that doesn't say much, as you can see in Figure 6-10. If you're sure that you want to delete the item, click the Delete button. If you dragged something to the Shredder by mistake, click the Cancel button to keep the Shredder from destroying your handiwork.

Figure 6-10:
Click the
Delete
button in
this box
after you
drag
something
to the
Shredder.

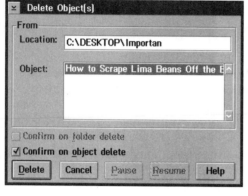

> ✔ If you get tired of seeing that little Delete box, you can tell OS/2 to stop sticking it in your face. Click in the little boxes next to Confirm on folder delete and Confirm on object delete, both seen in Figure 6-10. Then the Shredder simply destroys anything dropped on it — even if you dropped it there accidentally. It even destroys any objects mistakenly left inside shredded folders. Be careful with this one.

> ✔ The OS/2 Shredder isn't like the Trash Can in the Macintosh. The Shredder deletes items immediately. (The Macintosh Trash Can just stores unwanted stuff until you empty it.) Don't drag anything over to the Shredder unless you absolutely don't want it anymore.

> ✔ Anything you drag from your desktop to the Shredder is immediately deleted, except for program objects. If you drag a program object to the Shredder, you get rid of just the icon — the push button. The program file itself remains on the hard drive. No program files are deleted through the Drive folders.

> ✔ A quicker, but less fun, way to delete something is to click it with the right mouse button. Click Delete from the menu, and you see the same little *confirmation box,* just as though you had dragged it to the Shredder. Click Delete to finalize the deletion process and send the object scurrying to never-never land.

If you delete something accidentally, you may be able to undelete it. Move your eyes forward hastily to the next section for details.

Getting Stuff Back from the Shredder

Yes, OS/2 can undelete stuff you've accidentally deleted. Unfortunately, IBM disabled the *undelete* feature, so it doesn't work. I dunno why.

You can undo IBM's handiwork, however. Or, you can find a computer guru to undo IBM's handiwork for you. This process involves some fiddling with a file called CONFIG.SYS, one of your computer's most important files. A single typographical error can mess things up awful fierce. So hand this book to a computer guru and ask her to please fix your "undelete" feature.

If you accidentally delete a file, you can follow these steps to get it back. The following example retrieves the deleted file named I'M NOT A DUMMY.

The sooner you try to undelete a file, the better your chances of successfully snatching it back from the Realm of the Dead.

Undelete drivel

Greetings, Computer Guru. To make OS/2's undelete feature work, you have to load the C:\CONFIG.SYS file into OS/2's System Editor. Then look for the line in the CONFIG.SYS file that begins with the words REM SET DELDIR=C:\DELETE,512. (The part after the equal sign isn't important; it is different on different computers.)

Now remove the letters REM from the front of that line, save the CONFIG.SYS file, shut down OS/2, and reboot the computer. That makes OS/2's undelete feature begin working again. Collect the customary bags of snack cakes and move on.

1. **Double-click the OS/2 System object.**

2. **When the folder opens, double-click the Command Prompts folder.**

3. **When that folder opens, double-click the OS/2 Window object.**

4. **When the little box opens, type** UNDELETE /S **after the [C:\] thing, just as you see in Figure 6-11, and press Enter.**

   OS/2 ferrets through its entire list of deleted files and brings the name of the most recently deleted file to the screen first. In this case, OS/2 found your file right away, so it lists its name and asks, Do you wish to undelete this file (Y/N)?.

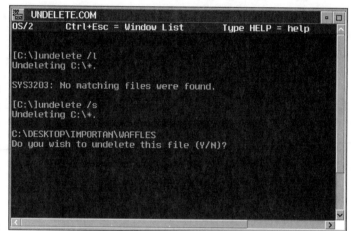

Figure 6-11:
After you
type
**UNDELETE /
S,** OS/2 lists
the files you
have
deleted.

5. **Press Y, and OS/2 brings the file back. If it didn't bring up the file you want to retrieve, press N. OS/2 brings up the names of other deleted files, one by one.**

   If, after you've pressed N dozens of times, OS/2 still doesn't find the file, it's probably gone for good. Perhaps OS/2 didn't have room to hang on to it, or perhaps you've deleted too many other files since you deleted that one.

   If Undelete found your file and retrieved it right away, it doesn't have to dredge up any more files. Make it stop searching the file graveyard by pressing Ctrl+C. OS/2 makes a rude remark about being interrupted and stops searching.

6. **When you're through with the UNDELETE program, type the word EXIT at the [C:\] thing.**

   The window disappears, and you're back to the desktop.

✔ When OS/2 undeletes a file, it puts it back where it was: The file reappears in the folder it used to live in. Give it a couple of seconds to show up, however.

✔ Your deleted file's name may look quite different from what you would expect — especially when it has a long title. For example, your data file called Inspirational Irrationalities might be called INSPIRAT when OS/2 dredges it back up from the netherworld. So if you see a filename that looks even remotely similar to the file you've shredded, press Y.

To make OS/2 quickly list all the files it has deleted, type **UNDELETE /L /S** at the [C:\] thing. OS/2 quickly lists the names of all the deleted files it can still retrieve. That can be a time-saver if you're trying to retrieve a file deleted a few days earlier.

Changing Names

Sometimes an icon looks too bizarre to give any clue about its function. To help you figure out their strange artwork, all icons have titles — little descriptive phrases beneath their pictures. Sometimes, however, long titles can bump into each other. And some titles aren't very descriptive.

To change an offending title, hold down Alt and click the title. The little box where the title appears turns white, as shown in Figure 6-12, indicating that you can start changing the words around.

Figure 6-12:
Hold down
Alt and click
an object's
title to
change it.

✔ Press the Delete or Backspace key to delete a title's old letters; then begin typing the new ones.

✔ To break a long title into two lines, place the cursor somewhere in the title's middle and press Enter. The first part of the title disappears, but don't be alarmed. Click any spot away from the title, and the newly split title snaps into place.

🖊 You also can change a title by using a less convenient method. Click the offending icon with the right mouse button and choose the Settings option. When the little *settings notebook* appears, click the General tab at the bottom right. Then you can edit the title as it appears at the top of the page. (Double-click the little symbol in the window's upper-left corner to close it and save the changes.)

Would Rembrandt Have Created His Own Icons?

One of the most popular pastimes in OS/2 is creating icons. You can waste some serious time, for example, touching up the DOS program icon — the ugly, gray square that says DOS. Or wouldn't it be nicer to have a picture of a golf ball represent your golf program?

OS/2 makes changing icons relatively easy — if you have an artistic bent, that is. First, click with the right mouse button the icon you want to change. When the menu shoots out of its head, choose Settings. When the *electronic settings notepad* appears, click General, the tab in the bottom corner. Figure 6-13 shows the System Setup Settings page that appears when you click General.

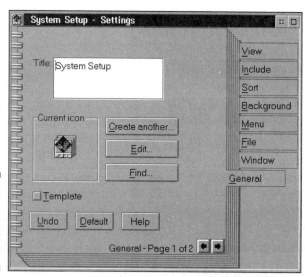

Figure 6-13: To edit an icon, click the Edit button.

The Icon Editor pops to the screen, ready for your creative input.

> ✔ The Icon Editor is described in more detail in Chapter 11.
>
> ✔ Windows icons don't work as OS/2 icons, unfortunately. You hear more about that dismal news in the first section of Chapter 5.

Shaving an Object's Head (and Other Useful Changes)

Sometimes dragging an object around isn't enough. To get some *hands-on control* over the little beggars, head for their settings. Click the object with the right mouse button, and click Settings. An electronic notebook pops up, similar to the one in Figure 6-14.

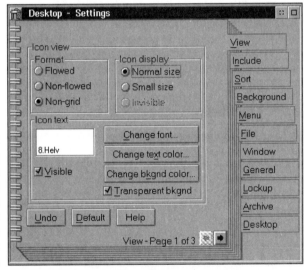

Figure 6-14: You can use an object's electronic notebook to tinker with its settings.

You can play with just about every aspect of an object. Fiddle with trite little things, such as the font it uses for its title. Or get your hands greasy by changing around its menus and adding your own favorite options.

To move from setting to setting in the *electronic notebook,* click the settings tabs along its right side.

Notice the arrows in the bottom-right corner of the notebook in Figure 6-14. Clicking those little arrows moves you through the notebook page by page; clicking the tabs along the right side moves you through the notebook section by section. Until you become familiar with the notebook, use the *page-by-page* flipping mode so that you don't miss any important pages.

Different types of objects offer different settings; the settings for a program object differ from those of a data file object or a folder object. You find a few other settings tucked away here and there among your objects, but the ones listed next are the only ones you really have to fiddle with. Or if you're not a fiddler, you can just leave them alone. They're really designed for people who like to play with their computers. They're not for people who like to play *away* from their computers.

Program: Found only in program objects, this page contains the name of the program and the directory (folder) it lives in.

Session: Found only in program objects, this page enables you to decide how a program should load when you select its object. You choose from a host of options, including loading in a window, filling the screen, and starting as a minimized window. DOS users will find special settings for their DOS programs here. (See Chapter 14 for more information about DOS.)

Association: You use this program object setting to assign the program that pops up when you click different types of data. You can tell the editor to pop up when you click a data file that ends with the letters *WRD,* for example.

Window: Found on both program and folder objects, this setting enables you to determine what happens when you click an object's Minimize button. Would you prefer it to hide itself in the Minimized Window Viewer? Or should it stay visible at the bottom of the screen? Or should it simply disappear, avoiding both those locations? Here's where you choose its invisibility level.

General: All objects have this setting. You can use it to change an object's icon and title; you can also transform the object into a template by clicking in the Template box.

If you've created a data file object that you want to use repeatedly — some letterhead with cool Egyptian fonts, for example, or a popular form — turn that data file object into a template with this setting. Then whenever you need that type of data, you can grab it from this template.

View: You use this setting, which is usually found in folder objects, to tell OS/2 how you want to view things in a folder. Normally you view things as icons. You can choose the *Small size* icons, however, so that they don't eat up so much room on the desktop. You can also tell OS/2 how you want it to *line up* the windows when you choose the <u>A</u>rrange option, which is described in Chapter 9; and you change the font used in the object's title or window. Change the font and size of your object title's and colors — go wild!

I<u>n</u>clude: You can use this setting to tell OS/2 to *filter out* objects you don't want to appear in a folder. You can filter out all the data files, for example, so that only program objects show up.

<u>S</u>ort: Do you want your folders' contents sorted alphabetically? by date? time? size? Do you want your programs sorted by size but your data files sorted by date? You can sorta get carried away with all these options. With this setting, you can determine the choices that appear on the <u>S</u>ort option when you click a folder with the right mouse button. (If you're nerdy enough to care about *attributes,* you can sort by those things here, too.)

To keep folders sorted automatically, click the <u>A</u>lways maintain sort order box on this page.

Background: Normally a folder uses a drab, gray backdrop. You can make it any color you want, however, by using this page. You can even use pictures or display the IBM OS/2 logo.

Yes, this is it — OS/2's equivalent to the Windows wallpaper setting. But it's much better. You can not only choose one piece of wallpaper for the desktop but also specify a different piece of wallpaper for every folder on the desktop! Ecstasy!

If changing to new colors and pictures make the icons' titles hard to read, head for the View page and choose the <u>T</u>ransparent bkgnd option.

<u>M</u>enu: Ever looked for a task on a menu, only to find that it wasn't listed? Search no more. You can use this page to add your own menu options to any object. It's even easier if you turn to Chapter 9 for the instructions.

<u>F</u>ile: These pages contain nitty-gritty information about your physical files: their size, creation times and dates, last access dates, and other information. You can even attach your own comments to a file, making it easier to find later.

Chapter 7

Opening and Closing Windows and Menus

*P*rogrammers and computer nerds, ecstatic about their new operating system, are beaming aboard the Starship OS/2 and traveling to distant nerdy galaxies at, well, Warp speed. Beginners, however, sometimes find it difficult to make this voyage as they try to navigate around the black hole of OS/2's buttons and switches.

This chapter hits the basics: how to make all those windows on the screen open, close, and face in the right direction.

Window Anatomy 101

A *window* is much more than a simple frame that keeps the stuff inside from falling out. All windows have bunches of hidden little buttons — places you click with the mouse — in order to make them carry out certain tasks.

You don't have to know the technical terms for all these *window parts,* but they're listed in Figure 7-1, just in case.

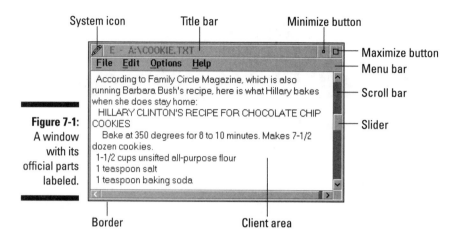

Figure 7-1:
A window
with its
official parts
labeled.

The window shown in Figure 7-2 is more important. It tells you which parts of a window to fiddle with when you want to make something happen. All these parts of a window are summarized next.

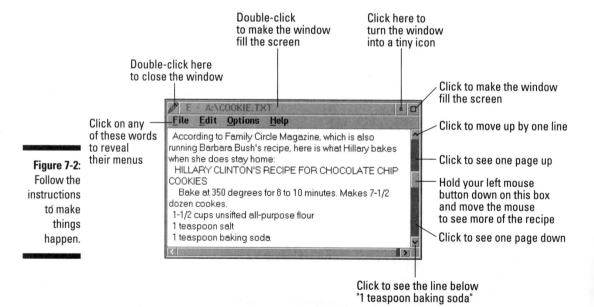

Figure 7-2:
Follow the
instructions
to make
things
happen.

Borders: Borders are simply the edges of a window. When you point at a border, the mouse pointer turns into a two-headed arrow. The two arrowheads stand for the two directions in which you can move the border to make the window larger or smaller. Hold down the left mouse button and drag the border inward to shrink the window (see Figure 7-3) or outward to expand it. Let go of the mouse button when you're finished, and the window will assume its new size.

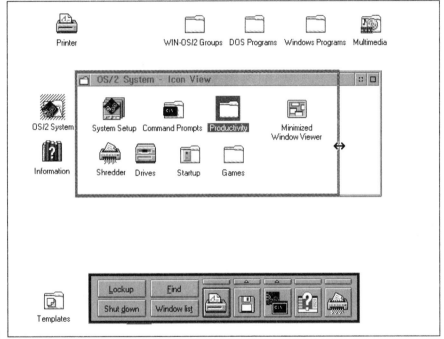

Figure 7-3:
The right border is being dragged inward to shrink the window.

Title bar: Don't confuse this element with the title you see underneath an icon. The title bar is the strip along the top of an open window. You usually see the window's title in there, along with some other pertinent information — the name of a file you're editing, for example.

Just as with Windows, you can double-click a window's title bar to make the window fill the entire screen. Want to put the window back where it was? Double-click the title bar again to return it to its former size.

A title bar makes a nice handle when you want to move a window. Simply point at the title bar with the mouse, hold down the left mouse button, and move the window to another location. When you let go of the mouse, the window stays put.

Menu bar: Everybody would prefer to see a restaurant's menu rather than try to remember what that restaurant serves. Same with computers. But because computers can do so much stuff, their menus would be bigger than a menu in a Vietnamese restaurant. So computer menus are hidden. Click in the right place, however, and the menus appear, offering more hints or instructions. Figure 7-4 shows a typical OS/2 menu.

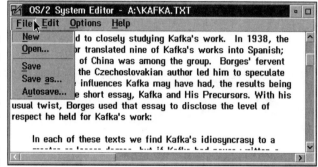

Figure 7-4:
Click File on the menu bar to see some file-related options.

Minimize/maximize buttons: These two buttons do four things because the buttons themselves change, depending on what they're doing. It's complicated, so here are some pictures. (You get more details about all this "moving windows stuff" later in this chapter.)

Click the *minimize button* to shrink a window into an icon:

Click the hide button to make the window disappear. (The window is still on the desktop; it's just invisible. Depending on the object's settings, however, it may be lurking inside the Minimized Window Viewer folder.)

Click the maximize button to make the window fill the entire screen:

The square symbol on the maximize button transforms into this stereo-TV-looking *restore symbol* when a window fills the screen. Click on the stereo TV to return the window to its normal size:

OS/2's minimize button works differently from the Windows minimize button. In Windows, minimized icons always line up along the bottom of the screen. OS/2 gives you three choices for minimized objects. You can line up the objects along the bottom of the screen as Windows does; put the objects inside the Minimized Window Viewer folder, where they're hidden from view; or simply make them disappear. (If you make them disappear, you can get them back by pressing Ctrl+Esc and plucking from a list the name of the one you want.)

Scroll bars: Sometimes not all the information fits inside a window: Parts of it scroll past the bottom or off the top. To scroll back and forth to see different parts of a page, click the little arrows on the scroll bar. Figure 7-5 explains how to use the scroll bars.

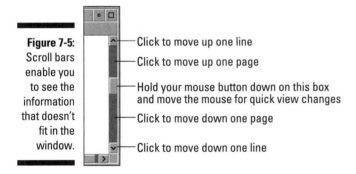

Figure 7-5: Scroll bars enable you to see the information that doesn't fit in the window.

Click to move up one line
Click to move up one page
Hold your mouse button down on this box and move the mouse for quick view changes
Click to move down one page
Click to move down one line

When the slider (that little elevator car riding in the scroll bar) is near the top of the scroll bar, you're near the top of the document. If it's at the bottom, you're near the bottom.

Because OS/2 uses graphics, using it is much easier than describing it. After all, saying "Press PgDn to move down one page" is easier than saying "Click the vertical scroll bar underneath the slider." But after you click a scroll bar, you'll say, "It's that easy? Golly!" Besides, the PgDn key still works. You don't have to use scroll bars if you think that they're dorky-looking.

Open a Window — It's Stuffy in Here!

Every time you double-click an object in OS/2, you open yet another window. It's that easy.

✔ The hard part is keeping track of all the windows after you open them. They all pile on top of each other. You learn how to move them around later in this chapter.

✔ Windows look slightly different, depending on what's inside them. For example, a folder window is just a big square with objects inside. A program window probably has some sort of menu bar across the top. Even if windows look different, however, they all behave the same. Click the same parts, and they all do the same thing.

✔ Some programs have even more windows inside them. You can keep several documents open inside some word processors, for example, each in its own window. You can play with these windows just as you play with any others. You can usually maximize or minimize them, and you can close them in the same way as you close any other window. (Move on to the next section to find out how to close them.)

Close the Window — It's Getting Chilly!

When a window has served its purpose (or is just plain getting in the way), you can close it.

Closing an *open folder window* makes that folder shrivel back down into an icon on the desktop. Or if you close a window that contains a program, the program closes too. (It gives you a chance to save your work.)

Regardless of what a window contains, you use the same method to close it. The simplest way to close a window is to double-click the little square in its upper-left corner, the one that is similar to what you see in Figure 7-6. (All those little squares look slightly different, however. They're supposed to look like miniaturized versions of their icons.)

Figure 7-6:
Double-click
this little
square to
close a
window.

Just as in Windows, you also can close a window by pressing Alt+F4.

If you're in an avant-garde mood, you can press Alt+spacebar. A menu shoots up, and then you press C to close the window.

✔ You also can close a window by calling up the *Window List,* a little pop-up box that lists every window that is open on the desktop. To call up the Window List, press Ctrl+Esc or point at a blank area on the desktop and click the left and right mouse buttons simultaneously. Then click the name of the window you want to close and press Delete.

✔ Sometimes you want to close several windows quickly. Call up the Window List and, while you hold down Ctrl, click the names of all the offending windows. Press Delete, and all the marked windows will close. This method can be a quick way to get rid of the *trail of windows* that remains when you are mousing your way to a program nested deeply within bunches of other folders.

✔ OS/2 remembers a window's last size and location when it's closed. When you open up that window again, it appears in the size you last made it and runs over to the same location it last used.

✔ If you're not using a window, keep it closed; OS/2 will run faster.

Changing a Windows Size

OS/2 is like a mansion on a cliff overlooking the sea: big windows, everywhere. In OS/2, however, you can change a window's size and location without worrying about getting bits of drywall stuck to the carpet.

To change a window's size, move one of its borders inward or outward. Try moving the mouse pointer over a window's edge and watch it transform into a two-headed mutant arrow, as shown in Figure 7-7, Figure 7-8, and Figure 7-9. Hold down the left mouse button while you move the mouse, and the window's size will change.

Figure 7-7:
When the mouse points at the window's bottom corner, the arrow grows a second head.

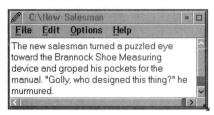

Figure 7-8:
As you move the mouse, the window's border changes to reflect its new shape.

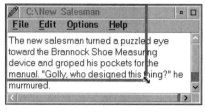

Figure 7-9:
Let go of the mouse button, and the window fills its newly adjusted border.

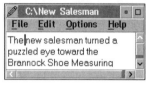

✔ Rather than drag a window's borders outward to make it fill the entire screen, you can just click its *maximize button,* that little square in its upper- right corner.

✔ Hold down Shift while you resize a window containing a DOS program to make the size change permanent. OS/2 remembers the new size the next time it brings up that window.

✔ If a window is already the right size but it's covering up another window, try moving the window out of the way, as described in the following section.

Moving a Window

On a normal desktop, you can spread out work across the desk. The OS/2 desktop is the size of the monitor, or barely 15 inches across. All the work piles up like pieces of paper skewered on a spike memo holder.

By moving the windows around on the desktop, you can sometimes get a better view of what's really going on. To move a window, point at the thick bar (title bar) across its top, hold down the left mouse button, and move the mouse around.

As the mouse moves, an outline of the window moves too. When you let go of the mouse button, the window hops over to where you moved its outline.

You don't have to keep all the parts of your windows visible. In fact, keeping most of a window dangling off the sides of the screen, with part of that thick title bar showing, is often easier. When you want to see the window's contents, you just drag it back to the top of the pile.

✔ Whenever you move a window, it automatically moves to the top of the pile on the desktop. When you let go of the mouse button, the window covers up anything you've set it on.

✔ To immediately bring a window to the top of the pile, click any part of it you see, no matter how small the part. OS/2 immediately shifts its attention to that window, effectively dredging it to the top of the pile.

✔ If you want to quickly access a window, yet you don't want it to take up room on the desktop, click its *minimize button,* the little square that sits next to the larger square in a window's upper-right corner. The window shrinks into a little icon or hides itself in the Minimized Window Viewer. To get it back, double-click the Minimized Window Viewer. When that folder opens, double-click the window's icon.

Opening Menus

Reading from a menu is often easier than trying to remember the happy hour special on a Wednesday. The same is true with OS/2. But where's the maître d'? By clicking in different places, you find different menus. Here's the scoop.

Menu bar: Programs often hide their menus on a menu bar: a thick strip with words on it near the top of a window. Click one of the words, and a menu falls from beneath the word, just as you see in Figure 7-10.

Title bar icon: See that little square symbol in every window's upper-left corner? Click there once, and a menu falls out, as shown in Figure 7-11. Most menu items listed there, however, can be accomplished more easily in other ways described in this chapter.

Object menu: If you're ever at a loss about what you can do with an object, click it with the right mouse button. A menu shoots out the top of its head, as shown in Figure 7-12.

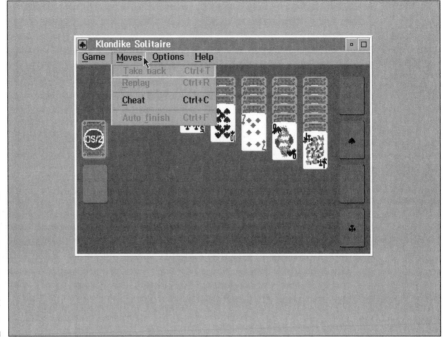

Figure 7-10:
Click the
word <u>M</u>oves
in Klondike
Solitaire to
find the
<u>C</u>heat
option.

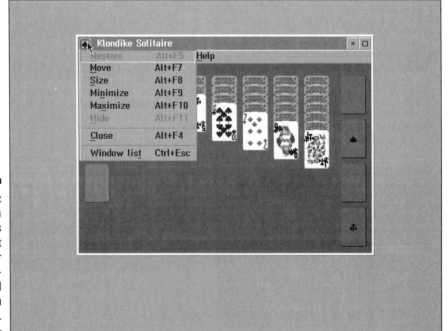

Figure 7-11:
Click a
window's
upper-left
corner for
window-
related
menu
options.

Figure 7-12:
Click an
object with
the right
mouse
button, and
a menu will
list stuff you
can do to
that object.

Notice how some of the words in a menu have underlined letters? Those letters are shortcut keys designed for people who think that mice are a bore. In the picture of Klondike in Figure 7-10, for example, see how the letter *G* in *Game* is underlined? Press Alt, and then press G. The *G*ame menu appears without a mouse. Quick, easy, and mouse-free.

There's more. See how the pull-down menu in Figure 7-10 has key combinations listed on it? For example, Ctrl+C is listed next to the Cheat option. That means that you don't have to bother with the menus. When you want to cheat, just hold down Ctrl and press C. You're immediately put into cheat mode. Not all menu items have such convenient shortcut keys, but keep an eye out for the ones that do.

 ✔ As these tips indicate, you can sometimes bypass menus by using shortcut keys. If you find yourself frequently mousing around to do the same things, check to see whether the shortcut keys are easier to use. They can save some time.

 ✔ If you press Alt accidentally, OS/2 thinks that you're trying to start a sneaky shortcut key. You get stuck in Menuland: Whenever you press an arrow key, you move from menu to menu. To get out of there, press Alt again, and you return to your regularly scheduled program.

Opening a Nested Menu

Sometimes OS/2 wants to dish out so much helpful information that the menu simply doesn't have room to show it all. So some crafty programmer with an organized shoe closet created *nested menus*. A little arrow sitting next to a menu item means that even *more* menu items are hidden inside there. Click the arrow next to Open, for example, and a nested menu flies out to the side, as shown in Figure 7-13.

Figure 7-13:
Click the
arrow next
to a menu
item to see
even more
related
options.

Nested menus provide options related to the word they leap out from. Under
Open, for example, you can choose between an Icon view, a Tree view, or a
Details view of the files living inside your folder.

You see two types of arrows in Figure 7-13. There's an arrow-in-a-button next to
Open, and a plain arrow next to Select. What gives? Well, buttoned arrows are
more difficult to open: You have to specifically point at the buttoned arrow next
to Open before it unleashes its nested menu.

The arrow next to Select, however, is an easy mark. Just point at the word
Select, and its nested menu shoots out to the side. Quick and easy.

✔ OK, there's an even bigger reason for the difference in arrows. See the little
check mark next to Icon view in Figure 7-13? That means that you can just
double-click Open and OS/2 will assume that you want the Icon view — it
doesn't bother shooting out the nested menu, asking for your order.
Because that check mark is next to Icon view, a double-click of Open
always gives you the Icon view.

✔ If you don't want an icon view, however, don't double-click Open. Instead,
click Open's little buttoned arrow. That brings up the nested menu, where
you can click one of the other, noncheck-marked items.

✔ You can change where the check mark sits, if you like fiddling with this
kind of stuff. In fact, you can even add your own menu items! This bit of fun
is covered in Chapter 9.

Keeping Your Desktop Neat or Messy

Like most programmers, OS/2 tends to enjoy a messy desk. Open windows
cover each other up, and objects live wherever they're haphazardly dropped.
You can tell OS/2 to clean up its act, however, and make the desktop tidy
enough to please your third-grade teacher.

Cascading

You can turn OS/2 into a card dealer who deals out open windows like a stack of cards. Here's how:

1. **Point at a vacant area of the desktop and press both mouse buttons at the same time. (If the desktop is completely covered up, press Ctrl+Esc to do the same thing.)**

   The Window List pops up.

2. **Click the name of the first window you want to extricate from the pile. Next, hold down Ctrl and click the names of the other windows you want to organize.**

   The Window List box looks similar to the one in Figure 7-14.

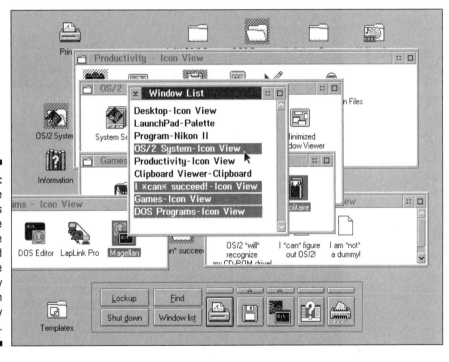

Figure 7-14: The windows whose names are darkened are miraculously pulled from this messy pile.

3. **After you choose the names of the windows, click a darkened name in the Window List box with the right mouse button. A menu pops up. Click Cascade and watch as OS/2 immediately deals the windows across the desktop, as shown in Figure 7-15.**

Figure 7-15:
Choosing
Cascade
makes OS/2
deal the
windows
across the
screen like
cards.

Tiling

Or perhaps you want the windows tiled across the desktop. In that case, repeat steps 1 through 3 in the preceding section but click the Tile option instead. The desktop looks similar to Figure 7-16.

OS/2 enables you to choose which windows you want to organize with the Tile or Cascade approach. The Windows Tile and Cascade commands, in contrast, organize all the open windows on the screen; you can't pick or choose.

- ✔ If you want only one window tiled or cascaded across the screen, call up the Window List and click that single window's name with the right mouse button. Then choose Tile or Cascade, and OS/2 will carry out your command.

- ✔ Tiling a single window is the same as clicking its Maximize button; cascading one window shrinks it down to playing-card size and sticks it in the screen's upper-left corner.

- ✔ You can find ways to organize the objects on the desktop in Chapter 9.

- ✔ Want to know how other people are organizing their desktops? Then flip ahead to Chapter 21 for some exemplary examples.

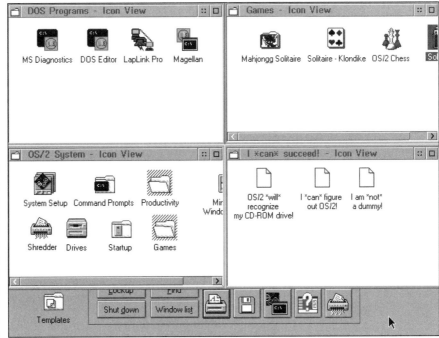

Figure 7-16:
Choosing
Tile makes
OS/2 spread
the
windows
across the
desk, giving
each one
equal room.

Chapter 8
Disks and Drives

. . . .

In This Chapter

▶ What's a file?

▶ Differentiating between object titles and filenames

▶ Naming files

▶ Getting information about files

▶ Finding out how much free space is on a disk or drive

▶ Formatting floppy disks

▶ Using CHKDSK

. . . .

*A*fter you pick a name for a child, you don't get any feedback for a few years. Then, six years down the line, the kid begins to hear "Jake, Jake, walks like a rake" or "Shelley, Shelley, with big worms in her belly."

But if you pick the wrong name for a computer file, OS/2 tells you immediately. OS/2's language isn't nearly as musical, though. It chants such things as "The requested path does not exist," or it uses the "Cover all the bases with one error message approach:" Invalid drive, path, or file.

Computer filenames clearly rank as one of the most boring things to talk about, even among close friends. Even OS/2 tries to cover up files by putting little pictures over them so that you don't fall asleep at the keyboard. Nonetheless, you eventually have to deal with the nitty-gritty of files and filenames, no matter how much OS/2 tries to pretty them up.

This chapter peels off some of the chocolate coating so that you can see the nuts inside more clearly.

What's a File?

A file is basically a collection of stuff on disk, usually information you want to keep around. Each collection of disk stuff gets a name, known as a *filename*. Some folks split the word in two and call it a *file name*. But no matter how many words you use, files come in two flavors: program files and data files.

Program files: Some files contain instructions for the computer — commands that make it bring a word processor to the screen, for example, or make it quack like a duck (if you've shelled out the cash for a sound card).

Data files: Other files contain information for you or the computer to use: a letter to Uncle Rhett asking him about his new batch of home-brewed bourbon, for example, or the collection of digitized sound waves that make up a duck's quack.

- A file is a collection of computerized information. You usually store the information on a floppy disk or on a hard disk. (Some of the cool, new *palmtop* computers can store files on RAM cards, but that's getting too complicated. Besides, OS/2 doesn't work on a Sharp Wizard. Or on a GameBoy, for that matter.)

- Files fit on disks the way songs fit on cassette tapes or CDs. You can fit only so many of them on a disk before it fills up and starts to complain.

- OS/2 deals with files in several ways. For example, a data file can show up as a Data File object sitting in a folder. Or the data file can appear as a filename listed on the hard drive.

- Although OS/2 usually shows you a view of icons when you open a folder, you can make OS/2 show you the names of the files in the folder if you want. Page ahead to the section, "Viewing Files on a Disk," later in this chapter.

- Program files already come with names thought up by their programmers. You have to think up your own names for the data files you create, however; OS/2 doesn't hesitate to tell you if it doesn't like the names.

What's the Difference between an Object's Title and Its Filename?

This subject gets a little complicated, so hang on to your ears to keep your head from spinning too quickly. OS/2's Program and Data File objects (those little icons in the folders) really have two names.

The first name is the *title* — that short, descriptive phrase underneath the little icon. You've probably changed a title or two in your day. You just hold down Alt and click the title (see Chapter 4 for details).

The second name is considered the file's *real name,* the name used by OS/2's file system for storing the chunk of information that makes up that program or data file.

To keep things simple, OS/2 tries to use the same name for both an object's title and its *real* filename. If you save a letter with the simple name LETTER, for example, OS/2 uses LETTER for both the object's title and its filename.

DOS, however, throws a wrench into the works. For more than a decade, DOS has refused to accept filenames longer than eight characters. The newer, more liberal-minded OS/2 accepts filenames that have as many as 254 characters.

Technical drivel: What's that EA on your FAT, buddy?

The old DOS standby, the File Allocation Table (FAT) system of storing files, allows for a little bit of information to be tacked on to a file. You can check a file's creation date, for example, to see whether you have the latest version. But FAT simply doesn't have much room for storing much information about a file.

OS/2 corrects that problem by adding *extended attributes* (EA). Files can store not only the information you enter but also information about themselves — an icon, for example, or a description of what's inside a file.

Although files can store this extra information easily on an HPFS system and on a hard drive, big problems surface on a FAT system or floppy disk. So OS/2 keeps the extra information in secret, hidden files. When you copy a file from a hard drive to a floppy drive, OS/2 sticks a secret, hidden EA file on the floppy as well. The EA file preserves the extra information that the FAT and the floppy just can't handle.

If you copy a file titled or named EXTREMELY BITING COMMENTARY to a floppy disk, for example, OS/2 renames the file EXTREMEL in order to get the disk's FAT system to accept it. It stores the leftover Y BITING COMMENTARY part in the EA file.

If a DOS program accesses that file, however, it doesn't know about the EA parts, so it doesn't always preserve them. It probably even wipes them out.

The ultracurious may see two hidden files on their FAT disks, EA DATA. SF and WP ROOT. SF. Those files are the EAs, and you can safely ignore them. (Just don't delete them, however, thinking that they are trash. And yes, they have spaces in the middle of their names. That makes them more difficult for people to delete.)

No problem exists if the hard drive uses OS/2's HPFS. You can name a new letter LETTER TO JEREMY ABOUT MUSTACHE WAX. OS/2 stores that information under the filename LETTER TO JEREMY ABOUT MUSTACHE WAX, and the lambs sleep peacefully. OS/2 uses that filename phrase as the title too. Simple, and no confusion.

But if the hard drive uses the older DOS FAT system — and you have to use FAT to use the Dual Boot system — OS/2 can't use that many letters. OS/2 doesn't even let you save the letter with the name MUSTACHEWAX because that name has 11 letters.

Yes, it's a problem. And until people stop relying on DOS programs, the problem isn't going to go away.

- ✔ If you're using OS/2's Dual Boot life-style (and if you chose the Easy Installation option, you're a Dual Booter), you're using the FAT system. That means that you're stuck with eight-character filenames.

- ✔ If your computer is expensive enough to have 6MB or more of RAM, you should seriously consider using HPFS rather than FAT. Thinking up descriptive filenames is much, much easier that way.

- ✔ If you name a file JMUSTWAX on a FAT drive under OS/2, you can still use LETTER TO JEREMY ABOUT MUSTACHE WAX as the title for its Data File object. Although using the same title and filename for an object is more convenient, OS/2 doesn't insist that they be the same.

- ✔ HPFS still chokes when you save files to a floppy disk, however. Floppy disks can't be formatted with HPFS, so OS/2 truncates the filenames down to eight characters. Yes, it's a bummer. But amazingly enough, if you copy a data file back to the HPFS hard drive from the floppy disk, its longer filename and title are resurrected (so long as the file hasn't been touched by a DOS program). If you want to know why, check out the nearby "Technical drivel" sidebar. Otherwise, nod your head, say "Well, that's convenient," and move on to the next section.

DOS programs don't know that extended attributes exist, so they don't make any special effort to preserve them. If you back up an HPFS hard drive with a DOS-based backup program, the program probably won't back up any extended attributes along with the rest of the hard drive. The files will be backed up, but any of their *extended attributes,* such as long filenames, icons, or other identifying information, will probably be lost. Make sure that the hard drive backup program is OS/2-compatible before you rely on it.

Giving a File a Name

Sooner or later, you create something useful in OS/2. For example, you whip out OS/2's System Editor, type a description of last night's ice cream cone nightmare, and click the Save option. A window like the one shown in Figure 8-1 leaps to the screen, giving you an opportunity to name your latest creation.

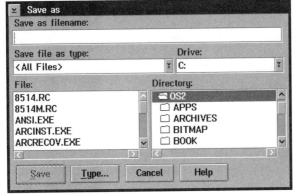

Figure 8-1:
You enter
the filename
in this
window.

You can't just type any old name, however; OS/2 forces you to follow certain rules. And, as with many things in OS/2, the rules change slightly, depending on whether the hard disk uses that HPFS stuff or that FAT stuff.

First, both FAT and HPFS freak out if you try to use any of the following characters when you name a file:

```
"   /   \   :   *   ?   |   <   >   [   ]   ;   =   +   ,
```

Second, you can't use the following names (although I doubt that they're on the tip of anybody's tongue):

```
KBD$
PRN
NUL
COM1
COM2
COM3
COM4
CLOCK$
```

```
LPT1
LPT2
LPT3
CON
SCREEN$
POINTER$
MOUSE$
```

Third, you can't use more than eight characters to name a file under the FAT system. If you feel like it, you can use eight characters, toss on a period, and type three more characters, like this: SUPERFAT.PIG.

Most OS/2 programs toss on their own three characters, however, so try to restrain yourself from adding your own.

Many OS/2 books and Help files tout the fact that you can use many periods in HPFS filenames. For example, you can use MR.ROGERS.NEIGHBORHOOD as a filename. But you can use MR ROGERS NEIGHBORHOOD just as easily without the periods, and it looks better. OS/2 folks just get carried away by the fact that FAT limits you to a single period in a filename. So don't feel that you have to use periods between words in an HPFS filename. Spaces work just as well.

✔ To find out whether the current drive you're using uses HPFS or FAT, find its *Drive object.* Begin by double-clicking the OS/2 System folder and then double-click the Drives folder (neither of these looks like a folder, by the way). The Drives folder contains an icon for each of the disk drives, whether they're floppy drives or hard drive partitions. Click the appropriate drive icon with the right mouse button and choose Settings. When the little *notebook* pops up, click Details. You see either HPFS or FAT in the top-right corner of the page.

✔ Sometimes OS/2's System Editor asks you to choose a file *type* in addition to a name. Unless you're doing some programming stuff, choose the Plain Text type and ignore the other two options, DOS Command File and OS/2 Command File.

✔ You don't have to remember those dorky characters that you can't use in filenames. If you accidentally try to use one of them, OS/2 sends you an error message. Just click the OK button and choose a different name.

✔ When OS/2 sends you an error message immediately after you choose a new filename, you probably used an illegal name. The error message probably won't be that succinct, however. It may say that the file is in use by another program or something less obvious. Nevertheless, try a new name, and the error message will probably disappear.

Don't bother with this command line stuff

Under HPFS you can use longer names for both directories (folders) and filenames. But if you're a DOS-head, you have to try something new at the command line. If you want to change to the directory FUN STUFF, for example, OS/2 makes you type the following at the command line:

```
[C:\] CD "FUN STUFF"
```

You need the quotation marks so that OS/2 can recognize both words as being part of the directory's name. Filenames that contain a space have to be enclosed in quotation marks as well.

Finally, if you create a folder called THE BEST on a FAT drive, OS/2 automatically converts it to THE_BEST. You don't need the quotation marks to access this one because there aren't any spaces.

Computers certainly are finicky when it comes to spaces.

Viewing Files on a Disk

Because OS/2 deals so heavily in graphics, it prefers to use little pictures to show you things. In a perfect world, this would be ideal. Pictures make it easy to identify things, and they can spice up a dull, dry computer world.

But this isn't a perfect world. One of the biggest concerns of most computer users is "Will that file fit on my hard drive?" Coming in a close second is "Will those files fit on my floppy drive?" Finally, there's "Is this file the latest version?"

OS/2 enables you to see files in varying levels of detail, from the pretty picture level to the encyclopedic level. By switching the file *views,* you can find all the file information you need.

First, find the icon for the drive you're interested in. (If there isn't a *shadow* of that drive on the desktop, you can find the real Drive object in the Drives folder of the OS/2 System folder.) Click the icon with the right mouse button, stand back as a menu shoots out the top of its head, and then click the arrow next to Open. A new menu appears, as shown in Figure 8-2.

Because you're curious about file details, click Details view. OS/2 brings a new window to the screen, showing you the files on that drive. But rather than show you the file icons, it shows you the filenames, sizes, and other more nerdy information, as shown in Figure 8-3.

Figure 8-2:
OS/2
normally
shows
objects in
Icon view;
click Details
view to see
the really
nerdy stuff,
like file sizes.

Drive C

Figure 8-3:
Click the
little arrows
on the
bottom of
this window
to see the
file details
that
currently lie
outside the
window's
edge.

Icon	Title	Object Cla	Real name	Size	Last write date	L.
	MMOS2	Folder	MMOS2	0	11-11-94	
	CONFIG.001	Data File	CONFIG.001	2,169	11-11-94	
	IBMVESA	Folder	IBMVESA	0	11-11-94	
	CONFIG.SYS	Data File	CONFIG.SYS	2,419	11-14-94	
	AUTOEXEC.BAT	OS/2 Comman	AUTOEXEC.BAT	268	11-11-94	
	DELETE	Folder	DELETE	0	11-13-94	
	SPOOL	Folder	SPOOL	0	11-11-94	
	WINA20.386	Data File	WINA20.386	9,349	9-30-93	
	ACLLOCK.LST	Data File	ACLLOCK.LST	71	11-11-94	
	PSFONTS	Folder	PSFONTS	0	11-11-94	
	WINDOWS	Folder	WINDOWS	0	11-11-94	
	UTIL	Folder	UTIL	0	11-11-94	
	DOS	Folder	DOS	0	11-11-94	
	README	Data File	README	15,519	10-10-94	
	Maintenance Desktop	Desktop	MAINTENA	0	11-11-94	
	OS2	Folder	OS2	0	11-11-94	
	Desktop	Desktop	DESKTOP	0	11-11-94	

Drive C - Details View

 OS/2 provides so many details that they don't all fit on the screen of a VGA monitor. You have to click the arrows on those little scroll bar things — the things along the edge — to see all the file information.

 The Details view shows you what a file's object looks like, its title, its *real name* in the file system, its size, and its birth date (the time and date you created it).

✔ OS/2 keeps track of a few more file details than DOS does. DOS just keeps track of when a file was created. Then, if you change a file, DOS forgets the creation date and saves the date you changed the file. OS/2, on the other hand, not only remembers when a file was created but also keeps track of the last time a file was changed, or accessed. This feature comes in handy if, perhaps, you're dying to know the last time you played with a program.

✔ Even though files are showing their <u>D</u>etails view rather than the customary <u>I</u>con view, you can play with them in the same way. You can drag a file-name to the Shredder to delete the file, for example, or drag several files to other folders. You can double-click a program's filename to rev it up. Or, if you see a directory listed, you can click it with the right mouse button, click the arrow next to <u>O</u>pen, and choose <u>D</u>etails view again. Yet another window opens, displaying details about the files in that other directory.

✔ Just as you see hash marks — little diagonal lines — running across an icon when its object is being used, you see little hash marks over the little icon in <u>D</u>etails view as well.

✔ An OS/2 folder is simply a directory, just like the directories in DOS. Near the bottom of Figure 8-3, in fact, you can see an icon with hash marks. That's the OS/2 Desktop directory, the desktop you've been working with on the screen since Day One.

✔ Unfortunately, the <u>D</u>etails view leaves out one important detail: the amount of space left on the disk drive. That brings us to yet another view, which is described in the following section.

How Much Space Do I Have on My Disk?

Disks can store only a certain amount of information before they fill up. Stuff doesn't spill over the edge as it does with a coffee cup, however. Instead, the computer tells you that it has had its fill before any data gets lost. When the disk is filled to the brim, OS/2 sends you a message like the one shown in Figure 8-4.

Figure 8-4:
OS/2 tells
you when
the disk
runs out of
room to
store
information.

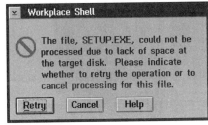

Although receiving the warning is better than having data spill out along the sides, it's still inconvenient. Your best bet is to plan ahead and make sure that you have plenty of room to begin with.

To see how much room you have on a floppy disk, click it with the right mouse button. When the menu shoots out from the top of its head, click the arrow next to <u>O</u>pen and choose <u>T</u>ree view from the other menu that pops up. The resulting view looks something like the one shown in Figure 8-5.

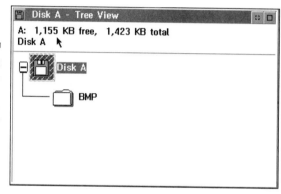

Figure 8-5:
The top line of the Tree view tells you how much space is left on the drive.

✔ The <u>T</u>ree view shows how the folders are arranged on the desktop. The farther out a folder appears on a *branch,* the more deeply it's stuck inside folders on the desktop.

✔ In OS/2, a folder can appear inside another folder. In DOS, a folder is a directory; a folder inside another folder is a subdirectory of the first directory.

✔ Choose the <u>T</u>ree view when you want to see the amount of room left on a disk; choose the <u>D</u>etails view when you want to see how much space each file takes up. Yes, this is inconvenient. When you delete old files to clear some space, you have to switch back and forth between views to see how much space you have left.

✔ For a more thorough (and slower) way of checking out the amount of space you have left on a disk, head to the sidebar, "What's this CHKDSK stuff?", later in this chapter.

✔ Opening a new view of a disk is similar to taking a snapshot. The window shows the information currently on the disk. But if you open another window of that disk, perhaps with a different view, and move some files around, the first window isn't updated to show the changes. To make sure that a view is up-to-date, use the Refresh option. Click the window with the right mouse button and choose <u>R</u>efresh now from the menu. OS/2 takes a second look and shows any changes in the window.

✔ When the hard drive begins to fill up, begin copying some lesser-used information to floppy disks for safekeeping. Don't have enough floppies? Well, buy some more. And remember, OS/2 enables you to format them in the background. (You can find formatting instructions in the next section of this chapter.)

✔ You can see information about files and available disk space much more quickly by bypassing OS/2's graphics stuff and heading for its heart, the OS/2 command line. That scary bit of viscera is described in, appropriately enough, Chapter 13.

✔ The Tree view looks a little different from the more oft-used Icon view. But they work the same. In fact, you can drag files to copy, move, or delete them, or to perform other chores, from any view of a disk.

✔ See the minus sign next to one of the folders in Figure 8-5? Click it, and the folder branching out from below it disappears. The minus sign turns into a plus sign. When you click the minus and plus signs in Tree view, you see the folders that are nested inside other folders.

Formatting Floppies

Most thank-you notes tend to look as though they were written on a ship during a thunderstorm. Without the guiding lines of ruled notebook paper, the sentences don't flow straight across the blank page; they waver up and down.

When computers write stuff on floppy disks (or hard drives, for that matter), they need little guiding lines too, or else their writing is too chaotic to retrieve.

That's where formatting comes in. When you buy a new box of floppy disks at the computer store, you can't use them right out of the box. You have to format them. Formatting is a computer's way of putting guiding lines on the disk so that it can write more-organized stuff to it later.

Luckily, OS/2 can format disks very easily, a feature that just about every OS/2 user worldwide points out repeatedly. Just follow these steps:

1. **Place the floppy disk in the floppy drive.**

2. **Click the right mouse button on the OS/2 object for that drive.**

   If you put the floppy in drive A, for example, click the Drive A object on the desktop.

3. **Click the Format disk option and stand back as a window leaps onto the screen.**

   It looks similar to the window shown in Figure 8-6.

4. **If the number listed as the Capacity is correct and you don't feel like giving the disk a name, just click the Format button. Or type a name in the Volume Label box and then click Format.**

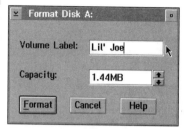

Figure 8-6:
OS/2
displays this
box when
you click the
Format disk
option.

That's all there is to it. OS/2 whirls into action and formats the floppy disk. If the word *Capacity* seems bizarre or foreign, flip back to Chapter 2 for a quick refresher.

Or if you want to avoid this task altogether, buy floppy disks that say "preformatted" on the box. You pay a little extra cash for this convenience, however.

✔ After you click the Format button, OS/2 begins formatting the disk. You can continue with other work on the desktop, however, because OS/2 formats the disk in the *background*. You can use this *background formatting* feature, in fact, as a reason to tell all your friends why you switched to OS/2. They have to twiddle their thumbs when they're formatting floppies. When you're formatting floppies, you can be practicing your putting on the third hole on the Mauna Kea golf course with Links386 Pro.

✔ The volume label simply gives a floppy disk an electronic name. That name doesn't appear on the floppy disk's outside label, though, so adding a volume label doesn't make the disk any easier to find.

✔ In fact, the volume label shows up only if you open the disk's Settings area and look at the Details page buried deep inside bunches of menus.

✔ If you want to give a disk a volume label, keep the name down to 11 characters. That's all you can use.

If you install OS/2 using Advanced Installation features such as HPFS or Boot Manager, OS/2 will probably format the hard drive, and that's the only time the hard drive needs to be formatted. Formatting a hard drive destroys whatever information is stored on it. Luckily, OS/2's user handcuffs are tight, so you don't have to worry about accidentally formatting the hard drive. DOS is much more lenient in this area. To be safe, stick to OS/2's menu method of formatting disks.

Formatting a floppy disk destroys any information on it. Format new floppies only when they first come out of the box. You don't have to format them again.

What's this CHKDSK stuff?

CHKDSK is a handy OS/2 program because it wears several hats. First, it can scan over a hard drive or a floppy disk and report back on how much space is left.

Second, while it's rooting around in the disk drive, it checks to see whether anything has been misplaced. If it finds anything wrong, it not only tells you so, it also fixes the mistakes.

Don't ever turn off your computer while you are running OS/2. And if you can help it, don't ever press Ctrl+Alt+Delete when you are running OS/2 either. Instead, use OS/2's Shut down command, which is described in Chapter 3. If OS/2 doesn't get a chance to shut itself down properly, it can lose track of where it has been storing files. Then you have to wade through all this CHKDSK stuff to get OS/2 going again.

To put CHKDSK to work, click any Drive object with the right mouse button and choose Check disk from the little pop-up menu.(Check disk is the civilized Menuland option that revs up OS/2's CHKDSK program.) OS/2 tosses a funny box in your face, like the one shown here:

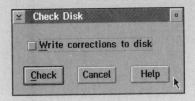

Normally, you click in the box to say "Yes, please, fix everything." If you're checking the hard drive, however, OS/2 rudely withdraws its offer and tosses in your face the box you see below:

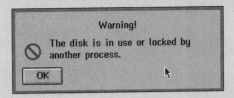

You see, you can't change files that OS/2 is already using. If you loaded OS/2 off the hard drive, OS/2 grabbed some files there for itself, and you can't do anything to change them — not even to fix any errors.

So click OK to get rid of the error message, click in the Write corrections to disk box to get rid of the check mark you put there earlier, and click Check to start checking the disk. The drive whirls as the program counts the files, looking for any stray bits of data.

It tells you whether it finds any errors, even though it doesn't fix them. (And if it does find errors, head for Chapter 23 for ways to beg OS/2 to fix them.) CHKDSK usually doesn't find any errors, however; it just reports back with a PacMan-looking box, like the one shown below:

(continued)

(continued)

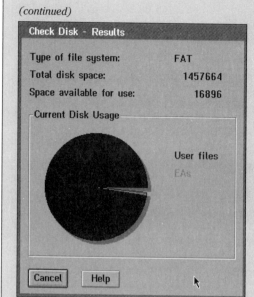

```
┌─────────────────────────────────────────┐
│ Check Disk - Results                     │
├─────────────────────────────────────────┤
│  Type of file system:        FAT         │
│  Total disk space:        1457664        │
│  Space available for use:    16896       │
│  ┌─Current Disk Usage─────────────────┐  │
│  │                                     │  │
│  │                         User files  │  │
│  │                         EAs         │  │
│  │                                     │  │
│  └─────────────────────────────────────┘ │
│  ┌────────┐  ┌────────┐                   │
│  │ Cancel │  │  Help  │              ▶    │
│  └────────┘  └────────┘                   │
└─────────────────────────────────────────┘
```

Depending on the type of disk (hard or floppy), the little pie chart shows four different things, each in its own color.

User files: This dark blue chunk of space, the biggest chunk, is taken up by files: programs and data files.

Reserved: The light blue chunk is the space OS/2 grabs for itself.

Directories: These little, yellow folders take up a tiny sliver of space.

EAs: A file's extended attributes, covered earlier in this chapter, are light green.

Finally, across the top of the window, you see whether the drive is HPFS or FAT, the amount of space it can hold, and the amount of space you have left over for important things, such as computer games.

✔ Even though computers are good with numbers, they're lousy with commas. The preceding figure shows the total disk space as 1457664. OS/2 is too lazy to say that you have 1,457,664 bytes of total storage space on that floppy disk. The other number, 16896, means that you have 16,896 bytes left to use for files.

✔ OS/2 isn't very accurate at checking disk space when you use it on a hard drive. You are better off with the View commands, described earlier in this chapter, in the section "How Much Space Do I Have on My Disk?"

✔ Feel free to check the *fix it* box when you're running CHKDSK on a floppy disk. OS/2 doesn't have any problems with that. If it finds any data that's not supposed to be there, it pours that data onto some files. (The files will end in CHK. Feel free to look inside them with the System Editor to see whether anything is worth saving. Chances are, you won't find anything to save, unfortunately.)

Chapter 9

Customizing OS/2 (Fiddling Around with the Settings Notebook)

- -

In This Chapter

▶ Adding *wallpaper* or new colors to OS/2's background

▶ Rearranging the desktop

▶ Changing video modes

▶ Setting up OS/2 work areas

▶ Starting the screen saver or locking up the system

▶ Changing the appearance of stuff on-screen

- -

*1*BM's power-hungry computer nerds created OS/2 to be a *powerful* system for *powerful* computers. That means that IBM's programmers couldn't resist tossing in dozens of *PFOs* (Powerful Fiddling Options).

Computer nerds relax by fiddling with their computers, whether that involves rearranging the computer's power cables to flow in a straight line or changing OS/2's desktop from its traditional dull gray to the livelier color of a Hostess Fruit Pie filling.

You won't turn into a nerd by fiddling on a small scale, however. For example, you can easily make OS/2's Shredder stop nagging you with that "Are you sure?" message every time you try to throw away some trash.

You don't have to fiddle at all. OS/2 works just fine when you leave it as is. But when you're ready for a little fiddling — turning your desktop's background into a swimming pool, for example — then this chapter is waiting.

Getting Rid of the Ugly Gray Background

IBM designed OS/2 for Boring Business Environments, so everything in OS/2 rests on a boring gray background.

But if you would rather liven things up, OS/2 is ready to party. You can not only transform that dull gray background into a sparkling new color but also hang a picture on the background wall.

In fact, OS/2 already sneaked a picture or two into the computer when you weren't looking. To see what IBMers call art, click the desktop with the right mouse button. When the menu pops up, choose Settings. An electronic *Settings* notebook pops up. Click the Background tab along the right, and you're ready to start some serious fiddling.

To hang a picture on the wall, click in the box next to the Color only setting, shown in Figure 9-1, to remove the check mark — that tells OS/2 that you want to see *more* than just colors. Then click the little downward-pointing arrow doohickey on the end of the File box to see the pictures you can use to decorate the desktop.

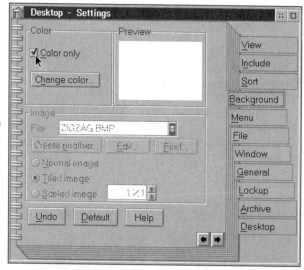

Figure 9-1:
You use this Background page to change the background of the desktop.

As soon as you click the name of a picture, OS/2 plasters the picture across the screen's background. Don't like any of the pictures? Then check the button next to the Color only setting and click the Change color button. You see a strange, telescope-looking thing, like the one shown in Figure 9-2.

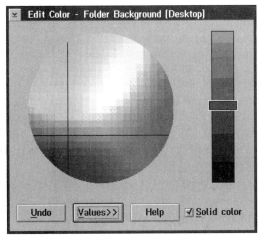

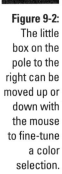

Figure 9-2:
The little box on the pole to the right can be moved up or down with the mouse to fine-tune a color selection.

To see the range of colors, move the mouse across the colorful circle while you hold down the left mouse button. As you move the mouse, the currently selected color is the one inside the little box on the pole to the right. In fact, when you find a color you like, move the mouse over to that little box. Then fine-tune the color by holding down the left mouse button and moving the mouse to slide the little box up and down.

Find the right color? Then double-click the upper-left corner of the window to close it. The color you left inside the box fills the entire screen.

✔ OS/2 comes with more than 40 *images* to choose from. If you've recently changed your resolution from VGA to Super VGA, the pictures will look much better.

✔ When you choose Image, you can decide how you want the images to appear on-screen. The Normal image setting sticks the image in the center of the screen. The Tiled image setting repeats the image across the screen until it completely covers the background. (If the image is big enough to fill the screen by itself, then the Normal and Tiled settings do the same thing.) Finally, the Scaled image setting places the picture across the screen in a square grid, using adjustable rows from 20×20 to 1×1. Unlike the Tiled setting, the Scaled setting shrinks or enlarges the picture to fit into the rows. (Yep, those are some powerful fiddling options.)

✔ Sometimes OS/2 uses *dithered* colors (colors with little patterns of dots or lines that make them look slightly more interesting). Don't like the dithers? Ditch 'em by selecting the Solid color box.

✔ To change colors even more quickly, double-click either of the Color Palette objects in the System Setup folder (which lives in the OS/2 System folder). Then simply drag those little color circles over to other windows and let go. Pow! The color of the windows changes instantly. You can use the Color Palette to edit colors too, if you would rather interior-decorate the screen than work.

✔ In Windows, most of the setting changes (when you fiddle with settings in the Control Panel, for example) take place *after* you close the window. In OS/2, however, most of the changes take place immediately. Because you can see the results of your OS/2 tweaks immediately, changing them back is easier if you choose something really lame.

✔ Here's the shocker: Unlike in Windows, in OS/2 you can use a different piece of wallpaper for each individual OS/2 window. For example, you can make the drive A window a bright red and the drive C window orange. Or you can display the butterfly picture in the OS/2 System folder and the OS/2 logo in the Games folder. Simply access the Settings menu from each window separately, just as you did with the desktop background, and choose a different picture or color for each one.

✔ Now here's the bad news: If you change the desktop's color, you may not be able to read the icon titles. Luckily, the Background settings page lets you choose Transparent bkgnd, an option that lets letters show up against just about any background.

✔ If you accidentally choose a background color that completely obliterates the icon titles, you can return to the dull gray color. Just click the Background page's Change color button, and change each of the Red, Green, and Blue values back to 204. Whew!

Rearranging the Desktop

When you first install OS/2, it dumps a bunch of objects on-screen. You don't have to keep the desktop looking as though you just moved in, however. You can easily rearrange things and get rid of the clutter.

When you're tired of looking at the Information object, for example, drag it to the OS/2 System Folder object and leave it there. Just click the Information object with the right mouse button and then hold down the button and move the mouse until the pointer rests over the OS/2 System object. Leggo, and OS/2 drops the Information object into the OS/2 System folder. That's a good first start in clearing some of the clutter off the desktop. (Open the OS/2 System folder, and you see the Information object in there, should you ever need it again.)

You may want to put *shadows* of frequently used stuff on the desktop. If you use the OS/2 System Editor frequently, for example, you don't want to waste time opening a bunch of folders just to grab the OS/2 System Editor object from the Productivity folder.

To make a shadow of the object, hold down both the Control and Shift keys while you drag the OS/2 System Editor object onto the desktop. A little line stretches, showing the connection between the real OS/2 System Editor and the shadow *button* you're making for it on the desktop.

Now you can start up the Editor by clicking it from the desktop instead of by rummaging through a bunch of folders.

Everybody's desktop looks different in real life. Your OS/2 desktop doesn't have to look like IBM's, either. Move things around until they suit your own needs.

✔ You can find more information about the more-practical-than-mysterious shadows in Chapter 5.

✔ For some desktop-arranging ideas, check out Chapter 21. There you can find pictures and descriptions of several eminently functional desktops.

✔ If you've spent hours organizing your desktop to make it look *just so,* don't ever click the Arrange option from the desktop's pull-down menu. Under the pretense of *arranging* the screen, OS/2 yanks the icons out of your *own* order and forces them into rows along either the screen's top or side. OS/2 Warp Version 3.0 finally adds an Undo command, however; click the desktop with your right mouse button, and you'll find the Undo Arrange command waiting for you at the bottom of the menu.

✔ If you like the icons arranged in neat little rows across the desktop, click the desktop with the right mouse button and choose Settings. The *electronic notebook* opens to the View page. Choose Flowed to line up the icons in rows across the screen. Choose Non-flowed to line up all the icons in a single column along the left side of the screen. Or choose Non-grid to make the icons stay wherever you drop them. (Who but a computer nerd would offer the options Non-flowed or Non-grid?)

I Want Super VGA Mode, Not VGA!

The more money you pay for the computer's video card, the more colors it can display on the monitor. OS/2 can't talk directly to the video card, however. The card needs a translator — a special OS/2 driver — before OS/2 can talk to it. (These *drivers* are just pieces of software, by the way.)

OS/2 comes with drivers for some video cards, and some video cards come with OS/2 drivers as well. If either OS/2 or your card has the right driver, you're in luck. You can switch between video modes and choose the one you like best.

Stop! Some brands of video cards make it easy to change video modes. To see whether you're among the lucky ones, double-click the System object. (It hides in the System Setup folder, which lurks in the OS/2 System folder.) If the System object has a Screen tab, click it: You see a list of available video modes. Click the one you want and use OS/2's Shut down command to reboot. When OS/2 starts up again, you see your new video mode on the screen. Don't have a *Screen* tab? Then you're stuck with the video mode you're using. Unless you buy a new video card, that is. If you've added a new video card, you have to tell OS/2 about your new card by using the robustly agonizing method described next:

First, open the OS/2 System folder with a double-click; from there, open the System Setup folder in the same way. Next, double-click the Selective Install object to make the window shown in Figure 9-3 appear on-screen.

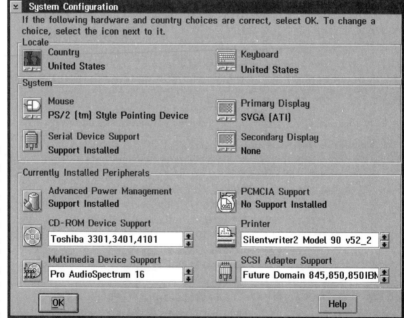

Figure 9-3: Click in the box next to Primary Display and click OK to get a list of video modes OS/2 can support.

Click in the box next to the Primary Display and click the OK button. OS/2 pops up a list of video modes it can support. Click the name of your new video card and click OK. (OS/2 sometimes identifies video cards by the chips on the card, not by the card's brand name. You might have to dig out the manual for this one. Or get a magnifying glass and start reading the names of the biggest chips on the video card.) Click OK in the next screen too. Click the Install buttons in the next two screens and click OK, and you're heading to town.

Now dig out the OS/2 installation disks. You have to feed some of those disks to OS/2 before it will switch to a different video mode. Depending on your particular brand of video card, you may have to insert one or two of OS/2's *Display Driver* disks as well.

When you've inserted the last disk, OS/2 says that you're finished but that you have to "restart the system in order for changes to take effect." In other words, you have to click the right mouse button on the desktop and choose Shut down. Then, when OS/2 says that it's OK, press Ctrl+Alt+Del to reboot the machine.

Ta da! OS/2 returns in its new video mode. If you like it, heavens be praised! You're all through. If you *don't* like it, you can change back to the old video mode. Unfortunately, you have to repeat the procedure and insert all those installation disks again.

✔ The higher the resolution, the more icons and windows you can pack on the desktop. Everything will look a little smaller, though.

✔ The Secondary Display option is for computer nerds with *two* monitors hooked up to a single computer.

✔ Some video modes aren't *seamless,* so you have to switch back and forth between a Windows desktop and an OS/2 desktop. A *seamless* video mode enables you to run a Windows program in a separate window on the OS/2 desktop. When you switch modes, OS/2 usually tells you whether you'll have seamless video in the new mode.

✔ If OS/2 doesn't include the correct drivers for your video card, you have to call up the people who manufactured the video card and bug them until they send you the drivers on a floppy disk.

OS/2's Housekeeper Work Areas

After you open a few folders on the desktop, things start to get crowded. Documents can get mixed up on-screen, and programs cover each other up.

To combat clutter, OS/2 comes with a built-in housekeeper that doesn't receive enough attention. You can put OS/2's housekeeper to work by making a folder an official *work area.*

When you double-click a work area folder, it opens up on-screen, just as any other folder does. You can open up any programs or documents you've put in that folder, just as you can with any other folder.

But to wipe your desk clear of all the stuff that came from that folder, you just close the folder. It automatically closes down any open programs that are stored in it, and it politely pauses to ask whether you want to save your work before it closes a window.

Later on down the road, you can reopen the work area folder with a double-click. OS/2 remembers all the stuff you had running the last time and puts it back on-screen.

For example, you can create a LEAKY REFRIGERATOR work area folder. Inside the folder, you can keep the spreadsheet that totals the damage, the letter to the refrigerator company, the letter to the insurance company, and the letter of apology to the guy who lives downstairs. You fill out the spreadsheet, write the letters, and close the work area folder.

When you close the work area folder, it takes the spreadsheet and letters with it, ready to spit them back up the next time you open it.

Or, if you *minimize* the work area folder, it minimizes all its associated desktop stuff as well.

You can keep your LEAKY REFRIGERATOR project in one work area folder, for example, and an OFFICE FOOTBALL POOL project in another work area folder. Minimizing first one work area folder and then the other is similar to switching between two quickly cleared-off desktops.

Imagine sitting in a swivel chair with a desktop that stretches all the way around you. Selectively minimizing work area folders is similar to turning your chair slightly to see different projects, one at a time.

- ✔ To designate a folder as an official *work area,* click it with the right mouse button and choose <u>S</u>ettings from the menu that squirts out. Click the <u>F</u>ile tab and then click in the inconspicuous box next to <u>W</u>ork area, near the bottom.

- ✔ Work areas work best with *shadows* of objects, not with the objects themselves. Shadows make work areas easier to manage. For example, you can put shadows of the *same* object into different work areas. If this shadow stuff still sounds goofy, hike back to Chapter 5.

✔ Rather than spend time opening and closing several folders, set up work areas to store all the related stuff for your projects. Work areas are great for containing special printer settings, for example, or views of past reports and charts. You can even stick a shadow of a work area folder in the Startup folder. Then, when you start OS/2, all your work starts up automatically.

✔ When you reopen a work area, it puts previously opened windows back where they were when you left them. If you left OS/2's free programs, Pulse or Clock, in the corner of the screen, for example, the work area folder puts them back there when you reopen it. In fact, your Desktop is a designated Work area. That's why OS/2 re-creates your desktop to look like it did when you last shut it down.

✔ Some programs don't tell OS/2 where they were last sitting, however. If you have a bunch of text files created by OS/2's System Editor in a work area folder, for example, they all are piled on top of each other when the work area folder brings them all back to life. They still open and close correctly; you just have to shuffle them around a little to see them all.

Looking for information in OS/2 Warp about work areas? When you're searching through its help system, be sure to search for *workarea, work-area,* and *work area.* OS/2 Warp Version 3.0 refers to the concept in three different spellings.

Starting the Screen Saver or Locking Up the Keyboard

In the dinosaur days of computing, cavemen worried about two things. First, programs that ran constantly on their computer screens caused *monitor burn-in.* That is, they left an ugly image on the monitor, even when the power was turned off.

Second, when cavemen left their computers unattended, other cavemen could sneak into their WOOLLY MAMMOTH SIGHTINGS database. They couldn't lock up their keyboards.

OS/2 solves both these problems with its Lockup now option. When you leave your desktop unattended for lunch, click a vacant area of the desktop with the right mouse button. When the little menu leaps to the screen, click Lockup now.

OS/2 throws an OS/2 beach blanket over the monitor, like the one shown in Figure 9-4.

Figure 9-4:
OS/2 throws this beach blanket over the monitor when you choose the Lockup now option.

If you haven't added a password, OS/2 asks you to think one up on the spot. When you're ready to return to work, just type your password; OS/2 pulls the beach blanket off your monitor.

To change a password or change the picture, click the desktop with the right mouse button and click Settings. Then choose the tab marked Lockup near the bottom-right corner of the electronic notebook.

On the first page, click Automatic lockup if you want OS/2 to toss the towel over the monitor after you haven't touched the keyboard for a certain number of minutes. (The number of minutes showing in the Timeout box, that is.) Otherwise, leave the No automatic lockup option selected.

Under Display, click Partial screen to skip the pictures; OS/2 simply puts a message on the screen saying that it's locked up — your work won't be hidden.

Click the little right-pointing arrow in the notebook's bottom-right corner to flip to page two. Click the little distorted arrow next to the File box to choose which picture you want OS/2 to stick on the monitor when you're away. If you don't like any of them, click Create another to make your own picture during a boring moment. Or click Edit to touch up an existing picture.

The Normal, Tiled, and Scaled image settings on this page work just like they do in the section, "Getting Rid of the Ugly Gray Background," at the beginning of this chapter; they either tile your picture across the screen or leave the picture at its normal size.

Finally, flip to the third page of the Settings notebook to change your password. Type something easy to remember in the Password box and then type it again in the second Password box to convince OS/2 that you know what you're doing. Then you have to type that password every time you or OS/2 locks up the screen.

If you forget the password, click the Help button. A message pops up, saying that you can break in to the computer by just turning it off and then on again. You lose any unsaved work, but you get your computer back.

Making OS/2 Display Everything Alphabetically

OS/2 is willing to be as sloppy or as organized as you are. Personally, I like to see everything in a window lined up in alphabetical order. For this sort of ABC regimentation, click the disorganized folder with the right mouse button, and choose Settings when the little menu flips toward you.

From the little electronic notebook, click the Sort tab and click the Always maintain sort order box. Then OS/2 always displays the contents of that window or folder in alphabetical order.

- ✒ OS/2 enables you to do some *very* powerful fiddling when you are sorting stuff. It usually figures that you want to sort everything alphabetically by name. That's why the word *Name* appears in the Default sort attribute box. If you want to sort by size instead, click the little arrow doohickey next to the Default sort attribute box. You can sort by Type (file, data, folder, and so on), Real name (the name of the file, not the object's title), and a host of other categories.

- ✒ If you want your most frequently used objects to appear at the top, consider sorting by Last access time.

How to Change Fonts

OS/2 normally chooses rather small letters when it labels stuff on-screen. You can make those letters bigger or different-looking by fiddling with OS/2's fonts. To make OS/2 use different letters for the icon titles, for example, whip out that electronic notebook. Click anywhere on the bare desktop with the right mouse button, and choose Settings.

The notebook opens right up to the page you want. When you click the Change font button, you see the Size box shown in Figure 9-5.

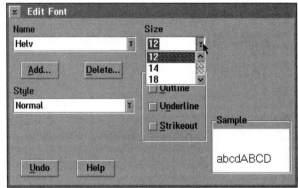

The size of a letter is measured in *points,* a topic you certainly don't want to learn about right now. Just remember that the bigger the *point size,* the bigger the letter. When you click the little arrow thing next to the box marked Size, OS/2 shows you the point sizes available for that font. Every time you click a different number, OS/2 shows the results in the Sample window. You can see the letters shrink or grow.

Done choosing? Then double-click that little symbol in the Edit Font box's upper-left corner. OS/2 immediately updates the desktop to reflect the changes.

✔ Want your letters to look different, like a typewriter's, perhaps? Then click the arrow next to the Name box. A menu drops down, just as one did for the Size box. When you click the name of a different font, OS/2 shows you in the Sample window what that font looks like.

✔ Fancy folks can underline letters by clicking in the Underline box. If you're weird enough to want letters crossed out, choose the Strikeout box. (The Outline box gives letters a hard-to-read 3-D look.)

✔ Even fancier folks can make the letters **bold** or *italic.* (Or even ***bold italic,*** for those very special days.)

✔ You can change the fonts in any window, not just in the main desktop. Simply choose a window's Settings notebook and start fiddling with the fonts section on the View tab.

✔ Fiddled things up so badly you can't read anything anymore? Then head for the Settings notebook and click the Default button at the bottom of the page. Things go back to the way OS/2 first looked.

Making OS/2 Recognize Your Mouse's Moves and Clicks

Some people can't click the mouse fast enough to make a double-click. OS/2 keeps thinking that they're making two *separate* clicks, not a bona fide double-click. To fix things, head for the System Setup folder (hidden in the OS/2 System folder). From inside the System Setup folder, double-click the Mouse object (for now, double-click as fast as you can; when you're inside, you can slow it down a little). The window shown in Figure 9-6 leaps to the screen.

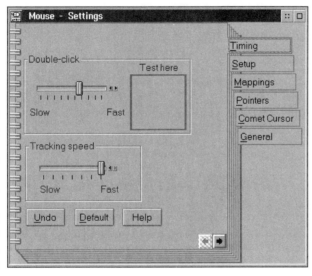

Figure 9-6:
Slide the little bars back and forth to fine-tune the way OS/2 listens to the mouse.

If OS/2 doesn't think that you're double-clicking fast enough, slide the Double-click bar toward the Slow side of the stick. If you want OS/2 to recognize only superfast double-clicks, move the bar toward the Fast side. To test how OS/2 is listening to your clicks, double-click in the little Test here box and then keep adjusting the bars until OS/2 gets your clicks right.

You can change the way OS/2 listens to the mouse's movements too. If a simple nudge sends the cursor flying, the *tracking speed* may be too fast. Slide the Tracking speed bar toward the Slow side and move the mouse around. When you find the right combination, double-click in the window's upper-left corner to close it and get back to work.

Left-handed mouse users can make OS/2 swap its buttons so that the left button works like the right button and so that the right button works like the left button. That option is on the notebook's Setup page.

✔ Normally, in OS/2, you use the mouse's right button to call up menus and its left button to select things. But you can change the way you use the mouse to anything you like. Click the Mappings tab on the notebook for a sea of options. For example, you can make OS/2 display a menu only when you double-click with the left button while you're holding down Shift.

✔ Don't know how to move those little bars back and forth by using the mouse? Trot back to Chapter 7; the bars work just like scroll bars.

✔ If you've played with the Mappings page and now you can't remember how OS/2 is supposed to work, click the Default button to bring everything back to normal.

✔ OS/2 had a bunch of sensitive (and militant) left-handed programmers. As a result, OS/2 doesn't refer to the left mouse button as the *left mouse button.* Instead it's known as *Button 1.* The right mouse button is always called *Button 2.* At least, that's the way it appears in all the OS/2 help screens and dialog boxes.

By all means, check out the Comet Cursor settings. The option creates puffs of smoke that follow your mouse pointer, making it easier to spot on laptops. However, it looks pretty darn groovy on desktop screens as well. Be sure to give it a shot.

Setting the Computer's Time and Date

Setting the computer's clock is sort of like setting the clock on a VCR or microwave. Actually, it's much simpler. If your computer's clock is off (or if it doesn't even show the correct date), head for the System Clock object. It's in the System Setup folder, which is nestled in the OS/2 System folder.

Click the System Clock object with the right mouse button and click Settings from the menu that shoots out. The Date/Time page comes to the screen, as shown in Figure 9-7.

See the little arrows next to the Hours, Minutes, and Seconds boxes? Click those arrows to change the numbers in the boxes. When the numbers are correct, double-click the notebook's upper-left corner to close it. OS/2 then updates the computer's clock.

✔ You may have to change the computer's clock during daylight saving time unless you live in one of those states, such as Arizona, that blows off the whole daylight saving time concept.

✔ You can change the date in the same way you change the time.

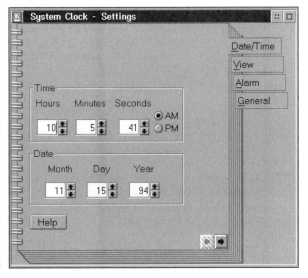

Figure 9-7:
If the
computer's
clock is a
little off, you
can reset it
on this
page.

> ✔ Oh, and don't forget to click the correct button for AM or PM, or else the
> computer's clock may be 12 hours off. Then anybody who reads the time
> on your computer files will think that you're a computer nerd who works
> all night.

Adjusting Your Keyboard

Typists notice the little things about a keyboard. If you hold down a key, for
example, it eventually starts doing thisssssssssssssssssssssssssss. But how long
does the computer wait before it repeats that key *for the first time?* And after it
begins repeating letters, how *quickly* do the newly repeated letters appear?

You can fine-tune OS/2's keyboard easily by heading for the Keyboard object.
It's in the System Setup folder, which is nestled in the OS/2 System folder.

Click the Keyboard object with the right mouse button and click Settings from
the menu that shoots out. Finally, click the Timing tab to start fine-tuning the
keyboard. The pop-up window looks like the one shown in Figure 9-8.

To make OS/2 begin repeating keypresses quickly, slide the Repeat delay rate
button toward Short. Move it to Long if you type slowly and don't want OS/2 to
think that you're trying to draw a line full of hyphens when you rest a finger on
the hyphen key a little too long.

Figure 9-8:
Slide the little adjustment levers by pointing at them with the mouse, holding down the left mouse button, and moving the mouse.

To make OS/2 spew out those repeated keys in a quick stream, slide the Repeat rate button toward Fast. Head for Slow if you prefer to see those keys repeat slowly, one key at a time.

While you're on this settings page, you also can adjust the cursor's blinking speed. The cursor, the little blinking line that shows your place in a text file, can flash more quickly than a K-Mart blue-light special or simply turn on and off very s-l-o-w-l-y. Move the Cursor blink rate lever toward Slow or Fast until the little guy beats to the sound of your own drummer.

✔ When you change any of the keyboard settings, click in the Test here box for a preview of how the changes will look.

✔ OS/2 sometimes asks you to press several keys at the same time. You press Ctrl+Alt+Delete, for example, to reset the computer. If you have difficulty pressing two or more keys at the same time, head for the Special Needs tab. You can use that page to make certain keys act *sticky,* which means that they act as though they are being held down. When you press Ctrl, then Alt, and then Delete, for example, OS/2 acts as though you're pressing those keys simultaneously. You also can adjust how long a key will be sticky.

✔ You can change some of the *hot keys* — also called *shortcut keys* — with the keyboard Mappings settings. In OS/2 you can press Shift+F10, for example, to call up an item's menu. (Or you can click that item with the right mouse button; both accomplish the same thing.) If you don't want to press Shift+F10, you can choose a different combination of keys — Ctrl+PgDn, for example. This fiddling option can mess up things, however. OS/2 may already be using Ctrl+PgDn for something else. At least you know that the options are available if you're looking for trouble.

Adding Your Own Stuff to Menus

Clicking the right mouse button on the desktop brings up a menu with bunches of options. Because it's so convenient, wouldn't it be fun to stick your own stuff on that menu? Then you could call up a favorite program just by clicking its name on the menu.

OS/2 is happy to oblige. Like most of the other fiddling, this fiddling takes place in the electronic notebook. To add Klondike to the desktop's menu, for example, call up the desktop's electronic notebook. Click the desktop with the right mouse button, and click Settings. Then click the Menu tab, and you see a page like the one shown in Figure 9-9.

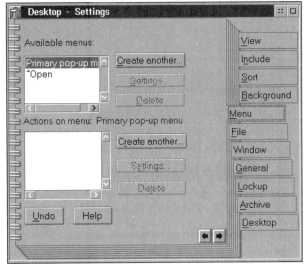

Figure 9-9:
You use this page to add your own stuff to OS/2 menus.

1. **Click the second Create another button — the one on the bottom half of the page.**

   A little box pops up, like the one shown in Figure 9-10.

2. **Type the following line in the Menu item name box:**

      Klondike game

   OS/2 puts Klondike game on the menu.

3. **Click the Find program button, then the Locate button, then the OK button, and then the Find button. Whew.**

   OS/2 ferrets out any programs on the desktop.

4. Yawn. Eventually, OS/2 brings up a list of available programs and shows you their objects. Click the scroll bar (or press PgDn) until you see the Solitaire-Klondike object. Give it a click and click the OK button. Click the OK button from the next window too.

5. Close the electronic notebook by double-clicking in its upper-left corner.

Figure 9-10:
Use this box
to get OS/2
to search
for
programs
and place
them on the
menu
automatically.

Klondike then appears as a menu option every time you click the desktop with the right mouse button. The desktop's menu looks like the menu shown in Figure 9-11.

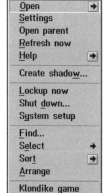

Figure 9-11:
Click
Klondike
game to
start a fresh
card game.

But I already know where the program is

If you know the path of the program you're after, don't bother with Step 3 in the preceding steps, where you press the Find program button. Instead, save some time by typing the program's name and path in the Name box. It looks something like this:

If you don't know the name of the program and where it's located, just make OS/2 find the program for you.

```
C:\OS2\APPS\KLONDIKE.EXE
```

✔ Although the OS/2 Desktop's menu is the handiest place to add menu items, you can add them to just about any menu by using the same method.

✔ If you're searching for other programs to stick on the menu (or if you've moved Klondike off the desktop and OS/2 can't find it), click the Drives tab on the Locate folder and root around for the folder you want to look through. To search for a misplaced file, use the Seek and Scan Files program, described in Chapter 11. When you know which folder the file is in, you can find it more easily. For information about rooting through file folders in a *tree,* head for Chapter 8.

Telling OS/2 Where to Send Minimized Windows

If you've used Windows, you're accustomed to *minimizing* a program or window. When you click the minimize button, the program shrinks itself into a small icon and places itself along the bottom edge of the monitor.

When you want that program or window to head back into view, you double-click its icon. Presto! It's back on the screen.

When you minimize programs or windows in OS/2, OS/2 gives you some choices. Sure, you can line up their icons along the bottom of the screen, just as you do in Windows. But until you instruct OS/2 otherwise, it sends icons to an *out-of-the-way* holding tank called the *Minimized Window Viewer.* The icon for the Minimized Window Viewer looks like this:

Minimized
Window Viewer

Double-click the Minimized Window Viewer folder, which hides in the OS/2 System Folder, and it hops to the screen, displaying all the icons for your minimized windows and programs. Give 'em a double-click to bring 'em back to life.

Unlike Windows, OS/2 normally tosses icons for all minimized windows into the Minimized Window Viewer. If you prefer to line them up along the bottom of the screen, try these steps:

1. **Click the Desktop with the right mouse button and choose $\underline{S}$ettings from the pop-up menu.**

   The Settings notebook opens.

2. **Click the $\underline{W}$indow tab to see your choices.**

If you want the icons lined up along the bottom of the screen, click the $\underline{M}$inimize button option and the Minimize $\underline{w}$indow to desktop option, as shown in Figure 9-12.

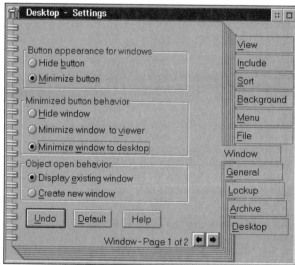

Figure 9-12: Click these settings to make OS/2's minimized windows line up along the bottom of the screen, just as they do in Microsoft Windows.

If you want the icons to head for the Minimized Window Viewer folder, click the $\underline{M}$inimize button option and the Minimize window to $\underline{v}$iewer option, as shown in Figure 9-13.

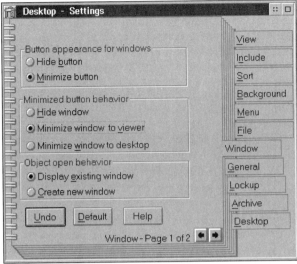

Figure 9-13: The Minimize window to viewer setting stashes minimized window icons in OS/2's Minimized Window Viewer folder.

Finally, if you want minimized windows to simply disappear, click the Hide window option, as shown in Figure 9-14.

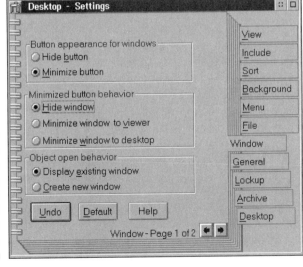

Figure 9-14: These settings make minimized icons simply disappear.

✔ If you choose the *simply disappear* option, you can retrieve minimized windows by clicking the desktop with both mouse buttons at the same time to bring up the Window List and then double-clicking the window's name on the list.

- ✔ You can mix and match, changing each program's settings separately, depending on that program's duties. Choose the *simply disappear* option, for example, for programs that run in the background, such as software that grabs faxes through fax cards. You don't need those icons cluttering up the desktop because you never need to access them.

- ✔ Use the Minimize window to desktop option for minimized windows you want to access easily: the icon for a notepad, for example, or a game of Mahjongg.

- ✔ The third set of options on the Window – Settings page enables you to control what happens when you click an object for a program that's already running. Choose Display existing window to make OS/2 bring the already running program to the screen. Choose Create new window to make OS/2 bring a second version of that program or object to the screen.

Silencing the Shredder

Every time you drag something over to the Shredder and let go, the Shredder pops up with a worried-mother "Are you sure?" question. Although being questioned is undoubtedly safer, some people like to live on the wild side. They want the Shredder to dispose of their trash without question.

To silence the Shredder, click the System object (hidden in the System Setup folder) with the right mouse button and choose Settings from the little squirt-out menu. Next, click the little notebook's Confirmations tab, and you see the page shown in Figure 9-15.

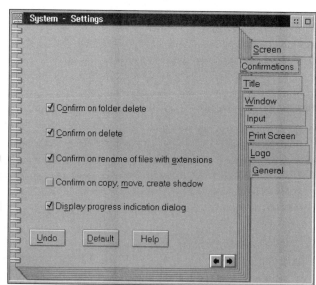

Figure 9-15: OS/2 warns you about everything that has a check mark next to it.

Click in the little boxes to toggle the check marks on or off. Here's what the options mean:

Confirm on folder delete: Put a check mark here if you like to be nagged every time you delete a folder.

Confirm on delete: Check here if you like a stern questioning whenever you delete *anything*.

Confirm on rename of files with extensions: Moving into more esoteric territory, this option warns you if you change a filename's *extension*. (An extension consists of the three letters that follow the period at the end of a filename.) Why be careful here? Because some programs (and almost all Windows programs) recognize their offspring by their extensions. If you change a filename's extension, you break its ties with the program that created it, and you can no longer load it by simply double-clicking its name.

Confirm on copy, move, create shadow: The actions for copying, moving, or creating a shadow of an object are quite similar. If you tend to forget which is which, put a check mark in the box for this option. Then, when you try to copy an object, OS/2 asks whether you're sure that you want to *copy* the object. (Using this option can keep you from accidentally moving the object or creating a shadow of it, either of which can make people laugh at you when you tell them about it over dinner.)

Display progress indication dialog: OS/2 puts a little *pause* button on the screen so that you can pause your copying, moving, or shadowing chores in an emergency — *if* you check this box.

✔ After you use OS/2 for a few months, you get that teenage urge to stifle OS/2's cautionary comments and brave it on your own.

✔ Or, if you're like me, you leave most of them on. It never hurts to have the computer keep you fully informed of what it's about to do next.

"LET ME GUESS — YOU'RE INSTALLING OS/2."

Chapter 10
Sharing Information

● ●

In This Chapter

▶ That cut-and-paste stuff

▶ What's the clipboard?

▶ Highlighting the important stuff

▶ Cutting, copying, or deleting highlighted stuff

▶ Pasting stuff into windows

▶ Private and public clipboard stuff

▶ The DOS version of cut, copy, and paste

● ●

*J*ust about everybody likes to share information at the water cooler.

A snippet of information about Bob and Jennifer, for example, can easily be passed to Steve, who passes it to Ethel, who passes it back to an embarrassed Bob.

OS/2 works like a giant water cooler. You can easily pass information between any on-screen windows. You can even lift words or pictures from a DOS program and shuttle them over to a Windows or OS/2 program.

And, like Bob and Jennifer, the programs don't even have to know that you are moving information around. OS/2 handles the entire process behind everybody's back.

This chapter shows you how to cut, copy, and paste information between programs without having any of them get riled up about it.

That Cut-and-Paste Stuff (and Copy, Too)

DOS programs used to be horribly selfish. When you created a chart in one program, for example, it was stuck there. You couldn't stick that fancy ice-cube-shaped chart into a word processor to illustrate a report on "Heating Costs in Igloos."

You simply couldn't shuffle information from one program to another. DOS programmers used different ways to save each program's information, and the programs couldn't read each other's formats.

Although DOS programmers eventually wised up, Microsoft's Windows didn't wait for them to start drinking diet soda together. Windows enables you to grab information from one DOS program's window and stick it into another DOS program's window. The programs (and programmers) don't even have to know what's going on. Windows simply freezes the DOS program on the screen so that you can pick out the good stuff for transferring.

OS/2 takes that concept one step farther. You can move information around freely between DOS, Windows, and OS/2 programs. Stealing information from windows works like this:

1. **Select the information you want.**

2. **Tell OS/2 to either copy or cut that information to its little clipboard.**

3. **Then tell OS/2 which program to paste the information in.**

It's a simple concept. Computers have finally reached kindergarten.

✔ When OS/2 *copies* information, it lifts a copy of whatever you've selected and sticks that copy in a special place called the *clipboard.* The clipboard, covered in the next section, acts as a temporary storage tank.

✔ When OS/2 *cuts* information, it surgically removes it. The information disappears from the first program and heads for its new, albeit temporary, home on the clipboard.

✔ When OS/2 *pastes* information, it takes a copy of whatever is currently sitting on the clipboard and sticks it in the program you're currently working with.

✔ OS/2 can cut or copy *text* — plain old words and letters — but the special formatting in that text rubs off during the move. If you try to copy a **bold-faced word** from one window to another, for example, the bold-faced part doesn't come with it. OS/2 copies only the words themselves.

✔ OS/2 can cut or copy graphics (pictures of things such as swans and lighthouses). However, you can't paste graphics into any program you choose. For example, you can't paste a graphic into the OS/2 System Editor. That program, as well as many others, simply isn't built to handle swans or lighthouses — or any other graphics, for that matter.

✔ Compared to Windows, OS/2 lags when it copies graphics to the clipboard. Pressing Alt+PrintScreen in Windows, for example, sends a copy of the current window to the clipboard. Pressing Alt+PrintScreen in OS/2 doesn't do anything at all. OS/2's version of Windows, WIN-OS/2, works just like

Windows does, though. Pressing Alt+PrintScreen while running WIN-OS/2 sends a copy of your current Windows program to the clipboard.

✔ OS/2 and its version of Windows (WIN-OS/2) both come with their own clipboard programs. To make it easier to figure out what's going on, OS/2 lets you make those two clipboards *public*, which means that anything that's copied to one automatically shows up on the other. There's much less fuss that way. (Public and private clipboards are covered later in this chapter.)

What's the Clipboard?

OS/2 learned something valuable from the kindergartners. As soon as a kindergartner cuts something out of something else, that new little scrap gets lost in the pile.

So as soon as you cut or copy something from a window in OS/2, OS/2 puts that information in a special holding tank called the *clipboard*. To see what's on the clipboard, use the Clipboard Viewer. Its object looks like this:

Clipboard Viewer

If you copy the word TWITCH from a text file, for example, that word heads for the clipboard. TWITCH stays on the clipboard, too, until you copy something else — another word, for example, or a picture. Then the incoming information replaces TWITCH.

To take a look at the clipboard's current contents, double-click the Clipboard Viewer object. For example, the clipboard shown in Figure 10-1 contains text, and the one shown in Figure 10-2 contains a picture.

When you are doing a great deal of cutting and pasting between windows, keep the Clipboard Viewer open at the bottom of the screen. Seeing what's currently inside the clipboard makes it easier to track exactly what you're cutting and pasting.

✔ OS/2's clipboard works behind the scenes. Your only contact with it is through the Clipboard Viewer. That's why OS/2's clipboard isn't capitalized and why the Clipboard Viewer, an actual program, is capitalized. It's a matter of capital importance.

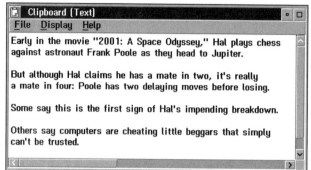

Figure 10-1:
Text on the OS/2 clipboard.

> **Clipboard (Text)**
>
> File   Display   Help
>
> Early in the movie "2001: A Space Odyssey," Hal plays chess against astronaut Frank Poole as they head to Jupiter.
>
> But although Hal claims he has a mate in two, it's really a mate in four: Poole has two delaying moves before losing.
>
> Some say this is the first sign of Hal's impending breakdown.
>
> Others say computers are cheating little beggars that simply can't be trusted.

Figure 10-2:
A picture of a flamingo on a beach is on the OS/2 clipboard.

✔ When the OS/2 clipboard contains a picture, it displays the picture in the bottom-left corner of the Clipboard Viewer. It looks weird sitting way down there rather than up along the top, where you find the Clipboard in Windows. Don't worry if the clipboard looks broken; the pictures are *supposed* to be down there.

✔ The clipboard usually holds text or pictures, but sometimes it contains something funky, such as a sound copied from the Windows Sound Recorder. Because no one can agree on what a sound should look like, you see a little picture of an oscilloscope showing a sound wave.

Rendering yourself silly over silly Render details

The clipboard shows a simple picture of your data — words or pictures — yet it often contains more than that. For example, if you use the Windows Paintbrush program to draw a picture of a housefly and then copy the picture to the clipboard, you see the housefly picture in the Clipboard Viewer.

However, the clipboard also contains that housefly picture in *other* computerized formats. Those other formats increase your chances of success when you try to dump the fly picture into other programs. But some of those other formats aren't visible to a human eye.

That's why you sometimes see weird, unrecognizable formats listed in the pull-down menu when you click the Render button in OS/2's Clipboard Viewer. The formats are usually called something like BITMAP, Native, OwnerLink, Metafile, or even something as weird as #9.

If you double-click formats that OS/2 can't put on the screen, OS/2 puts the following error message on the screen instead:

```
Error! Format not rendered.
```

It's no big deal. Click OK, and the error message disappears.

The Windows Clipboard works in pretty much the same way. If you click Display in the Windows Clipboard, the same formats are listed. Windows is a little more polite, however. The formats that aren't visible are *grayed out,* so you can't select them.

The moral? If you get an error message under Render, keep choosing a different format; eventually you get one you can see.

> ✔ The clipboard shows only one *view* of what it's holding. If you copy some artful squiggles from the Windows Paintbrush program, for example, those artful squiggles appear on the clipboard. But the clipboard holds more than just those artful squiggles, as you can see when you click Render, an option that pops up when you click Display. Most of the other formats can't be displayed, however, so ignore them. And ignore the boring technical sidebar, "Rendering yourself silly over silly Render details."

Highlighting the Important Stuff

Ready to grab some information from a window? Then tell OS/2 exactly what information you're after by *highlighting* it. Highlighted information usually turns a dark color, so when the words change color, you know that OS/2 recognizes them.

Unfortunately, the process of grabbing information differs slightly from window to window. Nevertheless, here are some pointers for grabbing most of the goodies:

✔ To grab text, click in front of the first desirable word and hold down the left mouse button. Then slide the mouse to the end of the words you're after. As you move the mouse, the words become darker, showing that they're highlighted. When the stuff you want changes color, let go of the mouse button to tell OS/2 the boundaries of the stuff you want to grab.

✔ You can highlight a single word, such as the word *Valuable* in Figure 10-3, by double-clicking it.

Figure 10-3:
The word
Valuable is
highlighted
and ready to
be cut,
copied, or
deleted.

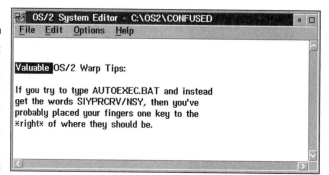

✔ In some windows, you can highlight a program's contents by clicking the word Edit on the menu bar, that word-filled strip that runs across the top of a window. Choose the Select <u>a</u>ll option to highlight *everything*.

✔ DOS and Windows programs make you run around a little differently when you're swiping stuff out of their windows. Check out their sections in this chapter for the full scoop.

✔ After you have highlighted the information you're after, you can either *cut it* (slice it out of the window) or *copy it* (make a copy of the information and leave the original in place). In either case, the highlighted information is sent to the clipboard. This *cut* and *copy* stuff is discussed in the very next section.

✔ After you have highlighted text, you have to either cut it or copy it right away. If you do anything else, such as absentmindedly click the mouse some-place else in the document, all the highlighted text reverts back to plain old regular text, much like a werewolf returning to normal after a full moon.

Copying, Cutting, Pasting, or Deleting Highlighted Stuff

After you highlight the information you're after, you have to tell OS/2 whether you want to grab a copy of it or simply cut it out of its current window. The following sections give you the scoop.

Copying

To copy highlighted information, hold down Ctrl and press Insert. At first it looks as though nothing has happened. Feel free to press Ctrl+Insert again, but there's no need. OS/2 has already copied the highlighted information to the clipboard. If you're doubtful, double-click the Clipboard Viewer. You see the information sitting on the clipboard, ready for action.

It may take you awhile to remember the Ctrl+Insert key combination to copy things, so until you do, just cheat by using the menus. After you highlight the information you're after, click the word Edit from the program's menu bar. A menu leaps out toward you. Click the word Copy to do the same thing as pressing Ctrl+Insert.

Not all programs have Edit and Copy menus, so you may be stuck with the Ctrl+Insert stuff.

Cutting

If you want to remove information from one place and stick it into another, choose *cut* rather than copy. To cut the highlighted information, hold down Shift and press Delete. The highlighted information disappears and then surfaces on the clipboard.

Can't remember Shift+Delete? If the program has a menu bar at the top, give this method a shot: Click Edit and then click Cut on the new menu that pops down.

Pasting

After you cut or copy something to the clipboard, you're ready to paste that information into its new home. Click in the window where you want to squirt that information. If you're pasting a paragraph into a letter, for example, click the spot in the letter where that paragraph should go.

Then, to paste, hold down Shift and press Insert. The clipboard then flings all its information into that spot.

Deleting

If you want to get rid of the highlighted information and never see it again, simply press Delete. OS/2 purges the information from the screen. Actually, it *looks* the same as though you had *cut* it — except that it doesn't show up on the clipboard.

Other trivia about copying, cutting, pasting, and deleting

Now that you have that straight, here's some more stuff to keep in mind when you're moving things around:

- ✔ If you accidentally cut the wrong thing, just press Shift+Insert to put it back where it belongs. If you accidentally *delete* the wrong thing, press Alt+Backspace to undo your last mistake. (That *undo trick* undoes only your last mistake, so if you discover that you've made two mistakes, you're out of luck.)

- ✔ Relax! All this Shift/Delete/Backspace nonsense can be found in the front of this book, on the "Cheat Sheet" tear-out card. Put away that Magic Marker.

- ✔ After you copy or cut something to the clipboard, it stays on the clipboard, even if you paste it into other windows. The information doesn't leave the clipboard until you copy or cut something else. Then the incoming stuff replaces the clipboard's older contents, which disappear forever.

- ✔ The Delete key is called *Del* on some keyboards; the Insert key is called *Ins* on some as well. Just about all keyboards say *Shift*, however.

Gads! How do I remember this stuff?

Yes, remembering the difference between Ctrl+Insert, Shift+Delete, and Shift+Insert is difficult. It's certainly too much for me to remember, so I don't even try. I just remember Shift+*Delete* to cut and Shift+*Insert* to paste. I leave copying right out of the picture.

I highlight the stuff I want to copy and press Shift+Delete to cut it. Wham! It disappears, so I'm pretty sure that it's on the clipboard. Then I imme-

diately press Shift+Insert to paste it back into the window again. Wham! The information is back in place. Plus, I'm *absolutely* sure that it left a copy of itself on the clipboard.

Sure, I have to take an extra step. Rather than simply copy and paste, I cut, paste, and paste. But remembering that *Delete* means *cut* and that *Insert* means *paste* is easier than trying to remember the Ctrl+Insert stuff. Right?

What's This Private and Public Clipboard Stuff?

Windows and OS/2 both grabbed the *clipboard* concept, so OS/2 and the version of Windows that comes with OS/2 have their own separate clipboards.

Normally, OS/2 treats those clipboards as *public,* meaning that what appears on one clipboard automatically appears on the other.

If you want to keep them separate for some reason, you can tell OS/2 to make the clipboards *private.* Then stuff that's on the OS/2 clipboard isn't affected by stuff on the Windows Clipboard, and vice versa.

To switch from public to private, head for the WIN-OS/2 Setup object. It's hiding in the System Setup folder, which is hiding in the OS/2 System folder.

Click the WIN-OS/2 Setup object with the right mouse button, click <u>S</u>ettings, and wait for the little Settings notebook to appear.

Then click the <u>D</u>ata Exchange tab. On the bottom of that page, underneath Clipboard, you see two options: Public and Private. Click the one you want, and OS/2 makes the change immediately.

- ✔ To get out of that Settings notebook thing, double-click in its upper-left corner. Poof! It disappears.

- ✔ If you're going to move information around among a number of Windows programs, go ahead and make the Windows Clipboard private. Then run those Windows programs in a full-screen Windows session to speed things up.

- ✔ To highlight a single word in any OS/2 or Windows program, point at it with the mouse and double-click. (In the Windows program Write, if you hold down the button on its second click, you can quickly highlight additional text word by word when you move the mouse around.)

- ✔ To highlight a portion of text in just about any OS/2 or Windows program, click at the beginning of the text, hold down Shift, and click at the end of the text you want. Everything between those two points is highlighted.

- ✔ Accidentally delete the wrong thing? Then hold down Alt and press Backspace to bring it back. (In Windows, try pressing Ctrl+Z for variety. Both do the same thing.)

- ✔ Going to be using Windows frequently? Then you may want to buy *Windows 3.1 For Dummies,* 2nd Edition, by Andy Rathbone (IDG Books, 1994). Almost every instruction in that book works equally well for the version of Windows that's built-in to OS/2.

The DOS Version of Cut, Copy, and Paste

The cut-and-paste stuff gets a little trickier when you are exchanging information with DOS programs. See, DOS programs always think that they're in complete control of the computer. They never expected that sneaky computer programmers would run several DOS programs on one computer at the *same time.*

So here's a dose of DOS exceptions to the normal OS/2 cut-and-paste stuff:

> **Rule 1:** First, you can't *cut* stuff from a DOS program. You can only *copy* stuff. The DOS program holds on to its information, no matter what.
>
> **Rule 2:** You can't paste anything but text into most DOS programs.
>
> **Rule 3:** You can't copy or paste anything into a DOS program when it's taking up the entire screen. You gotta put the DOS program in its own little window on the screen. (Press Alt+Home to *toggle* a DOS program from full-screen to window mode.)

✔ To *copy* information from a DOS window, click the window's upper-left corner and choose Mar<u>k</u> from the pull-down menu. Put the weird-looking mouse pointer at the beginning of the stuff you want to grab, hold down the left mouse button, and move the mouse to the end of what you want to grab. When the stuff you want is highlighted, press Enter, and OS/2 sticks it on the clipboard.

✔ To *paste* information into a DOS window, put the cursor where you want the information to appear. Then click the window's upper-left corner and choose <u>P</u>aste from the pull-down menu. (The Shift+Insert key combination doesn't work in a DOS program.)

✔ You can't paste graphics into most DOS programs. The <u>P</u>aste command in the menu is grayed out. That grayed-out stuff is OS/2's polite way of saying "Hey, don't even *think* about trying that, pal!"

Part III
OS/2 Applications (Those Free Programs)

The 5th Wave   By Rich Tennant

DARE TO BELIEVE YOUR EYES
HIPPOPOTAMUS MAN
Natures Strangest Joke!

MR. TWEETY
RAISED BY WILD
Parakeets!
DIRECT FROM THE
OUTBACK OF
AUSTRALIA!

GUY WHO BOUGHT
OS/2 BECAUSE HE
THOUGHT APPLICATIONS
RAN A WHOLE LOT
BETTER THAN UNDER
DOS!

SIDE SHOW
$1.00

In this part ...

First, the good news. OS/2 comes with a bunch of free programs that aren't even mentioned on the box.

Hidden away, inside OS/2's plethora of folders, are a free database, a spreadsheet, games, word processors, a tele-communications program, and even a program to send faxes.

Now, the bad news. Some of these free programs make life easier, but some of them are, well, pretty dopey.

This part of the book takes a good look at all the applications (IBM calls them *applets*) that come with OS/2. It describes how to use the good ones, points out the ones you can safely ignore, and singles out the applets that can be simply booted from the barrel.

Chapter 11

The OS/2 Applets, Er, Programs

● ●

In This Chapter

▶ Opening a file

▶ OS/2 System Editor

▶ Enhanced Editor

▶ Icon Editor

▶ Seek and Scan Files

▶ Pulse

▶ Klondike

▶ Mahjongg

▶ System Clock

▶ Enhanced Editor

▶ Picture Viewer

▶ Chess

● ●

*U*sing OS/2 is similar to moving into a luxury condominium complex: Both come with tons of features that sound great — for a month or two. But are you really going to pump iron in the condo's weight room, especially when the neighbors are watching? Will you really play tennis every day after work? Even after buying new tennis racquets, many newcomers find that their extra-curricular interest peaks with the Used Magazine Exchange box by the swimming pool.

Similarly, OS/2 comes with bunches of applets — cute-sounding little programs — that look great when you peek at their icons inside the Productivity folder. But which program does what? And which ones should you even bother trying to figure out?

This chapter tackles the programs OS/2 automatically adds to your desktop when you first install it. You'll want to keep some of them; others can probably be dragged to the Shredder. (Chapter 12 covers OS/2's BonusPak — a bunch of programs you have to install yourself.)

Opening a File

Most of OS/2's little programs work in pretty much the same way, so you don't have much to remember, and you have even less to learn. Chapter 7 covers the basics of windows: how to open menus, change their size, and move them around on the desktop. If you get stuck on that stuff, page through Chapter 7.

If you're comfortable with moving windows around, the next step is opening a file into an applet so that you can get some work done. (*Opening a file* involves plucking a collection of information off a disk and making it show up inside a program's window.)

The first step in opening a file from any OS/2 applet is to click File from the menu bar along its top. Then choose Open from the menu that dangles down.

The box shown in Figure 11-1 appears.

Click to filter out unwanted files

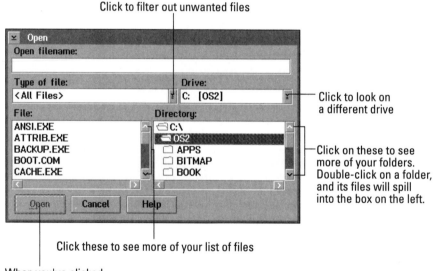

Figure 11-1:
Use this
screen to
open a file
from an
OS/2 applet.

Click to look on
a different drive

Click on these to see
more of your folders.
Double-click on a folder,
and its files will spill
into the box on the left.

Click these to see more of your list of files

When you've clicked
on the file you want,
click here to open it

What do those little labels mean?

Before you try to open a file, take a look at the screen that OS/2 throws at you. The following sections explain all the confusing labels that appear on the screen.

Open filename

If you know the name and folder location of the file you want to open, type that information in the box with the Open filename label. You can't use this box, however, unless you also know the file's path — its exact location on your disk. To open a file named OUCH.TXT, for example, that is stored on the OS/2 directory of drive C, you have to type the following line:

```
C:\OS2\OUCH.TXT
```

One typographical error and you're outta the game. Unless OS/2 has all the information it needs, it can't find the file. \OS2\ stands for the OS/2 folder. If the file you're after is nestled deeply inside a bunch of folders, you have to type the names of all those folders too. Unless you're familiar with paths, ignore this box and use the others instead.

Type of file

Some programs create certain types of files. If they do, those certain types of files show up here, letting you choose them more easily. Programs such as System Editor don't create any sort of special files, though, so you're stuck with <All Files>. That means that you'll see a list of all files, no matter what they contain. In fact, few of the programs that come with OS/2 use this feature.

Directory

Sometimes OS/2 refers to its folders as "directories," but "folders" and "directories" refer to the same thing: holding areas for files. The Directory box lists all the folders on a disk drive. Every time you double-click a folder, that folder's contents suddenly appear in the File box to its left.

To see more folders, click the little arrows on that scroll bar thing to the right. See how one folder in the Directory box looks as though it's open? That folder contains the files that are currently showing.

File

This box lists the names of files stored in the open folder. If you see the name of the file you're after in this box, double-click it. The file is then immediately sucked into the program, and you can quickly do away with this dumb box. If you don't see the file you want, click the scroll bar thing to the right of the box to see the filenames that are hiding from view above or below the box.

The files are listed alphabetically by name, so if the list is long, you have to click the down arrow for a long time to see files such as ZOUNDSO.FUN. Instead, just press Z. OS/2 jumps down the list to show you the files beginning with Z.

Drive

Some computers have more than one hard drive. To see drives other than plain ol' drive C, click the weird arrow thing in the Drive box. Then click the drive you want to explore and watch as OS/2 starts spelunking that drive, showing its folders and files.

You have to click in the Drive box to open a file from a floppy disk.

Help and Cancel

To read a few Official IBM Tips on file hunting, click the Help button. Or to give up and head for a refreshing beverage, click the Cancel button. (No, you don't get your file that way.)

How do I open a file?

Now that you have those labels under control, you can open a file. Generally, the steps for opening a file go like this:

1. **Make sure that the Drive box lists the drive on which you want to search.**

2. **Make sure that the Directory box lists the folder where the file lives.**

   You may have to click the little scroll bars to see all the folders. Also try going to the folder listed at the top of the list and double-clicking it. OS/2 then returns you to the top level of folders, where you can gradually begin burrowing your way down into them again.

3. **Click the little scroll bars to see an alphabetical list of files in the current folder.**

   If you're sick of scroll bars, the PgUp and PgDn keys work just as well.

4. **When you see the file you're after, double-click it.**

   Whew! Then put this book down and get back to work.

   ✔ If you feel more at home searching through folders with the Drives object, head over there. Double-click the OS/2 System folder, the Drives folder, and the object for the drive you're after. Then turn to Chapter 8 for the rundown on opening and closing folders. If you see the file you're interested in, double-click it. Most of the time, the program that created it then loads up the file and heads for the top of your desktop.

   ✔ If you can't find the file you're after, check out the cool Seek and Scan Files applet, described later in this chapter. If you can remember even a single word contained in the missing file, Seek and Scan can ferret out the file without the smell my sister's two ferrets had.

Reading and Editing Text Files

You'll probably find yourself using the official OS/2 System Editor quite a bit, whether you like it or not. In fact, if you double-click something OS/2 doesn't recognize, OS/2 automatically brings up OS/2 System Editor to process the unknown.

Despite its confusing name, OS/2 System Editor is merely a small word processor. You can use it to move words and sentences around. It's no WordPerfect, though. It doesn't let you change the margins. You can't compose and print fancy newsletters for the Girl Scout troop. You can't even make a single word bold or italicized — you have to boldface or italicize the entire document or none of it at all.

No, the System Editor is for simple writing chores: jotting down notes for yourself or reading ASCII files— bare-bones files containing only words and numbers and no fancy formatting. (It can read those strange files called READ.ME that you've probably seen lying around in some of your folders.)

OS/2's System Editor works almost exactly like Windows' Notepad. Both of them are for the same simple text-editing chores.

OS/2 System Editor

If you open a file containing words and sentences, all is well. OS/2 System Editor pops up with the file inside, as shown in Figure 11-2.

Figure 11-2:
OS/2 System
Editor
comes in
handy for
reading
explanatory
files called
README
that IBM
inserts in
folders for
you.

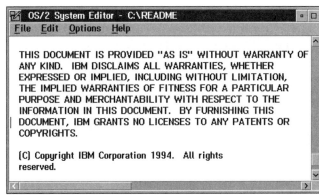

> **OS/2 System Editor — C:\README**
>
> File   Edit   Options   Help
>
> THIS DOCUMENT IS PROVIDED "AS IS" WITHOUT WARRANTY OF
> ANY KIND. IBM DISCLAIMS ALL WARRANTIES, WHETHER
> EXPRESSED OR IMPLIED, INCLUDING WITHOUT LIMITATION,
> THE IMPLIED WARRANTIES OF FITNESS FOR A PARTICULAR
> PURPOSE AND MERCHANTABILITY WITH RESPECT TO THE
> INFORMATION IN THIS DOCUMENT. BY FURNISHING THIS
> DOCUMENT, IBM GRANTS NO LICENSES TO ANY PATENTS OR
> COPYRIGHTS.
>
> (C) Copyright IBM Corporation 1994. All rights
> reserved.

If you double-click a filename that OS/2 doesn't recognize, though, OS/2 tries to load that file in OS/2 System Editor anyway. The screen looks similar to Figure 11-3.

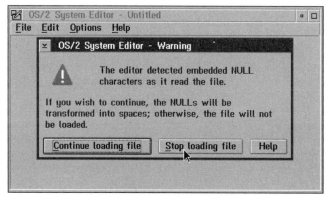

Figure 11-3: If you see this message, click the Stop loading file button.

The warning message you see in Figure 11-3 means that OS/2 System Editor is trying to read something that contains unreadable Japanese hieroglyphics or something similar. If you want to see this weird stuff, click Continue loading file. If you don't have time for mere curiosities, halt this nonsense by clicking Stop loading file.

OS/2 System Editor works fairly simply, with one exception. When you begin typing words, they don't break off and form a new line when they reach the end of the window. They keep right on going. You can see only the beginning of each paragraph in the window; all the rest of the words flow right off the right edge of the window.

To make sentences wrap themselves around to a new line so that they're always visible, turn on the Word wrap feature. Click Options, click Word wrap from the little menu that drops down, and click On. That's it.

✔ Can't figure out how to open a menu? Then flip back to Chapter 7 to the section, "Open a Window — It's Stuffy in Here!" for a quick briefing. The beginning of this chapter explains how to open a file.

✔ If you're ever told to edit important computer files called CONFIG.SYS or AUTOEXEC.BAT, OS/2 System Editor is the right tool for the job. (It's the right tool for REXX files or CMD files too, if you're heading down that path.)

✔ You can use OS/2 System Editor to change the font — the size and appearance of words — but only for the entire file. All the letters change equally. You can't use OS/2 System Editor to make a newsletter that has big headlines and smaller letters for the stories telling what the scouts did. For that fancy stuff, you have to head back to the store and buy a word processor or desktop publishing program.

✔ For simple newsletters or party fliers, check out the Windows program called Write. It's in your Windows Programs folder. Or, if you've installed the BonusPak, check out IBM Works' word processor.

✔ If the computer loses power before you can save your poems, they're lost forever. To prevent this tragedy, save your files often. Choose Save from the File menu, and after you click a folder in which to store the poems, type a name in the Save as filename box.

✔ Still paranoid about possibly losing unsaved files? Then choose Autosave from the File menu. Click in the Autosave on box to get OS/2 to save your file after every 100 changes — keystrokes, deletions, and other creative wangles.

✔ Need to find something in a text file? Click Find from the menu that drops down after you click the word Edit. Watch out for two check boxes, Case sensitive and Wrap. If you check Case sensitive, OS/2 makes sure that any capitalization matches. If you search for *Fat ducks,* a case-sensitive search doesn't find the words *fat ducks* or *fat Ducks.* Feel free to check the Wrap option, though. It just tells the editor to head back up and search the top of the file if it can't find *Fat ducks* near the bottom.

✔ *OS/2 System Editor* is a pretty long-winded icon title, and it often bumps into its neighbors. To shorten the title, hold down Alt and click the title. A little box appears around the title, and then you can change the words. Change the title to *Editor* so that it fits better in tight quarters.

Changing Those Boring Old Icons

Everybody loves a good icon, but OS/2's icons are pretty boring. Luckily, you can change them or create your own with OS/2's Icon Editor:

Icon Editor

Although you can open Icon Editor by double-clicking its object in the Productivity folder, the easiest way to change an object's icon is through the Settings page. The icon OS/2 tossed to my Links386 Pro golf game is pretty boring, for example, as you can see in the lower-left corner of Figure 11-4.

Figure 11-4:
Open an
icon's
Settings to
use Icon
Editor to
change it.

These steps show you how to edit a boring icon:

1. **Click the boring icon with the right mouse button and click Settings to bring up the electronic notebook. (Or hold down Alt and double-click the icon.)**

2. **Click the notebook's General tab and click the Edit button. Icon Editor leaps to action, as shown in Figure 11-5.**

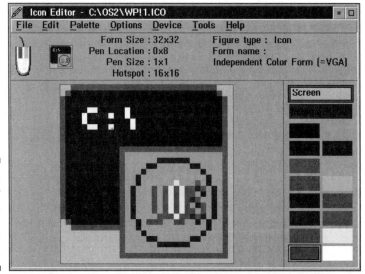

Figure 11-5:
Icon Editor
is ready to
change a
boring DOS
icon.

3. **Click the color you want and start smearing it around on the icon.**

   Soon, a new icon takes shape, as you can see in Figure 11-6. If you draw a splotch in the wrong place, remove that splotch with Alt+Backspace.

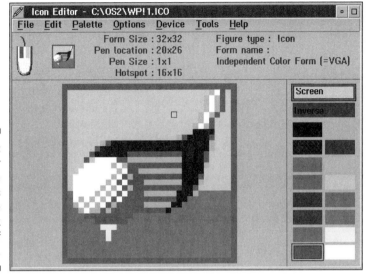

4. **When you're happy with your artistic creation, click File and choose Save from the menu that shoots out.**

   Then comes the hard part: figuring out what to do with the screen shown in Figure 11-7.

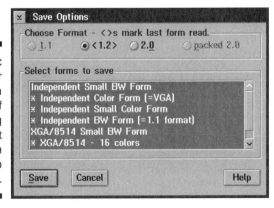

5. **The *forms* (video format) that OS/2 recommends for saving the icon have an asterisk next to them. So take all the *forms* that *don't* have an asterisk next to them off the list by clicking them.**

6. **After you choose the right form, click the** *version* **of OS/2 you're using. Here, OS/2 refers to the version as its** *Format*. **So click the button that comes closest to the version you're using and click <u>S</u>ave to save the newly created icon.**

7. **Finally, exit from the program by double-clicking in Icon Editor's upper-left corner. Do the same for the Settings page of the notebook as well, and the new icon appears in its folder. Fun!**

✔ If you create a miserable dud icon and accidentally save it, click the <u>U</u>ndo button when you return to the notebook's Settings page. <u>U</u>ndo brings back the boring old icon you started with, no matter how many times you've spruced it up since then.

✔ Although the Icon Editor has way too many options, one that comes in handy is holding down Ctrl and pressing the hyphen key (-). Then you can draw only straight lines. Press the same keys again to return to swirling squiggles.

✔ Another helpful option is Ctrl+F. This option turns the pointer into a can of spilling paint. Click on a putrid color in the icon to replace it with the color that is currently selected.

✔ Bad news: Even when you create a masterpiece of a new icon, OS/2 uses the new icon only in the program's folder. If you start the program and minimize it, OS/2 reverts to the boring original icon you tried to replace.

✔ You can open the Icon Editor by double-clicking its icon from the Productivity folder. When you create new icons, make a special ICON folder to keep them in. Then they're easier to find when you're assigning icons to new programs and files.

✔ Windows icons aren't always compatible with OS/2 icons and vice versa. Microsoft and IBM can't get together on something that important.

✔ You can copy the best ideas from other icons. Call up in the Icon Editor the icon that has the features you want to copy. Press Alt+A and Ctrl+Insert, in that order. The icon is copied onto OS/2's clipboard. Next, call up the icon you want to edit and press Shift+Insert. The icon that's on the clipboard is then pasted over the icon you want to change. Edit it a little, save it, and you're through.

✔ OS/2 confuses some people because its folders don't always *look* like folders. The Information folder, for example, is a bunch of books. To eliminate any confusion, use the Icon Editor to make that icon look more like a folder. First, copy an icon that looks like a plain old *folder* by using the trick in the preceding paragraph. Then edit the Information icon and paste the plain folder over the books icon. Next, draw a little book in the plain folder and save the new icon. Use this tip to replace any nonfolder-looking folder icons (such as the Drives folder and the System Setup folder).

✔ For the best-looking icons, use the screen color for the background to make the icons appear to be transparent. Go ahead — give it a shot before thinking, "That's a little too weird." It really makes your icons look great.

Using Seek and Scan Files

Sooner or later, you lose a file. No, the power doesn't go out, and the computer doesn't explode. You save the file *in a folder somewhere.* But which folder?

The time has come to hire the Seek and Scan Files program by double-clicking the Seek and Scan Files object lounging in the Productivity folder (which lives in the OS/2 System folder):

Seek and Scan Files

Seek and Scan Files can find any file on any disk. When the program pops to the screen, it looks similar to what's shown in Figure 11-8.

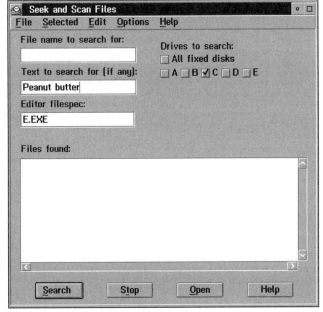

Figure 11-8:
Use this
screen to
tell the Seek
and Scan
Files
program
what to
fetch.

If you're searching for the file you saved as LUNCH.TXT, type **LUNCH.TXT** in the File name to search for box.

Or if you don't remember what you named the file but you remember typing PEANUT BUTTER in it somewhere, leave the File name to search for box blank; instead, type **PEANUT BUTTER** in the Text to search for (if any) box.

Click the Search button, and the program is on the hunt. It searches for the file on every disk that's checked below the Drives to search label.

If you have a particularly large disk drive, the program can take several minutes to gumshoe its way through each file. But that's not a problem. Minimize the program by clicking the little square next to the big square in the window's upper-right corner. The window gets off the screen so that you can work on other things during the search. (That's what all this *multitasking* stuff is good for.)

If Seek and Scan Files finds any files matching the search instructions, it lists them in the big Files found box at the bottom of the window.

- ✔ If you double-click any of the files listed in the big Files found box, OS/2 System Editor tries to read them. If they're plain old text files, OS/2 System Editor will succeed. If they're not text files, you see a sign warning you about *nulls* and stuff if you try to load it anyway. Don't bother trying to load them; click the Stop loading file button to restore order.

- ✔ If you find a *program,* you can start running it immediately by clicking Process. (Process is found on the menu that leaps down when you click Selected, one of those words in the menu bar at the top of the window.)

- ✔ If you load the wrong file in the OS/2 System Editor or if you *process* the wrong program, don't worry. The Seek and Scan Files list still is waiting for you. You don't have to make it search your drive again.

- ✔ The most hard-core OS/2 users format floppy disks while Seek and Scan Files does its search . . . just so that they can tell their friends that they can do both things at one time.

- ✔ The program can dig up a lost file much faster by searching for a filename than it can dig up a lost file by searching for words a file contains. If you think that you remember what name you called a missing file, try searching for it by name first; you may save a little time.

- ✔ Can't remember what you called your file but you know that the name begins with an *l?* Then type **l*.*** in the File name to search for box. The program then digs up all the files beginning with the letter *l.*

Taking the Computer's Pulse

Because of the zillions of TV doctor shows, most people have seen *pulse* meters (boxes with little lines that move around according to a person's heart rate).

In OS/2, you can take the computer's pulse with a program called Pulse. Double-click its object from the Productivity folder (stashed in the OS/2 System folder):

Pulse

Pulse leaps to the screen, complete with the little, pulsing line. (Unfortunately, there's no sound.)

When OS/2 sits there twiddling its thumbs, the little line stays pretty straight across the bottom. But when OS/2 is working hard to bring up folders, open files, or play a good game of chess, that little line rises near the top. Figure 11-9 shows the twiddling and the hard work.

Figure 11-9:
The high
marks on
the line
mean that
the
computer
has been
busy.

What's the point? Well, I like to keep Pulse running in the corner of my screen. If it ever freezes, I know that OS/2 has crashed and that I have to press Ctrl+Alt+Delete and let out a primal scream to get my screen back.

- By clicking Options, you can change Pulse's appearance. I like a black background with a solid-filled red graph. Watching it that way is more fun.

- If the graph is near the top of the screen, OS/2 is working pretty hard. You may want to think twice about running any more programs on top of what's already going on. Another program may run, but much more slowly, and it might take longer to load.

Playing Klondike

When IBM saw that Solitaire is the most-often-used Microsoft Windows program, it knew that it had to follow suit. So OS/2 comes with two games, and one of them, Klondike, works just like the Windows Solitaire program does.

Windows' Solitaire can display the cards in only one size. You can change the window's size, but some of the cards go off the screen.

Klondike, on the other hand, has scaling. *Scaling* isn't some gross affliction; it just means that when you change the size of the Klondike window, the cards change their own size to keep up. Unlike Solitaire, you can play Klondike in any size window.

Also, Klondike looks better than Solitaire when you use a high-resolution video mode, such as SuperVGA.

To play Klondike, double-click the Klondike object in the Games folder (neatly hidden away in the OS/2 System folder):

Solitaire - Klondike

When you click the object, OS/2 deals the cards. Feel free to change the window's size (that stuff's described in Chapter 7 if the window isn't in a good location or it covers up anything important.

Hoyle has detailed rules for playing Klondike. But I offer a few OS/2 tips nonetheless:

✔ When you're about to lose, cheat. Press Ctrl+C and you can make a game-saving illegal move. You can cheat as many times as you want, in fact — who's keeping track? Well, the computer is, and it tells you exactly how many times you cheated at the game's end. Take a look at Figure 11-10 to see how Klondike treats a winner.

✔ Make a bum move? Press Ctrl+T to take it back. In fact, immediately after you win a game, you can press Ctrl+T to play the last winning card once more. That way, you can see the fireworks again.

✔ If a card is ready to be played somewhere on the stack — an ace that can head straight over to the pile, for example — double-click it. That shortcut sends it automatically to the pile.

✔ As soon as you uncover all the face-down cards, you've won the game. You just have to stack the cards on the piles. OS/2 carries out these trivial details for you if you press Ctrl+F. You can't press Ctrl+F until you uncover all the face-down cards, though, so you can't use Ctrl+F to cheat.

✔ If you're using one of the high-resolution, expensive video modes, check out some of the different card backs. They look thousands of times better than they did in plain old VGA.

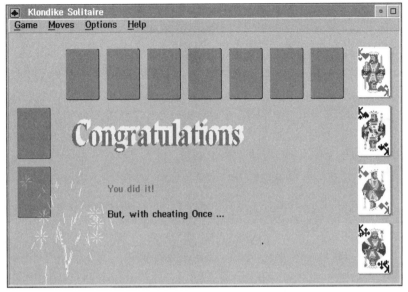

Figure 11-10:
When you
win at
Klondike,
OS/2
congratulates
you and tells
you how
many times
you
cheated.

✔ If the boss comes by, press Alt+F9 to shrink Klondike's window to an icon instantly. (The technical term for this process is *minimize.*) In fact, Alt+F9 minimizes any window into an icon. To get Klondike back when the boss moves on to the next desk, press Ctrl+Esc and double-click its name from the little box that pops up.

Telling Time with System Clock

If you don't wear a wristwatch, check out OS/2 System Clock. Double-click the System Clock object in the System Setup folder (which hides in the OS/2 System folder):

System Clock

A small clock, like the one shown in Figure 11-11, pops into the corner of the screen.

Figure 11-11:
System
Clock can
keep you on
schedule.

To tweak the clock, head for its Settings page. Click its icon with the right mouse button, click the arrow next to Open, and click Settings. Next, start fiddling.

- ✔ Click in Digital if you like to see computerized numbers on the screen. Or if you like hands and rotating second hands, click Analog.

- ✔ If you have trouble remembering the date, you can put it on the clock by clicking the Both date and time button.

- ✔ The Clock's Settings page has an Alarm tab you can use to set alarms. (You hear it go off if you're close enough to your computer when it goes off.)

Playing Mahjongg Solitaire

Way cool. Programmer Jürg von Känel has crafted a fine computer translation of the famous Chinese tile game. The concept is simple, the artwork excellent, and the animation fun.

Mahjongg Solitaire

In fact, there's only one problem: There's no on-the-fly volume setting, and it starts off pretty loud. For quick ear relief, head for the Volume Control object in the Multimedia folder and spin the little knob down to the 50s or 60s.

- ✔ Be sure to try out some of the other tile arrangements by clicking their icons — the ones with the cryptic, blue titles that read TOWERBRI or GIZEH.

- ✔ Also, be sure to save unfinished games before closing the application. If you just double-click the upper-left corner, the game simply disappears without asking whether you want to save the game.

Fiddling with Enhanced Editor

IBM didn't enhance this editor so that you could write nice reports with neatly centered titles and cool logos in the corners. No, IBM enhanced it for computer nerds who write long programs. So don't let the name fool you. The only thing that has been enhanced about this editor is its difficulty level.

Enhanced Editor

First, it borders the words with weird "Top of file" and "Bottom of file" sentences. They look dumb, and there's no way to get rid of them.

Second, it's awkward, with Card-Carrying Computer Nerd words such as "grep" on its menus.

Finally, its pull-down menus don't list normal, everyday chores such as Bold or Center. They say such things as A̲dvanced marking, C̲UA accelerators, and R̲ing enabled. Yuck.

Rather than fiddle with Enhanced Editor to write a letter or a report, buy a real OS/2 word processor, such as DeScribe, or check out the word processor in the BonusPak.

Looking at Picture Viewer

OS/2's Picture Viewer is a great concept. Most people have a few graphics files or pieces of clip art lying around on their hard drive. In fact, most of today's word processors come with art files, ready for you to spruce up your reports.

Picture Viewer

Unfortunately, Picture Viewer can't view most pictures. You see, various formats are used to store graphics in files. The most popular formats have arty names such as PCX, GIF, and BMP (short for bitmap). In fact, OS/2 uses BMP graphics files for its wallpaper — the pictures you can display on the back of the screen.

But Picture Viewer can't view the most popular types of graphics files. It supports only the more esoteric formats called MET, PIF, and SPL.

For a more realistic program, check out the Multimedia Viewer in the BonusPak, described in Chapter 12.

✔ Picture Viewer can't display PCX files, the most popular type of graphics files for the IBM-compatible PC. It can't even display OS/2's own BMP files or icons!

✔ Picture Viewer says that it can read the PIF format. In this case, *PIF* stands for *Picture Interchange Format*. It has nothing to do with a Windows PIF (*Program Information File*). You can *try* to read a Windows PIF with Picture Viewer, but OS/2 just slaps you with an error message that says "The file could not be opened."

✔ If you need to look at a PCX file for some reason, the Windows Paintbrush program can read it. Paintbrush can even save PCX files as BMP files. (Unfortunately, the BMP files in Windows aren't always compatible with the BMP files in OS/2. You can easily see that Microsoft and IBM don't really like each other.)

Mastering Chess

Chess plays a laughable beginner game but a reasonable advanced game. Unfortunately, it's painfully s - l - o - w, too slow to keep up much momentum — unless you're running on a Pentium, that is. After all, where's the joy in beating (or losing to) a computer, especially when it takes 45 minutes to make a move?

OS/2 Chess

The redeeming quality of Chess is that it comes with network support. If the computer is hooked up to the office network, you can play a game of chess against Jennifer in Accounting. If you're not hooked up to a network, though, you have to be pretty patient to play a game against OS/2's Chess.

Chapter 12

The Bogus, Er, BonusPak

- -

In This Chapter

▶ Installing the BonusPak

▶ CompuServe Information Manager

▶ FaxWorks

▶ HyperACCESS Lite

▶ Systems Information Tool

▶ Multimedia Viewer

▶ Video IN

▶ Person to Person

▶ IBM Works

▶ IBM Internet Connection

- -

*T*he BonusPak is a haphazard bunch of programs. Some of the programs have been kicking around IBM's offices for a while; others are programs that never went anywhere in their commercial versions. Still others are written by several smaller companies, purchased by IBM, and tossed into the BonusPak box to make the package sound more exciting.

The programs are a motley group, without a common look or feel. The installation programs differ from each other, as do their levels of dummy-friendliness. Some install themselves in a convenient new folder on your desktop. Others simply disappear, leaving you to forage through your desktop's folders to see where they've inserted themselves.

Much of the BonusPak, unfortunately, is pretty bogus. Why bother even mentioning it? So that you don't spend hours trying to make some of these programs do something useful and then wonder what's going wrong. No, you're not doing anything wrong. Some of these programs really *are* that bogus.

Installing the BonusPak

The programs in the BonusPak all come with their own separate installation programs. To bring everything together, OS/2 comes with a single installation program that lets you choose between all the other installation programs. It works like this:

1. **Insert the Installation Utility System Information Tool disk in Drive A.**

2. **Click the OS/2 Command Line icon from the Launch Pad.**

   It's the dark icon in the middle of the Launch Pad. Click it once, and an OS/2 command line pops up in a window.

3. **Type the following line and press Enter:**

   ```
   C:\ A:INSTALL
   ```

4. **Twiddle your thumbs and groove to the tunes.**

   Listen to the foot-tapping tunes the Install program plays in the background (if you have a sound card, that is).

5. **Click on the product you want to install and click Install.**

The BonusPak Installation Utility for OS/2, shown in Figure 12-1, lets you choose the applications you want to install. Unfortunately, you can't tell OS/2 to simply install them all at one time. No, you have to pick them one at a time. Also, you have to choose the Shut Down command and reboot your computer after you've installed each of the applications.

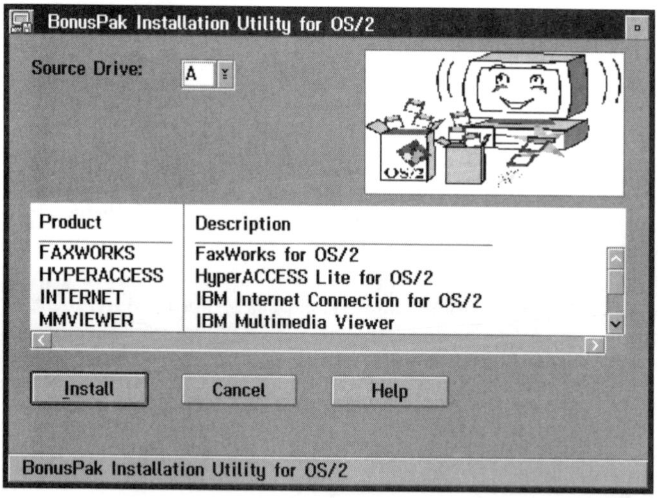

Figure 12-1: The BonusPak Installation Utility makes it easier to install the nine programs that make up OS/2's BonusPak.

Not only that, but IBM used a weird compression scheme to pack extra information on the disks. That means it takes a *long* time for most of these programs to extract themselves from the disks and lodge themselves on your hard drive. If you planned to install all the BonusPak programs, get a glass of orange juice; you're going to be here for a while.

The BonusPak Programs

The rest of this chapter tackles the individual programs in the BonusPak. Remember, IBM is tossing these in for free, so you get what you pay for. That means that some of the programs are difficult to use and difficult to set up. In addition, some of them are "teasers." They're whittled-down versions of real programs sold by mail order or in software stores.

To help you decide whether a program is worth the effort, be sure to check the IQ ratings next to each one.

FaxWorks

Configuration IQ: 130

Usability IQ: 100

Remember how easy it was to set up your printer when you installed OS/2 Warp? Sure, OS/2 couldn't figure out your brand of printer automatically. But at least it gave you a list of hundreds of printers to choose from. And when you chose your printer, OS/2 automatically chose the right settings for it.

FaxWorks gets lazy, however. It buries its list of modems inside a text file on your hard drive. To read the list, open the System Editor, press and release Alt, then F, and then O, and then type **C:\FAXWORKS\README.DOC** in the System Editor's Open filename box.

If you're lucky, you find your brand of modem listed in that README.DOC file. My Intel SatisFAXtion 400 internal modem was listed; unfortunately, the file said that that modem is supported only in the program's full *retail* version. Luckily, my USRobotics Courier HST Dual Std w/Fax *was* listed, so I used its recommended settings: Cls-1,Spc cmd &H2,Recv EOP delay.

FaxWorks isn't very dummy-friendly, unfortunately. After it's installed, though, it gets the job done (see Figure 12-2).

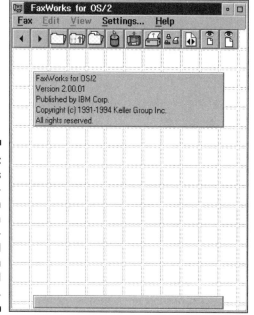

Figure 12-2:
FaxWorks is
a whittled-
down
version of a
more full-
featured
program
sold
separately.

The recommended settings listed for the USRobotics modem just mentioned are Warp's special coded way of saying to head for the Setting's Modem Type page, click the words "Class 1," type **&H2** in the Special Command box, and click in the little box next to Receive EOP delay. Don't let those abbreviations confuse you.

✔ Under the Ports section, choose whatever setting the program suggests. Chances are, it will recommend Port 1 (io=3F8 irq=4) — Send/Receive, and you should stick with it.

✔ When you're ready to fax something, drag its object to the FxPrint object on your desktop. FaxWorks pops up, asking you to fill in details about a cover sheet, the fax's recipient, and the phone number. When you've filled out the form, it sends the information to your fax modem to be whisked away to the recipient's fax machine.

✔ If your program has a Print command, look for its Printer Setup command and then choose the FxPrint printer as your default printer. To fax something from that program, choose its Print command, just as you would normally do to send something to the printer. This time, however, OS/2 routes the information to the fax modem.

✔ DOS fax programs rarely work well under OS/2; because of timing problems, pieces of the fax can drop off as it travels through the phone lines.
For more reliable faxing, you're better off with FaxWorks — if you can
stand its complicated setup options and lack of features. But if you're
looking for something a little more full-featured, you have to head for the
computer store.

CompuServe Information Manager

Configuration IQ: 120

Usability IQ: 110

OS/2 sticks the icon for CompuServe Information Manager in the Information
Superhighway folder, but CompuServe has been around much longer than the
trendy *information superhighway* marketing gimmick.

CompuServe is an on-line service: a bunch of big computers that supply
information over the phone lines to other computers. By connecting your
computer to a modem — and paying a monthly or hourly charge — you can call
CompuServe to check the weather or read the latest news. Plus, you can meet
people with similar interests on special forums — places to hang out and chat
about buying sailboats or solving COM port conflicts.

You can call CompuServe with any modem program. However, CompuServe
Information Manager is designed to make accessing CompuServe easier and
faster (see Figure 12-3). *Faster* is a key word because CompuServe charges by
the minute for some of its features.

If you don't have a CompuServe account, double-click the Member Sign-Up icon;
it's in the new CompuServe folder OS/2 leaves on your desktop. The program
guides you through the mechanics of signing up for a CompuServe account.

Already have a CompuServe account? Then open the program, click Session
Settings from its Special menu, and fill in the following info:

Modem: Click here and then click the menu's Modem setting to bring up a
list of popular modem brands. Click your brand, and the program automatically sets itself up for your modem.

Baud Rate: Choose not only the speed your modem uses but also the
speed your particular access phone number supports.

Name: Your name goes here.

User ID: Type your CompuServe ID here.

Figure 12-3:
CompuServe
Information
Manager
lets you
navigate
CompuServe
more
quickly,
saving
money in
per-minute
charges.

Password: When you type your password here, CompuServe puts aster-
isks in the box so that onlookers can't see your *real* password.

Phone: Type your local CompuServe access number.

Forgot your local access phone number for CompuServe? Then use a modem
program such as Windows Terminal or HyperACCESS Lite to dial CompuServe
by using its tollfree number, 1-800-346-3247. When CompuServe's computer
answers, type **GO PHONES** and press Enter. CompuServe asks for your local
area code and then spits out a phone number for your area.

✔ The CompuServe Information Manager for OS/2 works almost identically to
its Windows version. If you've used WinCIM, you'll feel right at home.

✔ Never used CompuServe? Then click the little green traffic light at the top
of the program, type **GO PRACTICE** in the box, and press Enter. That takes
you to CompuServe's practice area — a place to experiment with sending
messages and downloading files while CompuServe's pay-by-the-minute
clock isn't running.

> ✔ Have any questions about OS/2? Head for the OS/2 support forums on CompuServe. There's no extra charge beyond what you're paying CompuServe. For the Official IBM forum, type **GO OS2SUPPORT;** for advice from actual product users, type **GO OS2USER.** Both places are fantastic places to find ways to tweak OS/2 into working like it should.

HyperACCESS Lite

Configuration IQ: 120

Usability IQ: 100

HyperACCESS Lite just might be a keeper. It's another whittled-down version of a retail program, designed to make people want to upgrade to the full-featured version (see Figure 12-4). Sometimes a small modem program works better, however, than one with billions of bells and whistles.

Figure 12-4: HyperACCESS Lite is a small modem program, powerful enough to warrant keeping on your hard drive.

HyperACCESS Lite comes equipped to call most of the major on-line services and can be easily set up to call bulletin boards as well. It's about as easy to use as a modem program can be.

✔ Unlike FaxWorks, HyperACCESS Lite comes with a list of modems built into the program. Click the little arrow at the end of the <u>M</u>odem box, click your modem's brand name, and the program automatically sets itself up to use it.

✔ The program comes with little icons for calling CompuServe, BIX, ATT Mail, Delphi, Dow Jones, GEnie, and other on-line services. It doesn't come with the local phone numbers for those places, however. You need to find those phone numbers yourself and type them in.

System Information Tool

Configuration IQ: 70

Usability IQ: 90

This little program spits out information about your computer (see Figure 12-5). At least, it spits out information that OS/2 *thinks* is true about your computer. It often thinks that 486 computers are 386 computers, for example, and it simply listed Unknown for my 486. Still, the program is handy for occasional troubleshooting, even though it's not completely reliable.

Figure 12-5:
The System Information Tool can sometimes be handy for troubleshooting why OS/2 doesn't recognize parts of your computer.

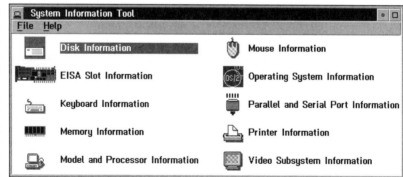

One more thing: OS/2's Install utility sticks the System Information Tool in your System Setup folder. That bit of information saves you some random folder searching until you stumble across it.

✔ The System Information Tool spits out information about your computer's disks, slots, keyboard, mouse, memory, CPU, parallel and serial ports, printer, and video card.

✔ Much of the information System Information ferrets out about your computer is technical, and much of it flies over most people's heads. Still, this utility is a good one to install: It's small, and it's handy for tech-heads to use when they're trying to figure out why your computer isn't working.

Multimedia Viewer

Configuration IQ: 70

Usability IQ: 90

This one's a winner; make sure that you install this part of the BonusPak, if nothing else. Multimedia Viewer gives you a way to view or hear files in a variety of formats: PCX, GIF, Kodak PhotoCD, Targa, WAV, AVI, and more.

The concept is simple, thank goodness. The program displays pictures as though they were photographic slides sitting on a photographer's light table. See a picture you want to blow up to full size? Then double-click its frame, and Multimedia Viewer enlarges it for easy viewing. Or if you've double-clicked a sound or video file, Multimedia Viewer plays it. Figure 12-6 shows Multimedia Viewer in action (as well as what a sound looks like).

✔ When the Multimedia Viewer is installed, it automatically adds support for PCX, GIF, and AU/SND files. It doesn't automatically install support for Targa, AIF (Apple Interchange Files), IFF (Amiga File Format), or TIF files. If you use those formats — or plan to use them in the future — be sure to click on their names while you're installing the program.

Used mostly by graphics professionals, Targa images are usually photographs containing millions of colors. TIF files were popularized by Aldus PageMaker for moving graphics between types of software and computers; they are often used by scanners.

✔ To add a picture, sound, or video object to the Multimedia Viewer's light table, click that object with your right mouse button and choose Create LT <u>R</u>eference from its pop-up menu. When the next window pops up, choose the Multimedia Viewer folder as the source for the image. That's it — the next time you open the Multimedia Viewer folder, your new multimedia object will be lying on the light table.

Figure 12-6:
Multimedia
Viewer
provides a
convenient
way to see
and hear
multimedia
files.

To see or hear an object, don't double-click the object *itself* while you're within Multimedia Viewer; that brings up an editor. Double-click the object's *frame,* and Multimedia Viewer lets you either see or hear it.

The plain white background Multimedia Viewer uses for its light table is pretty boring. Remember, you can change the background color of any folder to anything you want. For example, Figure 12-6 shows the Multimedia Viewer using the FERN.BMP image as a background.

Video-In for OS/2

Configuration IQ: 120

Usability IQ: 150

This program, says the little blue BonusPak manual, allows you to be your own movie producer and record digital video on your computer. The videos then can be played back on any computer that has OS/2 installed — no additional hardware required! That's a little misleading. True, you don't need any special hardware to play the videos, but you do need expensive video-recording hardware to *record* them.

You need not only special video-recording hardware — a video-capture card (see Figure 12-7)— but also a fast 486 with at least 12MB of memory. Plus, you need a decent video editor; hopefully, one came in the box with your video-capture card.

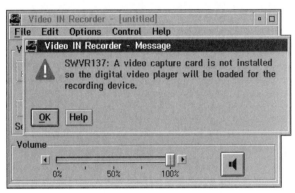

Figure 12-7:
You need a special video-capture card in your computer before you can use Video In.

✔ Video-In works with these video-capture cards:

- AITech International WaveWatcher

- CEI Video Clipper

- Creative Labs Video Blaster

- Hauppauge Win/TV

- IBM Video Capture Adapter/A

- Jovian SuperVia and QuickVia

- New Media Graphics Super VideoWindows and Super VideoWindows MC

- Omnicomp M&M Basic

- Samsung Video Magic

- Sigma Designs WinMovie

✔ You need a camcorder or VCR to connect to your video-capture card, too. Few video-capture cards let you simply plug in a TV antenna or cable and record TV shows.

✔ Don't bother trying to edit a video with the AVI File Utility, shown in Figure 12-8. Unlike video editors such as Video for Windows or Adobe's Premiere, AVI File Utility doesn't even display the video by using pictures. Instead, its menus are packed with options such as View Chunk ID and Length, Hexadecimal, and Change Audio Chunk Skew. Phew!

Figure 12-8:
Video-In's video editor doesn't display videos by using pictures; it displays them by using numbers.

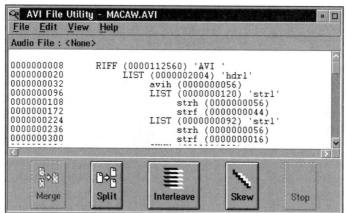

IBM Person to Person for OS/2

Configuration IQ: 170

Usability IQ: 130

Don't bother installing this 5-megabyte boondoggle. After the poor network person manages to set this program up, corporate executives are supposed to be able to talk to each other through their computers. The excited executives on one side of the country put data, files, graphics, images, or programs on their computer screens, and the executives on the other side of the country can see the same stuff on their screens.

Save this stuff for the executive's kids.

IBM Works

Configuration IQ: 90

Usability IQ: 110

IBM has stuck a huge 12$^1/_2$ megabytes worth of programs in a conglomeration called IBM Works (see Figure 12-9). For the most part, it's worth the disk space. The word processor is perhaps the best of the bunch; it has a spell checker and can create tables. It's also integrated with the rest of the programs, allowing you to easily insert charts and pictures. In fact, most of the programs in IBM Works work together as a team. Their jumble of overlapping features can be confusing at first but helpful when you finally understand them.

Figure 12-9:
IBM Works
contains a
scheduler,
spreadsheet,
word
processor,
database,
and chart
maker in
addition to
some
popular
forms.

- The programs are good about accepting data from other programs. For example, the spreadsheet can read not only Lotus 1-2-3 files but also files stored in formats from WordPerfect, Lotus Ami, Rich Text Format, older versions of Word for Windows, and Excel. It can also read files stored by its IBM Works teammates: the word processor, database, and chart maker.

- One folder contains preconstructed templates for making a balance sheet, bank record, budget, forecast, credit application, invoice, estimate, fax, and memo. That means that you can spend more time with your data and less time creating your own forms.

- If you're ready to give up your pen-and-paper address and appointment book, the IBM Works versions are ready to take over. You'll find a yearly calendar, daily scheduler, monthly planner, to-do list, phone book, and other goodies.

✔ Despite the hoopla, the program still has some rough edges — especially if everything's not set up correctly. For example, when I told the address book to auto-dial a phone number by using my modem, it didn't dial. Instead, it sent the dummy-unfriendly message shown in Figure 12-10. Count on spending several weeks to figure out how all the programs are supposed to work.

Figure 12-10:
IBM Works
isn't very
helpful
when
something
goes wrong.

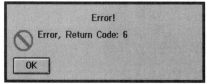

IBM Internet Connection for OS/2

Configuration IQ for IBM's provider: 80

Configuration IQ for your own provider: 160

Usability IQ: 130

This information superhighway metaphor is a little misleading. Scooting onto the Internet isn't as easy as hopping on a freeway on-ramp and putting the pedal to the metal. The Internet is a weird world filled with technogeekism and old-world computer lingo. It's not a friendly road through the countryside, with friendly people waving at you along the way. No, it's a drive through an underground tunnel, with deadends, road signs in foreign languages, and other drivers who make a point to tailgate newcomers.

First, it costs money. IBM's giving you an on-ramp to the information superhighway, but it's a toll road, with a $35 sign-up cost and a $6 hourly fee. When you sign up, IBM connects you to a *service provider.* That's a fancy word for a company that has a computer connected to bunches of phone lines. By calling the service provider, you can scoot around the phone lines, peeking into different computers around the world. Or, if you have your own provider, you can type it in the program, bypassing IBM's own service provider. (Of course, IBM can't pocket the hourly fees if you use your own provider, so it makes setting up your own provider much more difficult.)

After you've finally configured your computer to connect with the Internet, you can scoot fairly easily from computer to computer doing Internet stuff: copying pictures of birds (see Figure 12-11), joining in on discussions comparing Borges and Kafka, or dropping by Carlsbad, California, to watch the live surfing videos.

✔ You had better install the Multimedia Viewer before scooting down the information superhighway or else you won't be able to see (or hear) anything. OS/2 uses the Multimedia Viewer to display pictures on the Internet.

✔ Don't get too excited when you first log on. During the first call, the software updates itself, a process that takes as long as 20 minutes.

✔ Next, don't be surprised to reach some busy signals when you call. And remember that the Internet is a bunch of computers with no one in charge. If a computer doesn't answer, it just might kick you off-line. Be prepared to redial.

✔ All this modem stuff got you bamboozled? Pick up a copy of *Modems For Dummies,* by Tina Rathbone (IDG Books Worldwide). It's chock-full of ways to fight back against weird modem terms. Or, if the Internet's got you struck dumb, pick up *Internet For Dummies,* 2nd Edition, by John Levine and Margy Levine Young. Both are soothing balms for the balmy.

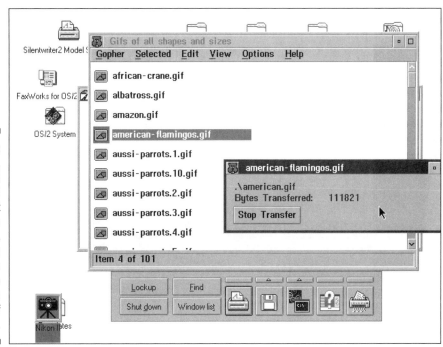

Figure 12-11: Gopher, included with IBM Internet Connection for OS/2, copies a picture of a flamingo from a database of bird pictures.

The 5th Wave

By Rich Tennant

"THAT'S RIGHT, DADDY WILL DOUBLE YOUR SALARY IF YOU MAKE HIM MORE OS/2 APPLICATIONS."

Chapter 13
Command Line Stuff

*1*magine walking into a restaurant and not finding any menus.

Far from being helpful, the waiters and waitresses are surly. They expect you to already know what you want to order. It's simply required knowledge. And if you mispronounce Dom Perignon, you don't get your champagne!

That surly attitude is what a computer's command line is all about. A computer's *command line* is simply a place for you to type computer-language instructions into the computer. There are no menus. If you misspell a word, the computer sulks and refuses to carry out your instructions.

Luckily, most OS/2 users can avoid the awkwardness of a command line. OS/2's little folders, boxes, and menus enable you to do just about everything you can do at the command line. But because OS/2 promises to do just about everything DOS can do, it includes the grunt-level awkwardness of a command line, too.

This chapter explains what that command line thing is and why you may have to use it in an emergency (or if you're ready to take your exploratory first steps down the Computer Nerd path).

What's a Command Line?

In the dark days of computing, people bossed their computers around through the command line. A command line is simply a *line of commands,* like these:

Halt.

Bring me a root beer.

And hurry!

Naturally, computers use a different language and don't care for soft drinks, especially on the keyboard. But the command line concept is the same. People type a command, and the computer carries out their wishes. (*If* they spelled the command right, that is. Computers are obnoxiously picky about spelling.)

> ✔ For years, IBM-compatible computer owners typed awkward commands into their computers. And they enjoyed it! It was easier than the old method of sticking in punch cards.

> ✔ People had to memorize all the computer commands. The computers didn't offer any help. In fact, most people taped little notes next to their keyboards so that they could remember everything. Then, if the janitor cleaned up a week later, they had to start from scratch.

> ✔ In OS/2, you boss around the computer by pushing little pictures around, so the system is a little more friendly than DOS. (If you want to know more about how DOS and OS/2 differ, head for Chapter 1.)

> ✔ OS/2 comes with two kinds of command lines: the traditional DOS command line and the newer OS/2 command line. They both work in pretty much the same way, causing about equal levels of confusion. You can find a comparison of the two prompts later in this chapter.

What's a Prompt?

Whether they're using OS/2 or DOS, command line aficionados type their commands at a little prompt on the screen. The *prompt* is usually a combination of a letter and symbols, and it looks something like: C:\ or [C:\].

To load the Klondike card game program by using OS/2's command line, for example, you type the following command at the prompt and press Enter:

```
[C:\] KLONDIKE
```

The computer reads the command KLONDIKE and loads the Klondike program in response. Of course, you have to know that KLONDIKE is the proper command to start the KLONDIKE program.

And if you type **CLONDIKE** by mistake, OS/2 retorts with the following reprimand:

```
C:\ CLONDIKE
SYS1041:
The name specified is not recognized as an internal or exter-
          nal command, an operable program or batch file.
```

With these words, OS/2 is simply saying, "I didn't understand what you typed."

It should add the words, "But you didn't hurt anything. Try again."

- ✔ In OS/2, a DOS prompt looks like this:

    ```
    C:\>
    ```

- ✔ An OS/2 prompt looks the same, except that it has little brackets around it, like this:

    ```
    [C:\]
    ```

- ✔ Sometimes an OS/2 prompt looks like this:

    ```
    [C:\OS2]
    ```

- ✔ The little OS2 after the slash mark means that you're currently working from inside the OS2 folder. The commands you type at that particular prompt are aimed at the files stored in the OS/2 folder. (A folder is also called a *directory*. If you double-click the Drive C object, in fact, you see the OS2 folder dangling from the tree for drive C. That *drive* stuff is covered in Chapter 8.)

- ✔ For most of the command lines discussed in this chapter, though, it doesn't matter what words come after the C:\ part of the prompt. The commands work from anywhere on the drive.

Why Should I Use a Command Line?

Computer nerds like the feeling of raw power they get from a command line. Rather than have to rustle through a bunch of folders to open a program, they just type the program's name at the command line and press Enter. The program leaps to the screen. Quick!

The nerds have usually memorized the exact names of all their programs. (The name is often different from the title below the program's object, by the way.) The nerds also know exactly where the programs are stored on the hard drive. Unless you tell OS/2 exactly where a program lives, OS/2 searches through only a few of its folders before it gives up.

The point? Stay away from the command line unless you *have* to use it. When OS/2 goes haywire, you have to put on your gloves and head for the command line to fix things.

If things are going smoothly for you, avoid the command line, and you can avoid a great deal of trouble.

How Does a DOS Command Line Differ from an OS/2 Command Line?

The DOS command line and the OS/2 command line are almost the same. Their *prompts* look a little different, as you can see in the section "What's a Prompt?" earlier in this chapter. The difference is subtle but noticeable.

The two prompts work almost identically, however. In fact, most OS/2 commands are based on the age-old DOS commands. And, believe it or not, most DOS commands will work at the OS/2 command line. You don't *have* to use a DOS command line to type a DOS command.

When you type something at an OS/2 command line, OS/2 grabs the words and tries to match them up with its own stable of programs and commands. If it finds a match, it carries out the instructions. If it doesn't find a match, it tries to match up the words with DOS's stable of programs and commands. If it finds a match there, it carries out your wishes.

- Because DOS commands work at the OS/2 command line, you may not have to use the DOS command line at all. When you type the name of a DOS program at an OS/2 prompt, OS/2 runs the DOS program. Or if you type a DOS command at an OS/2 prompt, OS/2 carries out the command.

- When you type *some* DOS commands at the OS/2 prompt, you run into some problems. If you type **MEM**, for example, which is a DOS command that displays a bunch of nerdy memory statistics, OS/2 loads up its *DOS prompt shell,* flashes the memory statistics on the screen, and jumps back to its own prompt. Unless your eyes are as quick as the computer, you'll have trouble reading the information as it flashes by.

✔ Don't try starting Windows at the command line by typing WIN. OS/2 has to prepare itself first for such a big chore. To start Windows, stick with double-clicking its little objects from inside the folders.

✔ In fact, don't start any DOS or Windows programs from the command line. These programs work much better when you double-click their objects to start them. If you want to know why, head for Chapter 14.

✔ Some persnickety DOS programs don't work if you install them at a DOS command line. Try installing them at an OS/2 command line instead, and your luck may change.

✔ You can run command lines for both DOS and OS/2 in their own little windows on the screen. Those little command prompts don't have to fill the entire screen. If you're exceptionally nerdy, you can run a DOS command line and an OS/2 command line at the same time, each in its own window.

Sometimes a window just isn't big enough. If you want to toggle a DOS window to fill the entire screen or head back to a window, press Alt+Home. You can't toggle the size of an OS/2 window, however. You're stuck with what you started with.

Where Can I Find a Command Line?

Although you can have a pleasurable OS/2 experience without ever venturing near the command line, you may need these commands someday. To call up a command line, double-click the Command Prompts folder (it lurks in the OS/2 System folder), and you see a window similar to Figure 13-1.

Figure 13-1:
Double-click the object that represents the command line you want, and OS/2 brings it to the screen.

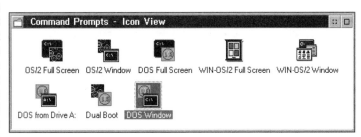

For a DOS command line, click the DOS Window object or the DOS Full Screen object.

For an OS/2 command line, click the OS/2 Window object or the OS/2 Full Screen object.

It doesn't really matter whether you choose the Full Screen version or the Window version of the command lines. The Window version is often a little handier because you can still see all the folders and other stuff on the desktop when the prompt is in its own window.

Don't click the DOS from Drive A object, however. That object is for people with DOS System *floppies* who want to *boot up* a version of DOS. Most of the time, that maneuver isn't necessary. Either avoid the DOS from Drive A object completely or head for Chapter 14 to see what a *DOS System floppy* is.

So, without further ado, this section discusses probably the only OS/2 commands you have to worry about. For all these commands, type exactly what you see after the prompt and press Enter to start the command.

How do I switch from DOS to OS/2 for my Dual Boot stuff?

If you used the Dual Boot method to install OS/2 — and most people do — you can use the command line to toggle between the two operating systems. Even when you double-click the Dual Boot object to switch to DOS from OS/2, for example, OS/2 tosses a command line at you. Here's the scoop.

To switch from DOS to OS/2, type this command at the DOS prompt:

```
C:\> BOOT /OS2
```

That is, type **BOOT**, followed by a space, a forward slash (found on the same key as the question mark), and **OS2**. Then press Enter.

If that command doesn't work, type the following line instead:

```
C:\> \OS2\BOOT /OS2
```

That is, type a *backward* slash (usually found near the Enter key), **OS2**, another *backward* slash, **BOOT**, a space, a *forward* slash, and **OS2**. Then press Enter.

To head for the DOS part of the *Dual Boot* computer from OS/2, type the following line at either a DOS prompt or an OS/2 prompt:

```
C:\> BOOT /DOS
```

That is, type **BOOT**, a space, a forward slash, and then **DOS**. Then press Enter. Or double-click the Dual Boot object in the Command Prompts folder. That trick does the same thing.

- ✔ When you type either of these BOOT commands to switch to the other operating system, OS/2 asks whether you're sure. Press Y if you're sure or N if you prefer to stay where you are.

- ✔ In its haste to do your bidding, OS/2 moves very quickly to switch operating systems when you use the BOOT command. In fact, it doesn't even save any work you have in progress. Be sure to save any important work before you head for a different operating system in Dual Boot. If you don't save the work, you'll lose it and feel upset.

- ✔ OS/2 always hops to the screen looking *exactly* the way it looked when you last left it. When you finish with DOS and head back to OS/2, for example, you see a command line window waiting for you. It's there because you were at the command line when you left OS/2. (It was asking whether you *really* wanted to switch to DOS.) When you get back to OS/2, though, you don't want to head back to DOS. So press N and then Enter. OS/2 closes the command line box, and all is well.

How do I get rid of a command line prompt?

When you're finished with a DOS or an OS/2 command line, don't just close the window as though it were a *normal* window. Close the command line session first. Closing the session is not as complicated as it sounds. Just type **EXIT** at the prompt and press Enter, as in the following:

```
[C:\] EXIT
```

The prompt disappears, followed quickly by its window. This command gets rid of both DOS and OS/2 command lines.

What version of OS/2 do I have?

As IBM's programmers keep laboring over OS/2, they keep patching the holes, pulling out loose threads, and adding new features. When they fix enough of the bad stuff and add enough of the good, they release a new version of OS/2. Which version of OS/2 do you have? To find out, type **VER** at the OS/2 prompt and then press Enter. OS/2 tosses back a sentence with the version number:

```
[C:\] VER
The Operating System/2 Version is 3.0
```

In this case, OS/2 says that you're using version 3.0 (you may have a different version, such as version 2.0 or 2.1).

What CSD level do I have?

When IBM's programmers discover how to fix something in OS/2 that has been kind of goofy, IBM sometimes releases update disks. Called Corrective Service Diskettes, or CSDs, these disks contain programs that help bring your version of OS/2 up to date.

Who cares? Well, the IBM Technical Support people will care when you call up to complain because something isn't working right.

To find out the exact *CSD level* of your copy of OS/2, type **SYSLEVEL** at the OS/2 prompt and press Enter:

```
[C:\] SYSLEVEL
```

The screen clears, and this information appears:

```
C:\OS2\INSTALL\SYSLEVEL.SDS
        Distributed SOM Framework
Version 2.01.1   Component ID 96F8647DS
Current CSD level: SM20004
Prior   CSD level: SM20003

C:\OS2\INSTALL\SYSLEVEL.SEM
        SOM Event Management Framework
Version 2.01.1   Component ID 96F8647EM
Current CSD level: SM20004
Prior   CSD level: SM20003

C:\OS2\INSTALL\SYSLEVEL.SUT
        SOMobjects Utility Classes
Version 2.01.1   Component ID 96F8647UT
Current CSD level: SM20004
Prior   CSD level: SM20003
```

```
C:\OS2\INSTALL\SYSLEVEL.SIR
          SOMobjects Interface Repository Framework
Version 2.01.1   Component ID 96F8647IR
Current CSD level: SM20004
Prior   CSD level: SM20003

C:\OS2\INSTALL\SYSLEVEL.SRK
          SOM Run-time Kernel
Version 2.01.1   Component ID 96F8647RK
Current CSD level: SM20004
Prior   CSD level: SM20003

C:\OS2\INSTALL\SYSLEVEL.GRE
          IBM OS/2 32-bit Graphics Engine
Version 3.00    Component ID 562260100
Type W
Current CSD level: XR03000
Prior   CSD level: XR03000

C:\OS2\INSTALL\SYSLEVEL.OS2
          IBM OS/2 Base Operating System
Version 3.00    Component ID 562260100
Type W
Current CSD level: XR03000
Prior   CSD level: XR03000

C:\MMOS2\INSTALL\SYSLEVEL.MPM
          IBM Multimedia Presentation Manager/2
Version 3.00    Component ID 562137400
Type W
Current CSD level: XR03000
Prior   CSD level: XR03000
```

Do you see the letters and numbers listed after the words "Current CSD level" and "Prior CSD level"? Those letters and numbers describe which version of OS/2's Corrective Service Diskettes has been installed on your computer. Your version is probably different from mine, so don't be surprised if the numbers aren't exactly the same.

The SYSLEVEL program also lists the version numbers of the IBM Multimedia Presentation Manager, the IBM OS/2 32-bit Graphics Engine, and the IBM OS/2 Base Operating System. Sometimes those prying technical-support folks want to know this information also.

When you load them up with all those facts, they should be able to diagnose your problem a little more easily.

I accidentally deleted the wrong file!

If you accidentally drag the wrong file to the Shredder, a glimmer of hope exists that you may be able to retrieve it.

Immediately after the accident, head for an OS/2 command line and type this command at the prompt:

```
[C:\] UNDELETE /S
```

That is, you type **UNDELETE**, a space, and a forward slash. Then you press **S**, followed by pressing Enter. You see one of two messages. First, the bad news:

```
[C:\] UNDELETE /S
Undeleting C:\*.
SYS3194: The DELDIR environment variable for the specified
          drive is missing or is incorrect.
```

Those cryptic words are really saying that the file is shredded beyond any hope of getting it back. Now for the good news. If you accidentally delete the file OHMY.TXT and you see this message, you're home free:

```
[C:\] UNDELETE /S
Undeleting C:\*.
C:\ DESKTOP\LETTERS\OHMY.TXT
Do you wish to undelete this file (Y/N)?
```

By all means, press Y and lean back as OS/2 retrieves the file. If OS/2 is trying to dredge up a different, unwanted file, press N. OS/2 keeps cycling through the names of all the files you've recently deleted. If you find the one you need and you want OS/2 to stop showing you names of deleted files, press Ctrl+C to shut it up.

If you get the bad-news message about the funny DELDIR environment variable, head for Chapter 6. That chapter explains how to tell OS/2 to begin *tracking* all the deleted files so that you can pull some of them back out of the graveyard.

What's that funny SYS error number?

Sometimes OS/2 gives you a weird *SYS* number, followed by a weird explanation. In the previous *bad-news message,* for example, OS/2 shot out this sentence:

```
SYS3194: The DELDIR environment variable for the specified
         drive is missing or is incorrect.
```

What the heck does that mean? To get a few more clues, try the Help command. At the OS/2 command prompt, type **HELP,** a space, and the weird SYS number. Then press Enter and see whether you can figure out what OS/2's message means:

```
[C:\] HELP SYS3194
SYS3194: The DELDIR environment variable for the specified
         drive is missing or is incorrect.
```

Explanation: The DELDIR environment variable specifies a temporary storage directory for each drive that supports the UNDELETE command. If this environment variable is not present or is entered incorrectly, the UNDELETE command is not active for the affected drive.

Action: To activate the UNDELETE command for a drive, add the appropriate DELDIR environment parameters to your CONFIG.SYS file. Refer to the Command Reference for more information. (You'll find the Command Reference waiting in the Information folder, by the way.)

Sometimes the information is pretty technical, but sometimes it gives you a clue about what's going on. When you beg a computer guru for help, you can say, "My environment variable is not present or is entered incorrectly. Can you help me?" Your local guru will appreciate that you tried to figure it out for yourself and will tell you that you need to come up with only two Hostess Pies with pudding filling, not the requisite three.

And, hey, anything is better than plain old SYS3194.

Part IV
Sticking with DOS and Windows Programs

The 5th Wave   By Rich Tennant

MODERN MARRIAGE

WE'RE AGREED ON THE SILVER PATTERN, WALLPAPER AND CARPET SCHEME, BUT WE'RE STILL HASHING OUT THE OPERATING SYSTEM.

In this part ...

People buy OS/2 to escape from dull, old DOS and
wimpy, old Windows.

But after OS/2 is installed, what does it do? It runs
everybody's DOS and Windows programs.

Sure, a few OS/2 programs are on the market. Just the other
day, somebody wrote a Robotic Arm Manipulator Controller
Application for OS/2. It works with all the standard robots
and mechanical devices on the market, its creator swears.

But for the robotless crowds, DOS and Windows programs
are where the action is. OS/2 can run bunches of them, and
at the same time. In fact, you'll soon be asking your neighbors to bring over their new floppy disks just so that you
can watch them being formatted while you're running
Windows.

When a few more OS/2 programs appear on the store
shelves, OS/2 buyers will certainly toss them into the mix.
But in the meantime, this part of the book can help you do
more with the computer than stick little folders on the
screen.

Chapter 14

Running DOS Programs in OS/2

In This Chapter

▶ Understanding what a DOS program is

▶ Starting a DOS program

▶ Understanding what all those *DOS settings* mean

▶ Changing a DOS program's setting

▶ Making DOS games run

▶ Changing DOS settings *on the fly*

▶ Changing a DOS window's fonts

▶ Making a DOS window open in the same size and place

▶ My DOS program froze up!

*D*OS programs always think that they have the entire computer to themselves. They're not used to bumping elbows with other DOS programs (or Windows programs or even an occasional OS/2 program).

To keep these isolationist programs happy at the OS/2 Inn, OS/2 tries to give each DOS program a separate room.

But one room rarely fits all. DOS programs yell for different things. Some want more memory; some want more time at the keyboard. Others want trendy southwestern shirts with New Mexico chili-pepper patterns.

When OS/2 can't keep DOS programs happy by being honest, it begins to lie. OS/2 can lie through its more than 40 different DOS settings.

Usually, DOS programs love the settings that OS/2 chooses for them automatically. But when a program starts yelling, you have to play nursemaid and tweak the settings until the program calms down. This chapter tells you what to tweak first.

What's a DOS Program?

DOS programs, simply put, are written for MS-DOS, which is the operating system a bunch of nerdy youngsters threw together for IBM's *new* line of personal computers more than ten years ago.

Just as a color TV can show black-and-white movies, OS/2 can run DOS programs. OS/2 has to work much harder, however, when it runs DOS programs. Because OS/2 runs a bunch of DOS programs on a single computer, it has to solve their quarrels: Which program gets to use the printer first? Which program gets which part of the screen? Which program gets to play with the mouse?

✔ To make sure that DOS programs work the way they're supposed to, OS/2 tosses each program its own computer. It's not a *real* computer. But the DOS program foolishly *thinks* that it's a real computer, so the program runs.

✔ IBM's Creative Acronym Department calls a DOS program's *fake* computer a *VDM*, or *Virtual DOS Machine*. Every time you open a DOS prompt or run a DOS program, you create a VDM. OS/2 tricks every DOS prompt or program into thinking that its VDM is the *only* VDM. So OS/2 is really just lying to all the DOS programs. But, hey, who cares about computer ethics as long as the DOS programs work?

✔ Sometimes a DOS program realizes that it's not *really* running on its own computer. When it thinks that something is fishy, it may stop running or just plain act weird. To restore order, OS/2 contains more than 50 different DOS settings. By fiddling with these settings, which are described later in this chapter, you can usually fool the DOS programs into thinking that they're back on their home turf and get them to start working again.

✔ Also, some DOS programs refuse to run under OS/2 at all. If you used the Dual Boot method to install OS/2, the solution is easy. Just boot to DOS and run the program there. Or politely ask a computer nerd to "VMDISK a DOS version on your hard drive."

Making a DOS Program Run

You don't have to pull a gun and curse to make a DOS program run. Just double-click its *object* (represented by a little picture in the DOS Programs folder). The DOS program leaps to the screen, either jumping inside its own window or filling the entire screen.

Sometimes, though, you can't even *find* the DOS program's object. Then it probably has to be migrated to the desktop. Migration is an animalistic process that's described in Chapter 16. When the program is migrated, it turns into an object. (Gads, does that sound boring, or what?)

You see, in OS/2, a DOS program is really three separate things:

The actual program: The program itself consists of the nerdy computer instructions that are stored in a file on the hard drive. (The file usually ends with EXE or COM.)

An object: The object holds any special settings for the DOS program. The *settings* contain your personal preferences, such as whether the program should start in its own on-screen window or take up the entire screen. Objects also contain *computer instructions* that make the DOS program feel at home. These instructions include the location of the computer's printer and information about which choice pieces of computer memory the program can nibble on.

An icon: The icon is just the little picture you see when you look at the object. A picture of a calculator, for example, represents the Calculator object (which in turn represents the actual Calculator program).

✔ So to start a DOS program (or any other program, for that matter), you double-click that program's *icon.* That double-click starts up the *object,* which in turn starts the program with the best possible settings for OS/2. Whew!

✔ This icon and object stuff works kind of like an elevator's button panel. The little number printed on the button's tiny face is its icon — a visual clue to its purpose. The button itself — the object — tells the elevator to move to the correct floor.

✔ So in OS/2 Land, are you double-clicking objects or icons? Well, you're really doing both: Pushing the button's picture also pushes the button — the object — which, hopefully, then activates the task you had in mind.

✔ Deleting a DOS program's object doesn't delete the actual DOS program. Doing so merely deletes that DOS program's settings. The program itself still exists on your hard drive. Likewise, if you pull Button 3 off the elevator panel, you haven't pulled the third floor off the hotel.

✔ If you want to delete a DOS program, call up your disk drive object and drag that DOS program's actual files over to the Shredder. (The Shredder is covered in Chapter 4.)

✔ If the program doesn't have an icon or an object, you have to create one yourself or tell OS/2 to create one. That stuff is pretty simple, but it gets its own section in Chapter 16 anyway.

✔ When a DOS program is finally up and running under OS/2, it might run a tad more slowly than it runs under *real* DOS. But, hey, that's the price you pay for running a bunch of programs at the same time.

✔ DOS users normally start a program by typing its name at the DOS command line. But when you try that method in OS/2, you bypass the special *settings* stored in the program's object. Without the settings, the program may not work under OS/2. It doesn't explode but it may crash, making you look silly in front of your friends who brought their floppies over to be formatted.

✔ Sometimes you can run a DOS program by double-clicking its name from the *directory tree* that sprouts from OS/2's Drives object. This method also bypasses all the special settings stored in the program's object, which can cause problems.

Gads! What Do All Those DOS Settings Do?

Most DOS programs run fine under OS/2. Just double-click their little object thing, and they start rolling.

In fact, IBM made one of its computer nerds sit down and write *OS/2 settings* for the most popular DOS programs. OS/2 recognizes many of the programs on the crowded hard drive and puts them in the DOS Programs folder, where they're ready for action.

And the programs OS/2 doesn't recognize? Well, IBM's computer nerds wrote a set of *generic* settings for 'em. Those generic settings usually do the job, just like *plain-wrap* sardines.

But just as plain-wrap sardines can sometimes do gross things to your stomach, generic settings can sometimes do gross things to DOS programs. The screen looks garbled, they run too slowly or too fast, or they start crying for more memory.

IBM's computer nerd isn't around, so you have to tweak the settings yourself. Tweaking, which is not as rough as it sounds, luckily, is described in the very next section.

✔ OS/2's special *DOS settings* change the way the DOS program reacts with the keyboard, memory, mouse, printer, monitor, and other DOS programs. All these options add up to about 40 different settings to choose from. Ouch!

✔ Don't be scared by all the choices, though. Chances are, you have to adjust only one or two settings out of the 40 to make a DOS program happy.

✔ Before you can begin tweaking, the DOS program has to have an object on the OS/2 desktop or in one of its folders. If the DOS program doesn't have an object, OS/2 doesn't *ever* know how to make it happy. Flip to Chapter 16 for the lowdown on *objectifying* DOS programs.

✔ If you tweak a program's settings and make things *worse,* don't fret. Just head back to the same DOS Settings page, click the settings you changed, and click the <u>D</u>efault button. The settings then return to normal.

✔ If you *really* screw things up, just drag the messed-up object to the Shredder to get rid of it. Then migrate that program, as described in Chapter 16, and start from scratch with the new object. Sooner or later, you'll get it right.

What Setting Do I Tweak to Make My Program Work?

All those DOS settings *look* scarier than an IRS form, but the IRS stuff is *much* more agonizing.

First, the DOS settings aren't *required.* Don't bother playing with a program's settings unless the program doesn't work right.

Second, after you tweak the program's settings, you're done! Unlike with IRS forms, you have to deal with the Settings page only *once.*

Slapped on your operating gloves? Here's how to tweak a DOS program's settings if it's not acting up to snuff:

1. **Click the DOS program's object with the right mouse button and then click Settings, as shown in Figure 14-1.**

   The object's Settings notebook leaps to the screen. (The rest of the Settings notebook gets its due, by the way, in Chapter 6.)

2. **Click the notebook's Session tab and click the DOS settings button. Click the OK button on the next window and stand back.**

   The incredibly huge list of confusing-looking settings leaps to the screen, as shown in Figure 14-2.

Figure 14-1:
Click
Settings to
bring up a
program's
Settings
notebook.

When you change a DOS setting, the changes take place *immediately.* Don't look for an OK button to click; there isn't one. Just double-click the Settings window's upper-left corner to close the window, and you're done.

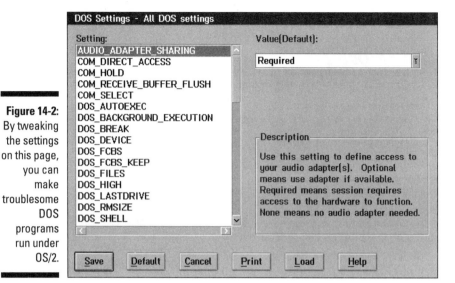

Figure 14-2:
By tweaking the settings on this page, you can make troublesome DOS programs run under OS/2.

Table 14-1 lists all the settings you have to pay attention to; Table 14-2 lists all the settings you can safely ignore most of the time. (You can ignore most settings, so don't go tweaking things randomly just to *see what happens.*)

There you have it; a rundown of the DOS settings. The key word for most of them is *ignore.* Also, if you don't want to bother with *hit or miss* setting tweaks, try giving the program's manufacturer a call. Chances are, the nerds there can tell you the specific settings that make the program run best.

Table 14-1   DOS Settings You Have to Pay Attention To

Setting	*How to Set It*
AUDIO_ADAPTER_SHARING	Does your program absolutely *have* to access your sound card? Then leave it set to Required. Otherwise, set it to Optional. Or if the program doesn't make sounds, set it to None. Only one program can use the sound card at the same time, so don't overuse the Required setting.
COM_DIRECT_ACCESS	Turn to On for programs that use the modem (unless you want to run more than one modem program at the same time). For programs that don't even know what a modem *is,* leave it at Off.

Setting	How to Set It
COM_HOLD	Leave it at Off, except for when you want to play cool modem games, such as Modem Wars or Stunt Driver, where you use a modem to call up somebody else's computer and then switch to the game program to start blowing each other up through the long-distance lines.
COM_RECEIVE_BUFFER_FLUSH	Don't fiddle with this one unless your modem program acts funny when you switch it back and forth from window to full-screen.
COM_SELECT	Leave it at All unless you want to run two modems or communications sessions at the same time.
DOS_AUTOEXEC	Leave it set as C:\AUTOEXEC.BAT unless you have a pressing reason for the DOS program to use a different, custom-made AUTOEXEC.BAT file. (In that case, type the name and location of the custom-made AUTOEXEC.BAT file here.)
DOS_BACKGROUND_EXECUTION	Leave it at On unless you *don't* want DOS programs to keep running in the background. For example, WordPerfect constantly asks the computer, "Have they pressed a key yet? Huh? Have they?" That pestering can slow down OS/2, so you may want to turn this setting to Off for WordPerfect's DOS version. (Don't ever turn this setting to Off for programs that use a modem.)
DOS_BREAK	Leave it at Off. (It enables you to press Ctrl+C to try to get a DOS program's attention, but Ctrl+C rarely does anything anyway.)
DOS_DEVICE	This box acts like a miniature CONFIG.SYS file. If you want OS/2 to load a device driver *only* when it loads this particular DOS program, type that device driver's name and location in this box. Leave out the customary DEVICE= part, however. For example, I typed the line D:\FAX\SATISFAX.SYS IOADDR=0350 into this box for each of my DOS telecommunications programs.
	(If I had wanted that driver to be loaded for *all* my DOS programs, I would have put it in OS/2's CONFIG.SYS file instead. For example, I would have typed the line DEVICE=D:\FAX\SATISFAX.SYS IOADDR=0350 and added the DEVICE= part.)

(continued)

Table 14-1 *(continued)*

Setting	*How to Set It*
DOS_HIGH	Leave it at Off unless the DOS program sends you error messages about needing more memory.
IDLE_SECONDS	Leave it at 0 unless you want OS/2 to concentrate on *this* DOS program more than on other programs; then increase the number. (You may want to increase this number for programs that use the modem.)
IDLE_SENSITIVITY	Leave it at 75 unless you want OS/2 to concentrate on *this* DOS program more than on other programs; then set the number to 100. (You may want to increase this number for programs that use the modem.)
KBD_ALTHOME_BYPASS	Leave it at Off unless you *don't* want Alt+Home to toggle a DOS program from a window to full-screen.
MOUSE_EXCLUSIVE_ACCESS	Leave it at Off unless you see *two* mouse pointers on the screen. Then choose On. (Then click the mouse in the DOS window to remove the extra mouse pointer.)
SESSION_PRIORITY	Want this particular DOS or Windows program to get more attention from OS/2? Then increase this number.
VIDEO_8514A_XGA_IOTRAP	Choose Off if you have an expensive 8514/A or XGA video card and want it to run a little faster. (You have to switch VIDEO_SWITCH_NOTIFICATION to On as well.) You can't run the program in a window, though, nor can you copy information from its screen to the clipboard. Ah, the sacrifices of high technology....
VIDEO_FASTPASTE	Switch it to On to speed up cutting and pasting stuff between the DOS and OS/2 clipboards. Switch it back to Off if the program acts weird, though.
VIDEO_ONDEMAND_MEMORY	Leave it at On unless you have trouble with some high-powered computer games.
VIDEO_RETRACE_EMULATION	Leave it at On unless you want to run computer games full-screen.
VIDEO_SWITCH_NOTIFICATION	Leave it at Off unless the screen acts weird when you toggle a DOS program between the desktop and the background.
VIDEO_WINDOW_REFRESH	Leave it at 1 unless the DOS program runs *jerky* when it's in a window. Then increase the number until the jerkiness disappears. The higher the number, however, the more OS/2 slows down.

Table 14-2   DOS Settings You Can Safely Ignore (Most of the Time)

DOS Setting	*Whether to Ignore*
DOS_FCBS	Ignore.
DOS_FCBS_KEEP	Ignore.
DOS_FILES	Ignore unless the program sends cryptic error messages about needing more *open files* or something. Then gradually increase the number until the error messages go away.
DOS_LAST_DRIVE	Ignore.
DOS_RMSIZE	Ignore.
DOS_SHELL	Ignore.
DOS_STARTUP_DRIVE	Ignore.
DOS_UMB	Ignore unless the DOS program sends messages about needing more memory or you need to load device drivers *high.*
DOS_VERSION	Ignore. A DOS program that needs this setting is usually on its last leg anyway. (It works just like the SETVER command in DOS 5 does, if you care about those things.)
DPMI_DOS_API	Ignore unless a program's manufacturer specifically tells you to change it.
DPMI_MEMORY_LIMIT	Ignore unless a program's manufacturer specifically tells you to change it.
DPMI_NETWORK_BUFF_SIZE	Ignore.
EMS_FRAME_LOCATION	Ignore.
EMS_HIGH_OS_MAP_REGION	Ignore.
EMS_LOW_OS_MAP_REGION	Ignore.
EMS_MEMORY_LIMIT	Ignore unless the program wants more *expanded memory.*
HW_NOSOUND	Ignore unless you don't want the DOS program to make little beeps. (This setting doesn't affect sound cards, however; it just stifles the beeping sounds that can come out of the PC's speaker.)
HW_ROM_TO_RAM	Ignore.
HW_TIMER	Ignore, except when some computer games and communications programs act weird.

(continued)

Table 14-2 *(continued)*

DOS Setting	Whether to Ignore
INT_DURING_IO	Ignore unless you're running fancy multimedia stuff with sound and video.
KBD_BUFFER_EXTEND	Ignore.
KBD_CTRL_BYPASS	Ignore unless you *don't* want Ctrl+Esc to put the DOS program in the background and call up OS/2's Window List, listing the programs that are running.
KBD_RATE_LOCK	Ignore.
MEM_EXCLUDE_REGIONS	Ignore.
MEM_INCLUDE_REGIONS	Ignore.
PRINT_SEPARATE_OUTPUT	Ignore.
PRINT_TIMEOUT	Ignore. (This setting controls the number of seconds OS/2 waits before telling you that it can't print anything because your printer's not turned on.)
VIDEO_MODE_RESTRICTION	Ignore.
VIDEO_ROM_EMULATION	Ignore (although some gamers report small speed gains when this setting is set to Off).
XMS_HANDLES	Ignore.
XMS_MEMORY_LIMIT	Ignore unless the program wants more *extended memory*.
XMS_MINIMUM_HMA	Ignore.

My Blast-O-Gas Missiles Don't Look As Cool When They Explode!

OS/2 chokes the most when you're trying to run DOS games. It gets distracted by all those exploding missiles, lightning bolts, and swarming ants. At other times, it just swings the golf club too darn fast or makes the monster's grunts stutter uncontrollably.

If a DOS game is giving you trouble, start by changing HW_TIMER to On and VIDEO_RETRACE_EMULATION to Off. Then close down all unnecessary windows in OS/2 and run the game by using the full screen. That solves 95 percent of DOS game troubles.

Table 14-3 tells you which games settings to tweak and how to tweak 'em.

Table 14-3	Settings for DOS Games
Setting	*How to Tweak It*
DOS full screen	Important! DOS games always run better on the full screen. This setting, unlike the others, is on the first page of a program's Session settings. (That page has the DOS settings button, which enables you to tweak all the other settings.)
DOS_HIGH	Important! Set this one to On. DOS games usually need all the memory they can get.
DOS_UMB	Set to On.
EMS_MEMORY_LIMIT	Check the DOS game's box. If it says that it uses *expanded memory,* keep adding 100 to this number until the program works right.
HW_ROM_TO_RAM	Setting this one to On can subtly speed up games such as Falcon 3.0.
HW_TIMER	Most important! Set this one to On, especially for games that run too fast or too slow or that use sound cards.
IDLE_SECONDS	Important! Set this one all the way to 60 so that OS/2 gives the game its full attention.
IDLE_SENSITIVITY	Important! Set this one all the way to 100. Like the preceding setting, it helps give the game all of OS/2's attention.
VIDEO_FASTPASTE	Turning this setting to On can subtly speed up a game.
VIDEO_RETRACE_EMULATION	Important! Turn this one to Off unless the game is running too fast.
VIDEO_ROM_EMULATION	Try this one in both the On and Off positions. Some games like it; others don't.
XMS_MEMORY_LIMIT	Set to at least 64K if you have set DOS_HIGH to On. Or if the computer game specifically uses *extended memory,* set to 1024K or higher.

✔ Start by changing the settings marked "Important!" and then start fiddling with some of the other ones. Sooner or later, you stumble on the right combination.

✔ Sound Blaster comes set up to use something called *IRQ7*. OS/2 doesn't like IRQ7, however, and prefers something called *IRQ5*. Because OS/2 is so picky, you have to turn off the computer, pull out the Sound Blaster card, and switch little *jumpers* on the card. If you're not comfortable with nerdy words such as *IRQ* and *jumpers*, you better holler for a computer guru for this one. (You also have to rerun Sound Blaster's installation program after you switch to IRQ5.)

Can I Change My DOS Settings "On the Fly"?

Just as everybody knows that they should be flossing their back molars, OS/2 gurus know that they should tweak the settings for DOS programs *before* they run the programs.

But who wants to be that efficient? With OS/2, you don't have to be. You can change many DOS settings *on the fly*, when the program is still on-screen.

With the DOS program running in a window (press Alt+Home if it's taking up the full screen), click the little box in its upper-left corner. Then click <u>D</u>OS Settings, as shown in Figure 14-3.

Figure 14-3:
Click <u>D</u>OS
Settings to
tweak the
settings
when the
program is
on-screen.

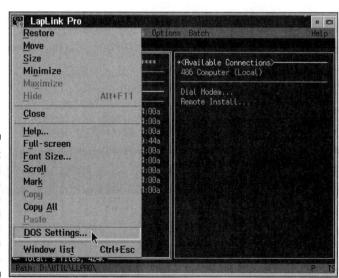

✔ Clicking DOS Settings from the window's menu brings up almost the same menu as the object's DOS Settings menu, which is described earlier in this chapter. It's a little more convenient, though.

✔ Clicking DOS Settings from the window's menu may be more convenient, but it comes with a big catch: Any changes you make apply _only to that particular DOS session._ When you close the program and open it again, the program reverts to normal, like Cinderella after the ball. To make changes _permanent,_ you have to change the program's object, as described earlier in this chapter.

Making a DOS Window Easier (or Harder) to Read

DOS programs are rude little buggers that can cover up nearly all the desktop, even when they're confined to a window. OS/2 can knock 'em into shape, though. It can make DOS programs use smaller letters and numbers (_smaller font sizes_) so that they take up less space.

To fiddle with the font sizes, click the program window's upper-left corner. When the menu tumbles down, click Font Size, and yet another menu pops up, as shown in Figure 14-4.

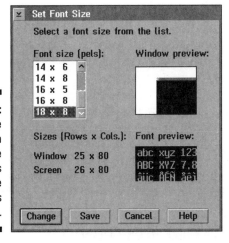

Figure 14-4: You can use this screen to change the font's size and the window's size.

Do you see the numbers listed in the Font size (pels) box? Click the bigger numbers to make the window's letters and numbers bigger. Click the smaller numbers to make the letters and numbers smaller.

The entire DOS window shrinks or grows, depending on the letter size you designate. Done? Then click the Change button to see the new window size.

When you click the numbers listed under Font size (pels), the Font preview box graciously gives you a sneak preview of how the new letters and numbers will look.

- ✔ One slight problem, though, is that this *font size stuff* works only for DOS programs that put mostly *text* on the screen. If a DOS program uses mostly *graphics,* you don't even see Font Size on the menu. (Instead, you see Scaled Image. Click that option to toggle the window between big and small.)

- ✔ Love the new size? Want to save it *permanently?* Then click the Set Font Size's Save button, not the Change button.

- ✔ Clicking the Save button, however, saves the new settings for *every* DOS window you open from then on. All the DOS windows open using the same font size and window size. Under OS/2, you can't use different fonts for different DOS windows. Something about typesetting unions. . . .

Making a DOS Window Open in the Same Place and Size

When you double-click a DOS program's icon, the program leaps obediently to the screen. But it usually leaps to the screen in the wrong place and size.

You can easily train it to get into shape and jump onto the right spot, though. To make the program jump through the right hoops, you have to jump through these hoops:

1. **Open the program.**

2. **Make the window your favorite size.**

   (This window-size adjusting stuff is covered in Chapter 7.)

3. **Now here's the secret: Hold down the Shift key while you move the window. When the window sits where you want it to open up for the rest of eternity, leggo of the mouse button and let go of the Shift key.**

That's the trick. The next time you double-click the DOS program's icon, its window pops up in the same spot, and it is the same size.

✔ Unfortunately, *all* the DOS programs open in the same spot and with the same-size windows.

✔ Every DOS program you open covers up the DOS program you opened before it. OS/2 can remember only *one* position, which it uses for *all* the DOS programs. Hey, nothing's perfect!

My DOS Program Froze Up!

Sometimes a DOS program just drops its job report and retreats up into the mountains. The program may freeze tauntingly while you're working on it. The keyboard doesn't work anymore, or the mouse pointer merely flies over the screen with no effect on the buttons beneath it.

If the miscreant DOS program is running in a window, click the little square in its upper-left corner. A menu shoots down. Click Close. When OS/2 asks whether you're sure, click the Yes button. Whoosh! The window closes, and the program disappears. Unfortunately, your unsaved work disappears too. All the other programs stay around, though, applauding your forcefulness.

If the misbehaving DOS program is taking up the entire screen, press Ctrl+Esc. OS/2's desktop heroically takes over the screen, showing you the Window List (a list of all the programs that are running, including the naughty DOS program). Click the DOS program's name with the *right* mouse button and choose Close from the menu that pops up. Click the Yes button when OS/2 asks whether you're sure, and the program disappears.

✔ If the program doesn't disappear, it's time to head for Chapter 19 for some troubleshooting. Bring your rifle.

✔ As another disciplinary measure, try pressing Alt+Home. That combination tells OS/2 to toggle the program from the full screen to an on-screen window, or vice versa. Sometimes it can shake the DOS program out of its stupor or make it easier to close.

Don't use the Close button unless the DOS program has wigged out beyond control. You lose any unsaved work in the program and create problems down the road. Instead, always try to close the DOS program the way the program intended, usually by pressing Alt+X, Alt+F4, or something similar. Sometimes pressing F1 brings helpful information about how to close the program.

"I'M WAITING FOR MY AUTOEXEC FILE TO RUN, SO I'M GONNA GRAB A CUP OF COFFEE, MAYBE MAKE A SANDWICH, CHECK THE SPORTS PAGE, REGRIND THE BRAKEDRUMS ON MY TRUCK, BALANCE MY CHECKBOOK FOR THE PAST 12 YEARS, LEARN SWAHILI, ..."

Chapter 15

Running Windows Programs in OS/2

You never know what to expect.

You can order Crème Brulée in a fancy restaurant, expecting a gourmet dessert, and the waiter can come back with an aerosol can of Redi-Whip and a match.

Microsoft Windows can be just as surprising under OS/2, although much less hot and sticky. You see, OS/2 Warp can deal with Windows in three different ways.

The "full" version of OS/2 Warp Version 3.0 comes with a copy of Windows 3.1 right inside the box. Warp doesn't call it "Windows 3.1," however; it calls it *WIN-OS/2*.

The other version of OS/2 Warp Version 3.0 — the one that *doesn't* come with a copy of Windows 3.1 — looks for a copy of Windows 3.1 already living on your hard drive. If OS/2 finds a copy, it uses that copy of Windows to run all your Windows programs.

Or some people simply use OS/2's Dual Boot feature to switch to DOS; then they can run their real version of Windows, without OS/2 having a hand in the action at all.

So which of those three types of Windows is best? Are they the same? What's Crème Brulée supposed to taste like anyway? This chapter provides the fire extinguisher to hose down all these burning Windows questions.

What Is Windows, Anyway?

OS/2 is not the first operating system to run programs in little windows on the screen. Microsoft wrote a program called Windows back in 1985 to do just that.

Everybody made fun of it. It was ugly, awkward, and slow. Microsoft kept plugging away, though, and five years later, everybody loved it.

But Windows has a big problem. It's not an *operating system*. It doesn't grab the computer's naked, shivering body at a blood-and-guts level. It's more like an overcoat that wraps around what's already there.

- ✔ Despite what Microsoft says on its box, Windows is merely a DOS program.

- ✔ Because Windows is a DOS program, it can't *multitask* other DOS programs very well. If one DOS program dies, the other programs often fall down like a stack of cards, and you lose any unsaved information that is hanging around.

- ✔ Even with its limitations, however, Windows can make computers easier to use. Windows has caught on so well, in fact, that people are buying more Windows programs than DOS programs.

- ✔ It has caught on *so* well that IBM knew that if OS/2 couldn't run Windows programs, no one would bother with OS/2. That's why one version of OS/2 Warp comes with Windows included and the other version uses a version of Windows already living on your hard drive. Either way lets OS/2 run Windows programs.

- ✔ You can find more Windows stuff (and a picture too) in Chapter 1.

- ✔ If you're going to use WIN-OS/2 much, check out *Windows 3.1 For Dummies*, 2nd Edition, by Andy Rathbone (IDG Books Worldwide). The Windows stuff in that book applies to WIN-OS/2 just as well. In fact, the next edition was going to be called *IBM OS/2 Warp Version 3.0's WIN-OS/2 and Microsoft's Windows For Dummies*, but that title wouldn't fit on the cover.

What's the Difference Between Windows and OS/2?

OS/2 and Windows look pretty similar, especially if you squint a little and turn your face sideways. If you've been using Windows for a while, in fact, you'll feel right at home with OS/2.

What's the same?

You do all this stuff the same way in both Windows and OS/2:

- ✔ You load a program by double-clicking its icon.

- ✔ You move a window around by dragging its *title bar,* that thick stripe across its top.

- ✔ You close a program or window by double-clicking the tiny box in its upper-left corner.

- ✔ You change a window's size by moving its borders back and forth.

- ✔ You boss programs around by clicking words that pop down from a menu along a window's top edge.

- ✔ You press Ctrl+Esc to see a list of programs that are running.

What's different?

Some of the differences between OS/2 and Windows can whack you a good one. Starting to use OS/2 is kind of like driving a rental car. You know what stuff is *supposed* to be on the dashboard, but you're not sure which knob does what. As long as you don't accidentally hit the windshield wiper switch, though, nobody else knows that you're confused.

Windows and OS/2 work differently when you are doing these things:

- ✔ In OS/2, you use the *right* mouse button to call up menus and move icons and objects around. In Windows, you ignore the right button completely.

- ✔ To see a list of running programs in OS/2, you click both mouse buttons on the background *simultaneously.* To do the same in Windows, you double-click in the background with the *left* mouse button.

- ✔ In Windows, you can drag icons around with the *left* mouse button. In OS/2, you use the *right* mouse button to drag objects around the desktop. (To confuse matters, OS/2 lets you use *either* button to drag a *minimized* object around the desktop.)

- ✔ Windows always lines up *minimized programs* along the bottom of the screen as icons. OS/2 hides minimized programs in the *Minimized Window Viewer* folder. (Again, to confuse matters, in OS/2 you can line them up along the desktop, if you prefer. Page back to the section "Telling OS/2 Where to Send Minimized Icons," in Chapter 9.)

These differences are the most unsettling, but a few other differences not worth mentioning here can bug you after a while.

Is WIN-OS/2 As Good As Windows?

Don't believe people who say that spaghetti squash tastes just like *real* spaghetti. Thick strands of vegetable fiber do *not* taste like Italian pasta.

But you *can* believe people who say that OS/2's version of Windows is just like the *real* Windows. Because of some bizarre legal technicality, IBM was able to grab the actual Windows program code stuff from Microsoft and stick it in OS/2. It's all there, even the bugs.

The only thing that's really different is the name. OS/2's version of Windows is called *WIN-OS/2*. IBM hired a crew of hungry programmers to search through the nooks and crannies in Windows, find all the references to Windows, and change those references to WIN-OS/2. (They missed a couple, though.)

- ✔ OS/2 2.0 came with Windows 3.0 built in. OS/2 Version 2.1 comes with Windows 3.1 built in. The latest version of OS/2 Warp comes in two packages, one with Windows 3.1 built in and the other without Windows 3.1 (but with the capability to use a version of Windows 3.1 on your hard drive.)

- ✔ In Britain during the 1800s, people were taxed by the number of windows they had in their houses. That's why many of the older houses still have bricked-up windows.

- ✔ WIN-OS/2 can run just about any Windows program that Windows itself can run.

You still don't believe that WIN-OS/2 is the same program as Windows? Then open up the Windows Calculator and type **4.000006**. After the first zero, the other zeros don't show up until you press 6. That bug is in Windows 3.1, so it's in WIN-OS/2 as well. (The errant young programmers still feel pretty goofy about it, too.)

- ✔ The Windows *secret hidden credits screen* doesn't show up in WIN-OS/2.

- ✔ You can run Windows and WIN-OS/2 in either *Standard* or *Enhanced* mode. If those terms don't mean anything to you, grunt approvingly and move on. If you want to grunt even more, check out the Enhanced-boring technical box.

Enhanced-boring technical box about the Windows Enhanced mode

Just like the program it's copying, WIN-OS/2 can run in either *Standard* or *Enhanced* mode. Most Windows users automatically assume that Enhanced mode works better, but that's not always true. In fact, Standard mode often runs faster, in both the *real* Windows and WIN-OS/2. Here's why:

The 386 Enhanced mode basically helps Windows work with *DOS* programs. You can keep DOS programs running in the background or in their own windows, and you can cut and paste graphics between DOS programs.

But the key words here are *DOS programs.* Because OS/2 already handles DOS programs better than Windows handles them, launching DOS

programs through WIN-OS/2 makes no sense. And because Standard mode runs faster than 386 Enhanced mode, there's not much point in bothering with 386 Enhanced mode.

In the rare case in which you need to make a single Windows program run in 386 Enhanced mode, open its Settings Notebook and head for the Session page, just as with DOS programs. Rather than a DOS settings button, you see a WIN-OS/2 settings button. Click that button and click the 3.1 ENHANCED button on the first page.

Enhanced mode may sound like more fun, but it's a misnomer, just like OS/2's Enhanced Editor. Yuck!

What Are Seamless Windows?

Seamless windows are all the rage in OS/2 today.

WIN-OS/2 can run in two ways. First, it can run just like Windows, taking up the entire screen for itself and its programs.

Second, it can run in *seamless* mode. You can start a Windows program (Microsoft Word, for example) and run it in a window right on the OS/2 desktop. No *Windows stuff* is in the background — just OS/2 stuff. The screen is much less cluttered, and you still have room to keep a few games going.

> ✔ By running Windows programs *seamlessly,* you get the best of both worlds. You get Windows' huge selection of programs, and you get to run the programs as though they were OS/2 programs. They run in their own windows, right next to all the other programs, as shown in Figure 15-1.

✔ You don't *have* to run Windows programs seamlessly. When you start a Windows full-screen session, OS/2 steps aside politely so that WIN-OS/2 can take over the display. For all practical purposes, the screen looks as though you're running Windows rather than OS/2. And programs run faster in a full-screen session than they do in seamless mode. (This *full-screen windows session* stuff gets dipped in the digestive juices in the next section.)

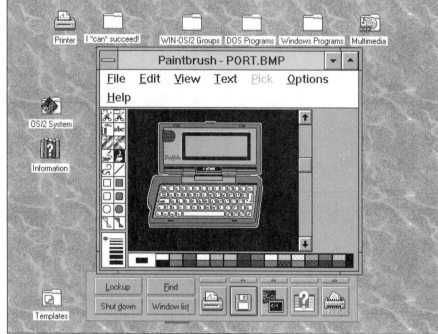

Figure 15-1:
The Windows Paintbrush program running seamlessly on the OS/2 desktop.

Running a Windows Session

As IBM's ads for OS/2 hasten to remind us, Windows occasionally crashes. When Windows hits the floor, choking on something called a *memory allocation error,* it usually takes *all* its programs down with it. The screen can freeze, or you can be rudely dumped at the DOS prompt. If you are running a bunch of programs at the same time, a crash can cause mild annoyance or screams of outrage.

WIN-OS/2 works just like Windows does, so it can gag too. You can run WIN-OS/2 stuff in *three* ways. They all have their pros and cons, which are described in this section.

Single full-screen Windows session

Figure 15-2 shows how the screen looks when you run WIN-OS/2 in a single, full-screen Windows session. (You can toggle back to OS/2's desktop by double-clicking the OS/2 Desktop icon at the bottom.)

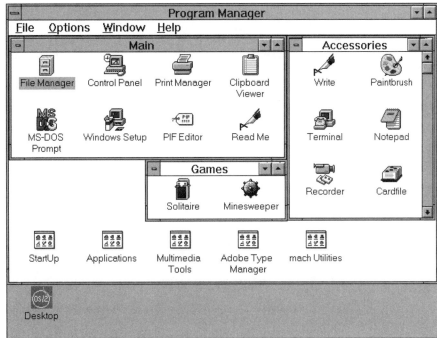

Figure 15-2:
OS/2 running a full-screen WIN-OS/2 session.

How: Double-click the WIN-OS/2 Full Screen object from the Command Prompts folder (found nestling in the OS/2 System folder). The OS/2 desktop is replaced by a WIN-OS/2 desktop that looks just like Windows.

Pros: This method is the *fastest* way to run a Windows program. It looks just like you're working in Windows. If you want to toggle back to OS/2 for some reference materials, double-click the OS/2 Desktop icon at the bottom of the screen.

Cons: Because you're essentially running *Windows,* you're also running the risks of Windows' limitations. If the Windows session crashes, all the Windows programs crash too. OS/2 steps in from the background and chuckles, but it doesn't help save any data you may have lost.

Seamless Windows sessions

Seamless windows enable you to bypass Windows' Program Manager. The Windows program simply appears on the screen, surrounded by your OS/2 desktop. That's how Windows Paintbrush appears as a separate window in Figure 15-1. It's running *seamlessly*.

How: Open the WIN-OS/2 or Windows Programs folder and double-click the object for the Windows program you want to run.

Pros: When you want to run only a single Windows program, seamless windows are the answer. By running a single program as a separate window on the OS/2 desktop, you don't have to keep Program Manager on the desktop, taking up space.

Cons: When OS/2 displays your seamless Windows program, it supports it with a Windows session hidden in the background. That makes the program run more slowly than if it were running under a full-screen Windows session. Also, if you open a second or third seamless Windows program, OS/2 runs them all through the same background Windows session. That means that if one seamless window crashes, it could bring down the other seamless windows too.

Separate seamless Windows sessions

Just as OS/2 can trick DOS programs into thinking that they're each running on their own computer, it can trick seamless Windows programs into thinking that they're each running under their own, separate Windows session.

You can make OS/2 open a new Windows session for each seamless window you want to run.

How: With your right mouse button, click the icon for the Windows program you want to run. When its menu pops up, click the arrow next to Open, and choose Settings. Next, click the tab marked Session. Finally, click the WIN-OS/2 window option, and click in the box underneath it that says Separate session. Done? Then double-click in the little box in the Settings page's upper-left corner to close it.

From then on, OS/2 always opens that Windows program by using a separate Windows session. To start that Windows program, just double-click its icon, just like any other program.

Pros: This is the safest way to run Windows programs. They each have their own full Windows session backing them, so they can't conflict with each other. And if one crashes, it doesn't bring down the others.

Cons: Separate Windows sessions can put a strain on OS/2's time, slowing everything down. And if your computer doesn't have a great deal of memory, the programs may not run at all. If you have a sound card, each session fights over it, dishing out errors unless you set the AUDIO_ADAPTER_SHARING setting in the WIN-OS/2 settings area to Optional or None. (That's described in Chapter 14.)

If you have gobs of memory, run each Windows program seamlessly in its own session. But if OS/2 complains about not having enough memory to carry on, you have to stick with a single Windows session and run all the Windows programs from it, whether seamlessly or all on the same Windows screen.

The moral to all this mess? Just make sure that you save your work often. No, more often than often. You're not considered paranoid if you save your words after every paragraph or save your spreadsheet after every entry.

Chapter 16

Installing a New Program or a New Computer Part

In This Chapter

▶ Making a backup archive

▶ Installing a new DOS, Windows, or OS/2 program

▶ Migrating a DOS, Windows, or OS/2 program

▶ Adding a new printer

▶ Salvaging a shredded Printer object

▶ Adding a new driver

*O*S/2 is supposed to be as easy to use as an elevator. Walk right in, push the button for the floor you want, and get out when your floor appears in front of you.

But what do you do if there isn't a button for the third floor? Or in OS/2's case, if there isn't a button for WordPerfect, Prodigy, or your other favorite programs?

And if you add something to OS/2, whether it's another program or something even more expensive, such as a sound card, how do you add a button for it?

This chapter tells you how to install your own buttons so that you don't have to swing from scaffolding ropes.

Making a Backup Archive for Safekeeping

OS/2's much-touted Crash Protection doesn't mean that the program never crashes. Naw, it crashes just as much as any other operating system does. Even more, actually, if you count the crashes in Windows and DOS programs, too.

OS/2's Crash Protection simply means that it's easier to get your work back —
and to get back to work — after the system crashes. By running Windows
programs in their own Windows session, for example, one program crash
doesn't bring down the rest. That's Crash Protection, because a program died,
but it didn't bring down the whole system.

One of the best ways to protect against crashes comes with OS/2's Archive
system. If OS/2 takes a dive and leaves you with a blank screen, OS/2's Archive
system can restore the screen to the way it was when you first began working
that day — if you've taken the time to turn on the Archive system.

These steps show you how to make OS/2 make an archive of itself every time
you turn it on:

1. **Click the desktop with the right mouse button and choose Settings.**

2. **When the Settings page appears, click the Archive tab.**

3. **Click the Create archive at each system restart option from the Archive
   page.**

That's it; close down the Settings notebook and breathe a sigh of "crash
protection" relief.

✔ Here's the good news: Every time you load OS/2, it keeps track of the files
it used to start itself. If OS/2 crashes and makes you press Ctrl+Alt+Delete,
try this trick: Press Alt+F1 when you see a little white box in the upper-left
corner of your screen while OS/2 is rebooting. OS/2 shows you a menu of
recovery choices. Simply choose the most recent archive, and you're set.
OS/2 rebuilds itself to the way it looked during its last archive.

✔ If you don't activate that Archive option, OS/2 still rebuilds itself — but
only to the way it looked when it was first installed. Chances are, you've
changed it a great deal since then.

✔ Now the bad news: OS/2 starts more slowly each time you load it. It takes
time to copy all those special configuration files to a special place on the
hard drive. But, hey, better to wait a little when you're loading OS/2 than
to spend hours trying to re-create your bungled desktop.

✔ OS/2 also uses some extra space on your hard drive to store those protec-
tive files. However, it saves only the last three archives — it doesn't keep
cluttering up your hard drive forever. After OS/2 has saved three archives,
it deletes the oldest archive to make room for an incoming copy.

The Easy Way to Install a New DOS, Windows, or OS/2 Program

For some reason, OS/2 offers six quadrillion ways to install a program.

But start with this method, the easiest way to install DOS, Windows, and OS/2 programs:

1. **Make sure that you have a recent archive of your desktop.**

   Check out the preceding section for complete instructions; by having an archive — a backup of OS/2's precious start-up files — you can restore order if something goofs up awful.

2. **Rummage around the box of the program you want to install for a disk marked Install or Disk 1 and stick it in the floppy drive.**

3. **Click the Floppy Disk object on the Launch Pad with your right mouse button, click the arrow next to Open, and choose Icon view.**

   A little window pops up, showing all the disk's objects. (If you stuck the floppy in drive B, do the same by clicking the Drive B object in the Drives folder, which hides in the OS/2 System folder. Oh, and if you're installing a program off a compact disc, click the CD-ROM object, which also lurks in the Drives folder.

4. **When you find the object called INSTALL.EXE, INSTALL.COM, SETUP.EXE, or SETUP.COM, double-click it.**

That's it. The SETUP or INSTALL program takes over, copying the necessary files to the right places.

✔ If the new program doesn't have any objects named INSTALL or something similar, don't give up hope. Head briskly for the next section.

✔ Even after you install the program, OS/2 is not clever enough to know that it's there. After you put the program on the hard disk, you still have to put its object on the desktop. That bit of weirdness, called *migrating*, is covered later in this chapter.

The Slightly Harder Way to Install a DOS, Windows, or OS/2 Program

If the software company was nice, it made an installation program that magically transfers the new program from its floppy disks to the computer's hard drive. But if it made an installation program, you wouldn't be reading this section.

Because the manufacturer was lazy, you have to do the grunt work yourself. You don't have to grunt too loudly, however; the fairly simple steps are listed here:

1. **Double-click the Templates folder and find the template marked Folder. Point at it with the mouse, hold down the right mouse button, and move the mouse to drag the Folder template to the desktop. Leggo of the mouse button when the new folder sits on the desktop.**

   Feel free to close the Templates folder now.

2. **With the program's first disk in the floppy drive, click the Drive A floppy disk icon on the Launch Pad. (Or if you stuck the floppy into drive B, double-click the Drive B object — it's in the Drives folder, which lives in the OS/2 System folder.)**

3. **When the floppy drive's window pops up on the screen, click in it. Then press Ctrl+/ to highlight all the objects.**

   Make sure that none of these new windows covers up the new folder you created in Step 1; if one of them does, move the folder out of the way, perhaps to an unobtrusive corner somewhere.

4. **Point at the highlighted objects, hold down the right mouse button, and drag them over to the new folder, just as you dragged the folder itself a minute ago. When a little square appears around the folder, leggo. OS/2 then copies all the floppy's objects to the folder.**

   Feel free to close the Drive B folder now so that it doesn't get in the way.

5. **Next, name the folder after the program. Point at the word Folder with the mouse and click it while you press Alt. Then type the name of the program — Robotic Arm Controller or whatever it's called.**

6. **Double-click the Drive C object that's sitting on the desktop. Then drag the new Robotic Arm Controller folder to an appropriate spot on the directory tree and leggo.**

   What's an appropriate spot? Well, you can drop the new folder inside any of the other folders. Or you can make it into its own little branch by dropping it on the box at the top of the directory tree. (What's this *tree* stuff doing in a book about a computer operating system? Find out in Chapter 8.)

Congratulations! You've installed the program!

✔ You have one more step, though. OS/2 was daydreaming while you were busy installing the program, so you have to tell OS/2 that the program is there. Then OS/2 can make an *object* — a push-button — for the program, and you can run it.

✔ To tell OS/2 to hurry up and make an object for the new program, check out the very next section, about migrating programs.

Making an OS/2 Object for a Program (or What Does All This Migrate Stuff Mean?)

At first, OS/2 says, "I'm a desktop." Therefore, you work by moving documents and folders around on the on-screen desktop.

Have you ever noticed how all your new pens and pencils eventually migrate to your coworkers' desks? OS/2 grabs that concept as well. When you want to add things to the desktop, you have to *migrate* them.

To create a desktop object for new DOS, Windows, or OS/2 programs, follow these steps:

1. **Double-click the Add Programs object.**

Add Programs

The Add Programs object lives in the System Setup folder (which rests peacefully in the OS/2 System folder, by the way).

You may recognize this migration stuff from when you installed OS/2. The same window you saw then suddenly returns to the screen, in fact, as you can see in Figure 16-1.

2. **For the most effortless method, just press Enter.**

This step tells OS/2 to snoop through your hard drive for any programs it recognizes and create objects for them on your desktop.

Figure 16-1:
When you
click the
Find button,
OS/2
displays this
window,
which
finds the
programs
you want to
migrate.

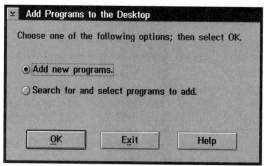

Choosing the Search for and select programs to add button is a little more complicated, letting you choose the places OS/2 searches, the types of programs it searches for (DOS, Windows, or OS/2), and the database it uses for recognizing programs. (Most people have only one database — the one that comes with OS/2.)

If OS/2 finds and recognizes your program, it tosses a preconfigured object for it in the appropriate folder, whether it's DOS Programs, OS/2 Programs, Windows Programs, or WIN-OS/2 Groups. You're done! If it didn't find your program, head for Step 3.

Because OS/2 recognizes your program and knows which folder to stash it in, OS/2 also knows which settings to use to make the program run right. OS/2 can recognize more than 100 games, for example; it recognizes them on the hard drive, creates objects for them in the right folders, and uses settings to optimize them for the OS/2 environment. The programs had fun with that one, eh?

3. **If OS/2 didn't find your program, you see a window like the one in Figure 16-2. Don't despair — click the Yes button.**

Figure 16-2:
If your new
program
isn't in
OS/2's
database,
OS/2 can't
find it, and
you see this
message.

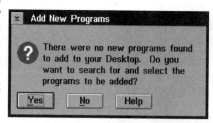

4. **Make sure that a check mark appears next to the type of program you're searching for (DOS, Windows, OS/2, or a Windows group), and make sure that the proper drive is highlighted. Then click the OK button to make OS/2 begin searching.**

For example, Figure 16-3 shows the settings that make OS/2 search drive C for Windows programs, Windows groups, and DOS programs. It doesn't search drive D, and it doesn't search for any OS/2 programs.

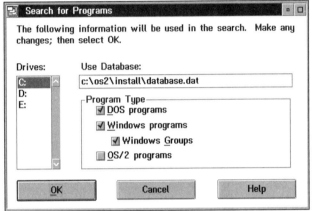

Figure 16-3: OS/2 searches drive C for Windows programs, Windows groups, or DOS programs.

When you click the OK button, OS/2 brings up a list of any of those programs it finds on that drive, as shown in Figure 16-4.

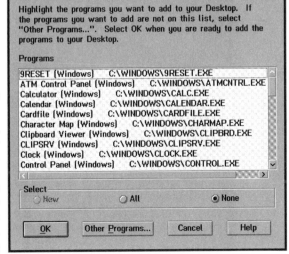

Figure 16-4: OS/2's quick search for Windows and DOS programs turned up these names.

5. Click the program names you want to bring to the desktop, and then click OK. If OS/2 didn't find your program, click the Other Programs button.

If OS/2 lists your program, you're through. But if OS/2 still hasn't found it, click the Other Programs button. Yet another window appears, as shown in Figure 16-5.

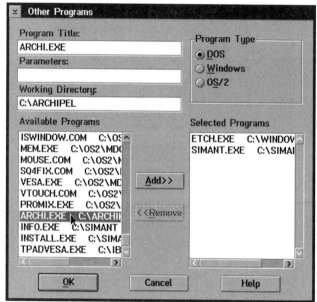

Figure 16-5:
OS/2 lists the names of every program it finds on the hard drive.

6. Click the name of your program or programs from the list of DOS, Windows, or OS/2 programs, and then choose OK.

OS/2 lists the name of every program on the drive it searched; yours should be there, if you recognize the program's filename. Yes, this is a laborious procedure.

✔ After the program called Search for and select programs to add (long name for a program, huh?) has migrated the new programs, it just sits there numbly. Click its Cancel button and then the Add Programs to the Desktop program's Exit button to gently remind them that they've fulfilled their mission in life.

✔ So where are the new objects? Well, OS/2 created new folders for them and plopped them on the desktop. They're called Additional DOS programs or Additional Windows programs or Additional OS/2 programs or something similar, depending on the programs you told OS/2 to add. When you double-click the folder, you see the objects inside, waiting for you.

✔ You don't have to leave those objects in those particular folders. For tips about arranging the desktop, check out Chapter 6 or Chapter 21.

✔ Now that you've *object-ified* the programs, double-click the objects to see whether the programs work. If they do, rub your stomach in satisfaction. If they don't or if a program does something weird, you have to tweak its settings. Scurry back to Chapter 14 for DOS program details; flip back to Chapter 15 for details about changing the settings in Windows programs. OS/2 programs don't have special settings, but you can tweak their objects anyway by checking out Chapter 6.

✔ Like many chores in OS/2, this one is pretty arduous. You have to do it only once, though (unless you accidentally drop some of the objects in the Shredder).

Yeah! I Bought a New Printer! Now How Do I Tell OS/2?

Congratulations on your new printer! Don't they have a fresh, invigorating smell when you take them out of the box?

Give the box an extra sniff for courage; then follow these steps to tell OS/2 about your new purchase:

1. **Double-click the Templates folder. When it opens, point at the Printer object. Hold down the right mouse button and point at the desktop. The Printer object follows, right to the desktop. Leggo of the mouse button, and a window similar to the one shown in Figure 16-6 leaps out at you ferociously.**

2. **Click the Install new printer driver button. Yet another window swoops down to fill the screen, as shown in Figure 16-7.**

3. **Click the Printer driver list and then press the PgDn or cursor keys until you see the printer's name. Click the name to highlight it, and then click the Install button. Another window pops up, as shown in Figure 16-8.**

4. **OS/2 asks you to insert one or more Printer driver disks that came packaged with OS/2, so start rummaging through the box until you find the one with the right label. Stick it in drive A and press Enter. (If you want to stick it in drive B, change OS/2's A:\ to B:\ before you press Enter.)**

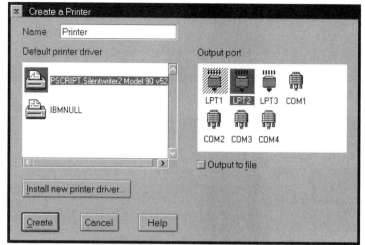

Figure 16-6:
Preparing
to install a
new printer
driver.

Figure 16-7:
When you
click the
Install
button, OS/2
grabs the
new drivers.

5. **When OS/2 says that it has successfully installed the new driver, praise it by clicking OK. Then choose the Printer port you've plugged your computer into by clicking the appropriate cable plug.**

   Big hint: Just about every computer user can safely click LPT1 and not worry about the other settings.

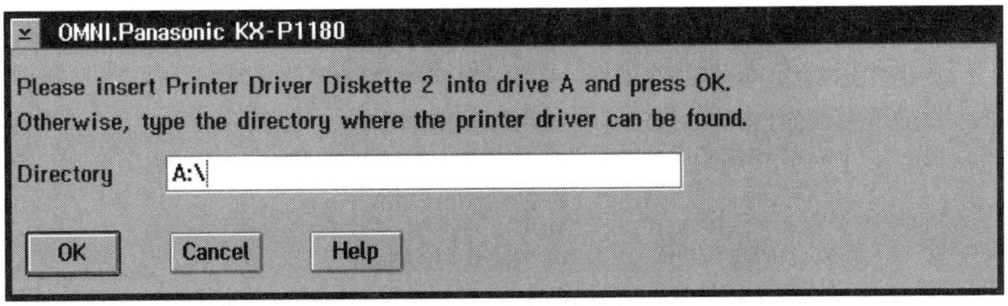

Figure 16-8:
OS/2 comes
with four
printer
driver disks,
and this box
asks you for
the disk it
needs.

❯ OMNI.Panasonic KX-P1180

Please insert Printer Driver Diskette 2 into drive A and press OK.
Otherwise, type the directory where the printer driver can be found.

Directory   A:\

[OK]   [Cancel]   [Help]

6. **Click the Create button, and OS/2 asks whether you want to install Windows drivers for the printer as well. If you're using Windows, click Yes and get out your Windows installation disks; you have to insert them into your disk drive as well. Not using Windows? Then click No.**

Either way, the window disappears, and you see the new Printer object on the desktop.

To tell the new printer to print stuff, drag file objects over to its new object and let go. If you remembered to plug in the new printer, remove all its packaging, *and* turn it on, it should squirt out the files in printed form.

✔ What should you do with the object for the old printer? Drag it to the Shredder. Or if you want to use the old printer later, leave its object on the desktop. If you want to use it, unplug the new printer from the computer's rump, plug in the old one, and drag your stuff to the old Printer object.

✔ If the computer has two printer ports, keep the old printer plugged in to the LPT1 port and plug in the new printer to the LPT2 port. When you install the new printer, click the LPT2 port. Then you can drag files to either printer. In fact, you can print things on both printers at the same time!

Help! I Accidentally Deleted My Printer Object!

It takes an exceptionally large elbow to knock a 35-pound laser printer off the desktop, but just one small slip of the mouse can knock the tiny little printer object off the OS/2 desktop.

If you accidentally drop the printer object into the Shredder, it's gone. Poof! You don't even hear any crunching sounds (other than the gnashing of your own teeth). But don't bother scrambling around for the quadrillion OS/2 installation disks; you don't need them. Putting the printer object back on the desktop is easy.

Open the Templates folder and drag a new Printer template to the desktop, as described in the first step in the preceding section.

Then click the Create button. That's it! The trusty printer object reappears, ready for use. If only all OS/2 problems were solved that easily. . . .

Adding a New Driver for a Sound Card, CD-ROM Drive, Robot, and Other Toys

Unfortunately, OS/2 doesn't always come with everything you need to make the computer work. Everybody's computer has different toys. Some computers have sound cards; others have weird laser light pens.

Before OS/2 can talk to these gizmos, it needs a translator — a driver. In fact, when you call a company's technical-support people and tell them that OS/2 isn't working right on your computer, they retort, "Why, you probably need an updated driver" and flap the fingers of their white gloves at the phone's mouthpiece.

If they have an updated driver, they mail it to you on a floppy disk. Then the fun begins:

1. **Stick the floppy that contains the updated driver in drive A and double-click the Device Driver Install object.**

   The Device Driver Install object lurks in the System Setup folder, which in turn hides in the OS/2 System folder.

   A window similar to the one shown in Figure 16-9 pops up on the screen.

2. **If you stuck the floppy in drive B, change A:\ to B:\ in the Source directory box. Click the Install button.**

   Yet another window pops up, listing the names of drivers on the disk.

3. **Click the drivers you want to install and then click OK.**

And here's where things start to unravel. Different companies install their drivers differently. Just follow the guidelines as best you can and keep your fingers crossed except when you're typing; that's too much of a challenge right now.

Figure 16-9:
Installing a
driver.

✔ When the Device Driver Install object is finished, close down all the OS/2 programs and windows. (Until you *shut down* OS/2 and start it back up again, it doesn't know about the new drivers.)

✔ Don't use the Device Driver Install object to install any drivers that came on the quadrillion OS/2 disks. Use the Selective Install object instead, or else OS/2 may get confused.

Just one more device driver in the CONFIG.SYS file

It's not uncommon for a DOS program to demand a change to your computer's CONFIG.SYS file. The problem? OS/2 and DOS share a single CONFIG.SYS file; if a DOS program starts adding device drivers to the CONFIG.SYS file, those lines not only disturb OS/2, but they also apply to every DOS program on your computer.

The solution? Don't let the DOS program make the changes to the CONFIG.SYS file. Instead, write down the lines it wants to add to the file. Then head to that particular program's Object and add the changes to the Session Settings.

For example, my modem wants this line in the CONFIG.SYS file:

`DEVICE=C:\UTIL\SFAX\SATISFAX.SYS`

Unless that line is in the CONFIG.SYS file, my DOS modem program doesn't work. So I typed these words into the DOS_DEVICE area of my modem program's DOS Settings page:

`C:\UTIL\SFAX\SATISFAX.SYS`

Whenever I load my modem program, it thinks that that line has been added to the CONFIG.SYS file, and everything's fine.

Part V
Help!

"YOU'VE PLUGGED YOUR MOUSE INTO THE ELECTRIC SHAVER OUTLET AGAIN."

In this part ...

$\mathcal{B}$y the time most people start fiddling with computers, they've realized that problems pop up now and then. They're part of life, in fact. Problems are *supposed* to happen all the time. It's how we deal with our problems that make us feel human.

For example, what do you do in a crowded theater when you sneeze and the toupee of the man in front of you flops off, obstructing your view of the screen? Even Miss Manners isn't likely to be of much help.

In the world of OS/2, problems are a little easier to deal with, thankfully. OS/2 comes with a built-in help manual (the one you didn't find in the box). Push a button, and OS/2 racks its brain to figure out what you've done wrong. If you're lucky, it brings the right page to your screen, leading you by the hand to higher ground.

And if you're not lucky? Well, this part of the book explains how to kick OS/2 in the right places when it's not moving in the right direction.

Chapter 17

Help with OS/2's Help System

*O*S/2 comes with a 400-page manual. But who reads manuals anyway? Most people would rather have the ends of their fingernails folded backward than read about stuffy technical stuff such as "object manipulation patterns."

So IBM pulled a fast one: It turned the manual into a computer program and stuck it inside Warp, ready for some *virtual* page turning. That means that you can't stick it on your lap. But then again, you can't lose it either.

This chapter shows you not only how to find OS/2's computerized manual but also how to make it automatically turn itself to the right page.

Help! What Do I Do Now?

When OS/2 throws you for a loop, pound your fists on your desk in frustrated outrage and bellow like a bull.

Then extend one finger and gently press the F1 key, which is usually located near the keyboard's upper-left corner. OS/2 responds with a helpful suggestion. If you click the Printer object and then press F1, for example, the window shown in Figure 17-1 pops up on the screen.

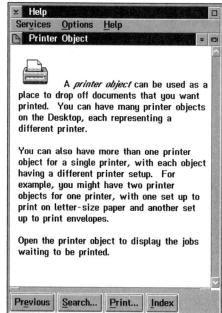

Figure 17-1:
OS/2's own
Computer
Guru pops to
the screen
when you
press F1.

You see, OS/2 is smart enough to figure out two things. First, that you clicked the Printer object. Second, that you pushed the "Help! I give up!" button (also known as F1). OS/2 racked its brains for a connection between the two events and then placed a window on the desktop with some helpful information about printers. Smart stuff, eh?

Whenever you're confused about something in OS/2, press F1. OS/2 attempts to figure out what you're trying to do, and then it brings up some information that may be helpful in your current dilemma.

✔ When the page with the helpful information is on the screen, you can press the PgUp or PgDn keys to see more helpful information.

✔ If OS/2 brings up some information that's *incredibly* helpful, turn on the printer and press the Print button. Press the Print button on the menu that pops up, and OS/2 shuttles that helpful page off to the printer.

✔ If the Help window contains a word you don't understand, look to see whether it's *highlighted* — darkened with a box. If so, double-click it. OS/2 immediately brings up that word's definition or other information pertaining to the word. Nod your head knowingly and then click the Previous button at the bottom of the window to return to your place in line. (Sometimes you have to click the Previous button twice.)

✔ At the bottom of the Help page, you sometimes see some phrases filed under Related Information. If one of those phrases looks spicy enough, double-click it. OS/2's Help program flips to the pages containing that spicy information. Are you confused about all the *jumping around* from page to page? Then jump right to the next section.

Why Do the Help Pages Jump Around So Much?

In a normal, paperbound manual, you flip the pages to search for the right section. You flip them over and over, until you give up and turn to the index in the back.

OS/2 is nice enough to turn the pages for you. As a result, it jumps around a lot, which can be distracting until you get the hang of it.

Blue words: Double-click these words to get OS/2 to jump to a new page that gives information about the blue word or phrase.

Highlighted words: These words are just blue words that have been *highlighted,* either because you clicked them once or because they're the only blue words on the page. Just press Enter to jump to helpful information about these topics. (Or double-click them; the results are the same.)

✔ If you jump around so much that you lose the only page that *was* helpful, keep clicking the Previous button until you see the page again.

✔ If you're *still* confused, try pressing Ctrl+H. That combination brings up a list of most of the Help pages you've seen. If you spot the helpful page on the list, give it a double-click to get OS/2 to bring it back to the screen.

✔ Still can't find anything helpful? Try pressing Ctrl+C. That combination brings up a Table of Contents. You may be able to narrow the search by double-clicking one of the subjects that are listed.

✔ Programmers who search for ways to glamorize their profession call this "jumping around" stuff *hypertext.*

✔ If you still can't find a shred of helpful information, check out the next section for instructions on how to *force* OS/2 to find your information so that you don't have to discipline it by pouring chocolate syrup over its keyboard. Well, *your* keyboard. Actually, strike that syrup part altogether.

Bring Me Help on My Problem Now! (Sound of Fist Striking Table)

IBM is quick to point out that the OS/2 Help program contains 5,000 nuggets of helpful information.

And you'll believe it, especially when you're trying to extract your particular nugget from the other 4,999. Make OS/2 do all the searching and spare yourself the hassle. Press F1 to bring up the Help program and click the <u>S</u>earch button at the bottom of its window. A window similar to the one shown in Figure 17-2 jumps to attention.

Figure 17-2:
To make OS/2 search for a topic in every nook and cranny, click the All libraries button.

See the Search for box? Type the subject that has left you grasping for straws — objects, for example. Then click in the area you want OS/2 to search. Here's a rundown on the areas, in order of importance.

All li<u>b</u>raries: This option is the winner, hands down. Choosing this option tells OS/2 to search everywhere and bring up a list of pages — sections — that mention the word you're baffled by. If OS/2 brings up too many sections, press PgDn until you see one that looks relevant. Then double-click it.

<u>I</u>ndex: Just like a book, OS/2's Help system comes with a *Master Help Index.* Click here to get OS/2 to rummage through that index — it's just like a book's index, really — and bring up any sections that mention your topic. Double-click the section you want, and OS/2 pops it to the screen.

<u>A</u>ll sections: This one searches all the sections in *one* library — the one that's open. It's handy but frustrating if your sought-after information lives in a different library. (Stick with the All li<u>b</u>raries search, which was just described.)

<u>T</u>his section: Ignore this one. OS/2 merely searches the single page you're already looking at. Very lazy.

The Marked sections and Marked libraries buttons take too much legwork. You have to press Ctrl+C (to bring up a list of sections) or Ctrl+H (to bring up a list of libraries) and then hold down Ctrl and click the sections or libraries you think will be helpful. Too much trouble. Choose one of the other settings and make OS/2 do the work.

Why Bother with the Master Help Index?

The Master Help Index object lives in the Information folder, unless you've dragged it someplace else.

If it isn't in that folder, however, don't bother looking for it.

Whenever you press F1, OS/2 shoots a Help window to the screen. The window has an Index button at its bottom, as shown in Figure 17-1. When you give the Index button a click, OS/2 brings up the same index the Master Help Index uses.

Using the Index button is faster and more convenient than rooting around the desktop and double-clicking the Master Help Index.

What the, Uh, Heck . . . Is a Pel?

When OS/2 shoots you with a funky word such as *pel,* fight back with *Glossary.* Glossary, part of OS/2's *electronic manual,* hides in the Information folder.

To find out what those *pel* things are, give the Glossary object a double-click and stand back as Glossary leaps to the screen, looking like the window shown in Figure 17-3.

Figure 17-3:
Double-click the word that has you stumped, and OS/2's Glossary defines it for you.

See the little alphabet tabs in Figure 17-3? You can click these tabs to flip to different pages, but a quicker way to get to the word you want is described in the following paragraph. (We get to use up one of those TIP icons too.)

To browse through the Glossary book, press the first letter of the word you're looking for. Glossary immediately jumps to the words beginning with that letter.

When you press P, for example, Glossary heads to the words beginning with *P.* Keep pressing the PgDn or down-arrow key until you see *pel;* then double-click it. The window shown in Figure 17-4 pops up with all the information you ever wanted to know about pels.

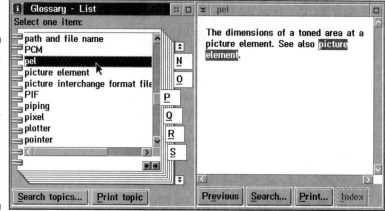

Figure 17-4:
When you double-click pel, Glossary tells you what the heck pel is supposed to mean.

✔ Just as with the other parts of the Help program, Glossary enables you to jump around. For example, see how the words *picture element* are highlighted in Figure 17-4? You can double-click them to see some nerd-level geekism about picture elements and their kind.

✔ For an even quicker way to look up a baffling word, click Glossary's Search topics button. When a box pops up, type the confusing word and press Enter. OS/2 lists all the words that even remotely resemble what you typed. Double-click any of those words to see their definition.

✔ Glossary can be a life-saver when you are confronted with the thick streams of Computer Geek Lingo that flow through OS/2's veins. It's not much help with acronyms, however. For help in doing battle with IBM's Society for Creative Acronyms, march swiftly to Chapter 24. (And check out this book's own glossary, near the back.)

What's an Error Message?

Sometimes when you're plugging along normally, dragging icons around nonchalantly, a window pops up on the desktop, like a prairie dog peeking from its hole (or like the window shown in Figure 17-5).

Figure 17-5:
An error message such as this one means that OS/2 is upset but isn't sure why.

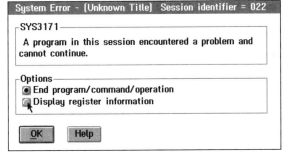

Unlike most windows, this one can't be moved. And if you click the Help button, OS/2 responds with the following:

> **Explanation:** The process was terminated without running exception handlers because there was not enough room left on the stack to dispatch the exception. This is typically caused by exceptions occurring in exception handlers.

Translated to more human language, that explanation says, "A program screwed up, and we don't know why."

The solution? Write down the error number of the message, in this case, SYS3171. Then click the Display register information button. When a new window appears with even *more* nerdy information, press the Print Screen key to send a *snapshot* of the screen to the printer. Then you can show the page to a computer nerd who can read hieroglyphics.

Then try to avoid doing what you were doing when you got the error message. Especially if you see the message shown in Figure 17-6.

✔ Some error messages are simple to figure out. You forgot to stick a floppy disk in drive A, for example, or you forgot to turn the printer on. For these error messages, OS/2 usually describes the solution: Stick a floppy disk in the drive, or turn on the printer. Follow the directions and then click the Retry command or operation button, and OS/2 keeps going.

```
TRAP 000d        ERRCD=0bdc  ERACC=****  ERLIM=********
EAX=00000000  EBX=abd53f34  ECX=00000000  EDX=00000063
ESI=00120013  EDI=0000001f  EBP=0000513c  FLG=00013246
CS:EIP=0160:fff9960f  CSACC=c09b  CSLIM=ffffffff
SS:ESP=0030:00005028  SSACC=1097  SSLIM=0000421b
DS=0158   DSACC=c093  DSLIM=ffffffff  CR0=8001001b
ES=0158   ESACC=c093  ESLIM=ffffffff  CR2=12b6efe8
FS=0158   FSACC=c093  FSLIM=ffffffff
GS=0000   GSACC=****  GSLIM=********

The system detected an internal processing error at
location ##0160:fff5c34c - 000d:a34c.
60000, 9084

048600b4
Internal revision 8.162, 94/09/19

The system is stopped.  Record all of the above information and
contact your service representative.
```

Figure 17-6:
Grab your pencil and paper; here's what OS/2 looks like when it has crashed.

✔ Other error messages are more dastardly. The language may be difficult to understand, or the machine may freeze up solid. Sometimes everything is working fine, and you don't know why an error message appeared at all. To help troubleshoot these perplexities, part the pages to Chapter 19.

✔ Keep track of the error messages' numbers, though, and if possible send the messages to the printer for later reference. If you end up on the phone with IBM's technical-support crew, you can read the little numbers to them so that they can look up the numbers in their big book. Perhaps they can come up with a cure.

Getting Help from IBM

Realizing how befuddling OS/2 can be for new users, IBM offers to help in several ways.

First, you can call IBM's tollfree technical-support line; the current number is written in fine print on one of those cards that come in the box. Unfortunately, the tollfree number only gets you through to a voice-mail system that gives you the toll number to call for your particular problem.

The technical-support staff is a decent bunch of nerds, and they can answer many of your questions — after they call you back. They're often too busy to take calls as they arrive. (Just remember to write down the *problem number* they assign you. They use it to track the problem if it grows worse.)

Finally, the technical-support staff stops talking to you 60 days after your first call. At that point, you have to start paying for help.

Or you may want to buy a modem and join CompuServe. A mixture of IBM support staff and diehard OS/2 fans hang out on special OS/2 *forums* to talk about OS/2 stuff. After you join CompuServe, type **GO OS2USER** or **GO OS2SUPPORT** for the latest scoop on OS/2.

Finally, don't be afraid to talk to some computer nerds in your area. Chances are, a group of them meets for OS/2 user group meetings. They're usually held in the evenings, so your neighbors won't see you going in or out.

Also check to see whether IBM is still offering its *Fax back* program, which provides information seven days a week, 24 hours a day. Call this number and follow the computerized instructions:

1-800-426-4329 (1-800-IBM-4FAX)

After you push bunches of touchtones, IBM sends you a fax with the information you requested. It's kind of slow, but hey, it's open Sundays.

Chapter 18

I'm Lost!

*W*hat's my most common nightmare? Unpaid mortgages? Credit card hounds knocking on my front door? Crashing into a turn signal while trying to retrieve the french fry that fell under my driver's seat?

No, it's that I'm back in high school, walking through a maze of halls, anxiously trying to find my locker, and hearing the tardy bell ring three times.

OS/2 is not *that* terrifying, but you eventually find yourself wandering lost in a maze of folders and objects. You may forget which folder holds your favorite object. Or files can sometimes *disappear,* stored in long-forgotten areas. Sometimes the desktop itself is nowhere to be found.

I eventually painted my high school locker door purple so that I could find it more easily. If you want to paint your most-used folders purple, head for Chapter 11. For other ways of finding that lost folder (or object or file or anything else), stick with this chapter.

I Can't Find the Window I Opened Two Minutes Ago!

Just about anything you do in OS/2 involves opening a window. And the more windows you open, the more windows you cover up. Pretty soon, the desktop is covered with trash.

And like recently received faxes that roll into little tubes and fall off the sides of your desk, opened windows can fall into the pile and bury themselves past recognition. How can you retrieve them? Try these tricks, in this order:

1. **Press Ctrl+Esc. This combination brings up the Window List that, appropriately enough, lists all your windows. Double-click the missing window's name, and OS/2 pulls it to the top of the pile.**

   Still don't see it? Try Step 2.

2. **Press Ctrl+Esc. This time, however, click the missing window's name with the *right* mouse button and choose Tile from the little pop-up menu.**

   OS/2 not only brings the window to the top of the pile, it also stretches it to fill most of the screen.

This technique can retrieve windows that are hovering off the edge of the screen, where they're almost invisible even when OS/2 pulls them to the top of the pile. It also retrieves *minimized windows* and their icons, whether they've been sitting in the Minimized Window Viewer, hanging from the walls of churches, or hiding in the corners of the screen.

I Can't Find the Report I Wrote Last Week!

Because OS/2 can consume about 50MB of a hard drive, most OS/2 users have whoppingly large hard drives. As a result, *lots* of room is left for stuff to get lost in.

If you misplace a file, perhaps a report you wrote last week, head for OS/2's Seek and Scan Files applet.

It's free, it came bundled with OS/2, it's sitting in the Productivity folder, and it's described completely in Chapter 11.

- The Seek and Scan Files program can whip through the entire hard drive, dredging up all the files that contain the word *thyme,* for example. (The program isn't popular just with French chefs. You can type your *own* words to search for.)

- Seek and Scan Files also can search for files by name — if you remember what you called the file. Searching by name is a little faster than other methods.

- If you're prone to misplacing files, put a shadow of the Seek and Scan Files object on the desktop. Then you don't have to keep flipping through folders to rev it up. (Head for Chapter 5 to shed some more light on shadows.)

I Can't Find My Object!

Do you know exactly which of your kitchen drawers holds the little spikes you use for eating corn-on-the-cob? Do you know which drawer has your nut-cracker? Your microwaveable vegetable steamer?

Similarly, can you tell at a glance which OS/2 folder holds Clipboard Viewer? If not, use the handy Find command to make OS/2 rummage around for it, no matter where it's stashed.

First, click the desktop with the right mouse button and choose Find from the menu that leaps up from the desktop like bubbling crude, as shown in Figure 18-1. (Or you can click the Find button on the Launch Pad — that does the same thing.)

Figure 18-1:
Choosing the Find command displays this menu, in which you tell OS/2 what your lost item looks like and where to look for it.

Now check out the Find window's little boxes. You have to tweak a few of them before OS/2 knows what to look for.

> **Name:** Anything you type here speeds up the search. Because Clipboard Viewer begins with the word *CLIP*, for example, type **CLIP***. (The asterisk stands for *anything*, so OS/2 searches for any object beginning with *CLIP*, no matter what the object ends with.)

> **Start Folder:** Find comes set up to search all your hard drives; if you prefer that it also search floppies or CD-ROM drives, click the little arrow to the right of this box and choose the new search areas from the little menu that drops down.

Locate: Don't bother with this one. It lets you limit the search to certain folders or select areas of your hard drive. If you've lost something, chances are, you don't know where to tell OS/2 to search. So just ignore this button, and OS/2 searches everywhere on all your hard drives.

More: You probably won't want to bother with this one, either. In intricate engineer-approved fashion, it lets you conduct detail-oriented searches by an object's size, creation date, last access date, extended attribute size, and other mind-boggling details.

Options: Keep the Search All Subfolders box checked; that makes OS/2 search all the folders in addition to any folders *inside* those folders. Planning to put a shadow of the found object on your desktop? Then click in the Save Results box; OS/2 creates a folder containing a shadow of every object it found during the search.

Then click the Find button at the bottom of the screen. The hard drive whirs merrily as OS/2 starts rooting through everything on the desktop. Then a hush falls over the computer, and you see a new window, named Find Results - clip*, on the desktop.

The window shows everything OS/2 found that matched your criteria. In this case, OS/2 found the Clipboard Viewer, both OS/2's and Windows (in addition to a shadow and a icon), as shown in Figure 18-2.

Figure 18-2:
OS/2 has
created
shadows of
all the
objects
beginning
with CLIP
that it found
on the
desktop and
in its folders.

> ✔ After OS/2 has found the object you're after, you have several options. You can simply double-click it to launch it. Or put a shadow of it on the desktop by dragging it there while holding down Ctrl+Shift. Or if you're sick of it, drag it to the Shredder to delete it.

✔ OS/2's Find program finds not only objects but also shadows of objects and the actual files. That's why the Find Results window contains two objects, a shadow, two clipboard program files, and two clipboard program help files.

✔ Like trying to charm large cobras with an Indian reed instrument, this Find command stuff is kind of complicated until you've fiddled with it for a while. OS/2 gives you *many* options to narrow the search, only adding to the confusion factor.

✔ What do you do with that *Find Results* window when you're finished? Just click the Close button to get rid of it. If you *know* that the object you're looking for is sitting on the desktop somewhere, try this quick trick: Click the background with the right mouse button and choose Arrange from the pop-up menu. OS/2 rounds up every object on the desktop and organizes all of them into neat little rows. It wipes out the orderly arrangement you've spent hours creating, but it also fetches any icons hiding off the edge of the screen.

Here are the nitty-gritty details on what OS/2 found and displayed in the Find Results window, listed from left to right: OS/2's Clipboard Viewer object from the Productivity folder; the Windows Clipboard Viewer icon from the Windows directory; the shadow of OS/2's Clipboard Viewer object from the Launch Pad; OS/2's actual file for the Clipboard Viewer; the help file for OS/2's Clipboard Viewer; the help file for Windows Clipboard Viewer; and the actual file for Windows Clipboard Viewer from the Windows directory.

I Can't Even Find My Desktop!

If a real desktop disappears, people start shoveling off all the Book-of-the-Month Club offers and other junk mail. Eventually, the base-level layer of desktop appears.

OS/2's desktop, however, sometimes disappears completely, even when no windows are on top. Sometimes it's *supposed* to disappear. Other times, it's simply broken. Here's how to tell the difference:

Windows fills the screen: If you're running a full-screen Windows or WIN-OS/2 session, OS/2's desktop is *supposed* to sit in the background, leaving only Windows stuff on the screen. To get back to OS/2, shut down Windows (or WIN-OS/2) by closing down the Program Manager. (A double-click in the Program Manager's upper-left corner closes it down, just as with any other window.)

A weird C: **thing fills the screen:** If you're running a full-screen DOS or OS/2 command line session, you may see just a prompt on the screen, like this:

        C:\>

or this:

        [C:\]

You can get rid of either of these *command line sessions* in the same way. Type **EXIT** at the C:\> thing and press Enter. They are closed down, and OS/2's desktop returns to the forefront.

Nothing fills the screen: If you see nothing but a sea of gray (or black or, with version 3.0, just about any color), OS/2 has probably crashed, most likely because of the video driver. Try waiting about a minute to see whether OS/2 appears. If not, press Ctrl+Alt+Delete and see whether OS/2 comes back to life. No? Then head for Chapter 19 for some troubleshooting tips or start yowling for the help of a computer guru. This problem can be rough to fix.

✔ Sometimes, pressing Alt+Esc makes OS/2 drop what it's doing and return to the desktop. If that combination doesn't work, try Ctrl+Esc as well.

✔ If the screen turns black and a message says, "Your system has stopped," OS/2 is not going to return. Some error messages are described in Chapter 17, but be forewarned: You can't do much about them except write down what they say and show them to a computer guru. An OS/2 guru may be able to figure out what's going wrong. Chapter 19 has some troubleshooting tips to try if you can't pry any gurus away from their keyboards.

✔ As a last resort for a crashed computer, push its Reset button, usually located in the front of the computer. If that still doesn't work, turn off the computer. Count slowly to ten, and turn it back on. Strangely enough, this technique fixes many frozen computers. And printers too. And modems.

Chapter 19
Something Weird Happens!

. . . .

In This Chapter

▶ When I minimize a window, it disappears!

▶ My icons don't always show up in my folders!

▶ My floppies don't have as much room as they used to!

▶ The window keeps opening up to fill my whole screen!

▶ All my icons cover each other up in the folder!

▶ I have two mouse pointers at the same time!

▶ I accidentally deleted my bundled OS/2 applications!

▶ Oh, no! I forgot the password to OS/2's Lockup screen!

▶ My DOS program looks weird on OS/2's Desktop!

. . . .

During the first few months you use OS/2, something weird will happen, no doubt about it.

Much of the weirdness is built in. OS/2's Comet Cursor is *supposed* to shoot psychedelic bullet holes across your screen.

At other times, the weirdness resembles the knocking in a car's engine. It signals the beginning of something that could be just awful.

This chapter helps you separate the harmless psychedelia from the bad car knocks.

When I Minimize a Window, It Disappears!

If you've used Microsoft Windows, you're familiar with minimizing a window. You click a little square in the window's upper-right corner, and the window turns into a little icon at the bottom of the screen.

That doesn't happen in OS/2. The window disappears! Relax. It's supposed to disappear. In fact, OS/2 *does* turn the window into an icon. It just doesn't put the icon at the bottom of the screen. OS/2 sticks the icons for minimized windows in the Minimized Window Viewer folder, which rests in the OS/2 System folder:

Minimized
Window Viewer

When you double-click the Minimized Window Viewer folder, it opens up on the screen, showing all the icons for minimized windows.

- ✔ If you prefer to see the icons lined up along the bottom of the desktop, head for Chapter 9 for directions.

- ✔ Chapter 9 tells you how to make the icons *really* disappear, in fact, if you don't want them sent to the desktop or to the Minimized Window Viewer. OS/2 can hide them until you press Ctrl+Esc and click their names from the pop-up Window List.

My Icons Don't Always Show Up in My Folders!

Sometimes when you open a folder, it looks empty — or else just a few icons line up along the bottom. But when you press PgDn or click the scroll bar, you see the rest of the icons that were hiding from view.

Why don't icons line themselves up from the top down? I dunno. The problem seems to happen with full folders, though. To put all the icons in plain sight, click in the folder with the right mouse button and choose Arrange from the pop-up menu.

My Floppies Don't Have As Much Room As They Used To!

After you use OS/2 for a while, you notice something strange about all your floppy disks, especially if you've been moving files back and forth between OS/2 and DOS. The disks don't have as much room on them as they usually do. For example, 3 1/2-inch disks that used to hold 1.44MB now hold only 1.42MB.

Secret, hidden, and excruciatingly boring files

The first time OS/2 copies a file to a floppy disk, it writes *three* files to the disk. First it copies the file you told it to copy. Then it sticks in two secret hidden files called EA DATA.SF and WP ROOT.SF.

You see, the meticulous OS/2 keeps track of more file information than DOS does. The most obvious extra information is the filename. An HPFS name can be something like MAXIMUM EARTHWORM STRETCHING PARAMETERS. But floppy disks are stuck with the FAT system. So when you write the file to a floppy disk, HPFS shortens the filename to something FAT can handle, usually taking just the first eight characters (EARTHWOR, for example).

It dumps the rest of the information in the hidden EA DATA.SF file. (The WP ROOT.SF file stores even more boring information about how the desktop is set up.)

After you use a floppy disk to shuffle a bunch of files around, the EA DATA.SF file can get pretty full of leftovers. If leftovers bother you, reformat the disk and start over. Otherwise, ignore them; these leftovers won't sprout green mold hairs.

Oh, and be sure to copy all your important files off your floppy disks before you reformat them, or else you'll lose your important stuff in addition to the leftovers.

But there's nothing really wrong with the disks, so don't bother with the technical box. Just reformat the disks if the loss of space bothers you. (Be sure to save any important files on a different floppy, though. Formatting a disk erases *everything*.)

The Window Keeps Opening Up to Fill My Whole Screen!

Just one wrong click, and a window stops being a window. It expands to cover the entire screen. And it won't leave! It just sits there, covering up everything on the desktop.

To turn it back into a window, double-click its *title bar* — that long strip across its top that has the window's *title* written on it. When it's a window again, you can drag its edges in or out to make it the right size. Whew!

All My Icons Cover Each Other Up in the Folder!

OS/2 can be sloppier than its users. When you drag a bunch of objects over to a folder and let go, for example, OS/2 obediently moves those objects into the folder.

But when you double-click the folder and look inside, you'll probably see a mess. Like a cat that's bored with a toy, OS/2 merely drops the objects haphazardly on top of other objects, as shown in Figure 19-1.

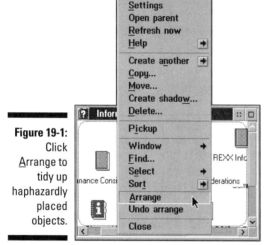

Figure 19-1:
Click
Arrange to
tidy up
haphazardly
placed
objects.

To make OS/2 tidy everything up, click anywhere on the folder's background with the right mouse button and choose Arrange from the pop-up menu. OS/2 moves the objects into neat, orderly rows. (For ways to make OS/2 this tidy *all* the time, head for the section "Rearranging Your Workplace Shell," in Chapter 9.)

I Have Two Mouse Pointers at the Same Time!

In this situation, you definitely have too much of a good thing. You start up a DOS program in a window, and you see *two* mouse pointers on the screen. One is OS/2's mouse pointer, and the other is the DOS program's mouse pointer. Usually they are different sizes and shapes.

When you move the mouse, both pointers move, one following the other. You can ignore OS/2's mouse pointer, in fact, and watch the DOS program's mouse pointer. With some subtle wrist swipes, you can still point and click buttons on the DOS program's screen. But who needs this kind of *double mouse pointer* aggravation? Get rid of the OS/2 mouse pointer like this:

Press and release the Alt key. When the menu dangles down, click DOS Settings (or just press D), and then press Enter at the next page. Finally, click MOUSE_EXCLUSIVE_ACCESS and click the On button. Got it? Then click the Save button at the bottom of the screen.

When that *setting menu* stuff disappears, click in the DOS window. The OS/2 mouse pointer disappears, leaving a good-looking DOS pointer stuck inside its own window where it belongs.

✔ The OS/2 pointer comes back to life when you close the DOS program.

✔ Or, if you want the OS/2 pointer back sooner than that, press and release Alt again. Then you're back to having two mouse pointers. Click in the DOS program's window, and you're back to one.

✔ To make these changes permanent, you have to change the DOS settings on the program's object. Changing the settings while the program is on the screen affects only the currently running window. (You can learn more about this DOS settings stuff in Chapter 14.

I Accidentally Deleted My Bundled OS/2 Applications!

If you accidentally drag one of the bundled OS/2 programs to the Shredder, relax. Check out Chapter 11 and Chapter 12; the program may not be worth salvaging. Many of OS/2's bundled programs are as much fun as spilling Spaghetti-Os on a white T-shirt.

If you *really* want the program back, take heart in knowing that you've probably just deleted the program's *object* — its settings — not the actual program. The program itself is still sitting on the hard drive.

To get the object back, you have to *migrate* it back to the desktop. (Migration is described fully in Chapter 16.) You can speed up the migration process by asking OS/2 to migrate only OS/2 programs. (Also, you have to click the Search for and select programs to add button because OS/2 doesn't automatically find its own bundled applications.)

✔ The Add Programs program identifies programs only by their filenames. If you accidentally delete the System Editor object, for example, OS/2's Migrate Applications program lists the System Editor as E.EXE. That's not very intuitive at all.

✔ So if you don't know the filename of a particular bundled application, tell OS/2 to migrate all of 'em. OS/2 creates an object for *every* OS/2 program it finds and places the objects in a folder called Additional OS/2 Programs. Open that folder, and you can spot your cherished application by its familiar-looking icon. Just drag the object back over to the folder where it belongs. Then drag the Additional OS/2 Programs folder to the Shredder to get rid of it.

✔ Dragging the Additional OS/2 Programs folder to the Shredder doesn't delete any program files. It deletes just the *objects.* No harm done.

✔ If you really *did* delete some of OS/2's bundled files from the hard drive, you can still resurrect them. Double-click the Selective Install object in the System Setup folder to rev up OS/2's installation program, which is described (and pictured) in Chapter 3. Click O̲K on the first page, and on the second page click the names or types of programs you want to reinstall.

Oh, No! I Forgot the Password to OS/2's Lockup Screen!

When you choose L̲ockup now from the desktop's main menu, OS/2 follows your instructions. It gift-wraps your desktop with OS/2 logos, keeping away prying eyes and fingers.

To get your desktop back, type the password and press Enter. Forgot the password? Then click the screen's Help button for the Official IBM solution:

If you forget your password, turn the computer off and then on.

When you turn off the computer, of course, you wipe out any work you haven't saved, so you were probably hoping to find a less drastic solution here. There isn't one. After OS/2 boots back up, don't forget to change the password to something a little easier to remember.

My DOS Program Looks Weird on OS/2's Desktop!

DOS programs always think that they have the entire screen to themselves. If the program doesn't have the whole screen, it can look weird. The colors may not look normal, and some of the graphics may be weird. The program may look so weird, in fact, that you can't use it!

Try making OS/2 give the entire screen to the program. Click inside the DOS program's window and then press Alt+Home.

When the DOS program fills the whole screen, it should look and act normal. As normal as a program can be, anyway.

Part VI
Tons of Tens

"GENTLEMEN, I SAY RATHER THAN FIX THE 'BUGS', WE CHANGE THE DOCUMENTATION AND CALL THEM 'FEATURES'."

In this part ...

Normally, nobody really cares about waffle irons. If you saw a newspaper story about waffle irons, you would probably skip right over it.

But if that newspaper story were titled "The Ten Best Waffle Irons," your eyes would wander over to see which one was at the top. There's something about a list that's, that's, well, that's more appealing than a waffle iron.

This part of the book is a time-honored tradition in the *...For Dummies* series — the Lists of Tens. It includes lists of suggestions, tips, and other helpful information for people with OS/2 staring back at them from their computers.

Some lists have more than ten items; others have fewer. But who's counting? At least you don't have to read about waffle irons....

Chapter 20

Ten Aggravating Things about OS/2 (and How to Fix Them)

*S*witching a computer over to OS/2 is similar to moving into a new house. When the realtor (or the OS/2 picture collection on the software box) first romances you, you think that everything will be perfect — that it's just what you've been looking for.

Then, after you move in, a few little things start to bug you. Water may drip down the fireplace shaft when it rains, or those once-handy folders may seem crowded and distracting.

This chapter lists the subtle (or not so subtle) things about OS/2 that can get on your nerves after a while. And, more important, it tells you how to fix the annoyances without hiring a chimney sweep.

It Won't Leave My Num Lock Key Alone!

For some reason, OS/2 has an unhealthy fixation on the Num Lock key, and it really aggravates people who type numbers with the numeric keypad (that calculator-looking batch of keys on the right side of the keyboard).

When you first load OS/2, it turns Num Lock off. You have to press the Num Lock key if you want it back on. Pressing the key is usually no big deal. Distracting, but livable.

But if you head for a DOS session, OS/2 turns Num Lock off again. In fact, every time you head for another full-screen DOS, OS/2, or Windows (or WIN-OS/2) session, OS/2 instantly turns the Num Lock key off. A rumor was going around that OS/2 programmers wanted to get back at their accountants or something. . . .

You can't fix this problem from within OS/2, unfortunately. Just get used to it and keep pressing Num Lock to turn it back on every time you start another full-screen program.

- ✔ Actually, you can fix it. Give a floppy disk to a computer guru and ask for a copy of a little utility program that automatically turns Num Lock on every time you start a DOS session. Many frustrated OS/2 programmers have written these programs.

- ✔ If you have a modem, you can find several Num Lock utilities on CompuServe, one of those dial-up information services.

Those Zillions of Mouse Menus Take Forever!

Just like Windows, OS/2 comes with zillions of menus that pull down, drop down, or squirt out of just about any place you click.

At first, clicking File and then Save to save a file in System Editor (or in any other OS/2 or Windows program) is kinda fun.

But after a while, you can get frustrated by having to stop your work, grab the mouse, click on File, wait for the menu to fall down, and click Save to complete the process.

You can save a file much more quickly. See how some of the letters on the menus are underlined? (And see how some of the letters in this book are underlined, too?) The underlined letters are *hot keys,* and you can press them for instant action.

The Alt key triggers the whole thing. So to Save a File in System Editor, press Alt, F, and S, in that order. The Alt key tells OS/2 that you're ready to use a hot key; F stands for File, and S stands for Save.

Now you know why the menu keys are underlined, and you can sympathize with this book's poor editors, who had to make sure that all the corresponding letters in the book were underlined, too. Send 'em a beer (and a magnifying glass)!

- ✔ You can bypass the mouse when you load an object, too. Whenever you open a folder, one of the objects is already highlighted. Press Enter, and that highlighted object leaps into action. Or press the cursor keys to move the highlighting from object to object. Press Enter when your favorite object is highlighted.

- ✔ You can find other *shortcut keys* in Chapter 2; the handiest ones are on the Cheat Sheet tear-out card at the front of this book. Unless a coworker has already pulled yours out from the binding, that is.

It's Too Slow!

OS/2 is not always speedy. In fact, booting up can take as long as two minutes on some of the older 386 computers out there. The easy solution? Don't ever shut it down. Here are a few other tips that speed up OS/2 a little:

Dump the exploding animation: When you open a folder or window in OS/2, it *explodes* onto the screen. Those little moving lines look cool, but they slow things down. To get rid of 'em, head for the System object (in the System Setup folder, which lives in the OS/2 System folder). Open the Settings notebook, click the Window tab, and click the Disabled button under Animation.

Buy more RAM: OS/2's box says that it needs 4MB of RAM, but it's *much* faster with 8MB. Give it 16MB, and you'll hear it roar with appreciation. If the price of RAM drops, consider dropping some cash on extra RAM.

Close down extra windows: When you're done with a window, close it. Then OS/2 can wipe the window from its "things to keep track of" list.

Keep track of background programs: Because OS/2 doesn't put icons for minimized windows on the desktop, you can easily forget that you have seven DOS programs and three Windows sessions going on in the background. If you're no longer using something, close it down.

Use OS/2's HPFS: OS/2's cool, new High Performance File System runs faster than the system it replaces. But not unless you have at least 6MB of RAM and at least a 100MB hard drive. (To be more realistic, stick with at least 8MB and a 340MB or 500MB hard drive.)

Buy an accelerator card: The latest video cards not only stick graphics on the computer's screen, but they also do it quickly. Because OS/2 is so graphics-hungry, an accelerator card can speed things up. Make sure that the card has OS/2 *drivers,* though. To be sure, ask the salesperson. (Then make sure that you can return it if it doesn't work.)

I Can't Back Up My Hard Drive!

Everybody knows that you're supposed to back up the hard drive. When your hard drive eventually fails, you don't scream as loudly if you backed it up just 12 hours ago.

OS/2, like MS-DOS, comes with a Backup and Restore program for copying the hard drive's contents to floppy disks. But considering that many OS/2 users would need 100 floppy disks for this chore, OS/2's program is not really practical. The best solution is to get a tape backup unit. It looks like a tiny VCR, and it copies all the stuff on the hard drive to a videotape-looking thing.

Traditional DOS tape backup units can't reliably back up OS/2 files. OS/2 saves files with weird names and attributes that DOS can't handle. Make sure that your tape backup unit is compatible with OS/2 before relying on it.

✔ A tape backup unit costs more than floppy disks, but which do you prefer: inserting 100 disks, one by one, or putting in a backup tape, pushing a button, and going to a Thai restaurant for lunch?

✔ More and more companies are releasing OS/2 versions of their software. If you have an older tape backup unit, call the manufacturer and find out when the OS/2 version is going to be ready.

My Mouse Died! How Can I Shut Down OS/2?

Why, by carrying out this seemingly random series of keystrokes:

1. **Press Ctrl+Esc.**

2. **Press the up-arrow key to highlight the Desktop - Icon View line.**

3. **Press Enter.**

4. **Press the spacebar.**

5. **Press Shift+F10.**

6. **Press D.**

7. **Press Enter.**

That should do it.

I Gotta Close a Long Trail of Open Folders!

Anybody who has worked with a filing cabinet knows how deeply that important piece of information can be filed. It's probably the third piece of paper in
the second file within the top drawer's fifth folder.

The same is true with OS/2's desktop. By the time you've rummaged your way
through to the object you want, three or four open folders clutter the screen. Is
there any way to make a folder close automatically when you grab something
out of it?

Yep. Work areas, described in Chapter 9, come close because they let you open
and close bunches of related folders with a single mouse click. However, here's
a way to make a folder close automatically whenever you open a folder or
program from inside it:

1. **Open the System object.**

   You can double-click the System object from within the System Setup
   folder (which lives in the OS/2 System folder). A faster way, however, is to
   click your right mouse button while pointing at a blank area of your
   desktop; when the menu pops up, click System setup — and *then* double-
   click the System object.

2. **Click the <u>W</u>indow tab, and then click the little right-pointing arrow at
   the page's bottom.**

3. **Click the <u>A</u>ll Objects setting.**

   OS/2 closes down a folder when you open a folder or object from within it.
   It's a handy way to keep a trail of open folders from cluttering your
   desktop.

Make the Shredder Stop Nagging Me!

The Shredder knows how deadly it is, so it's overly cautious with warning
messages. Every time you try to delete something, it shouts a warning message.
Then you have to stop and click the "OK, I know what I'm doing" button before
you can shred your trash.

To shut it up, double-click the Setup object (which hides in the System Setup folder, which hides in the OS/2 System folder). Click the Confirmations tab, and then remove the check mark from the Confirm on folder delete line. Remove the check mark from the Confirm on delete line as well.

The Shredder then just shreds your garbage and keeps its mouth shut. For another handy Shredder tip, flip through to Chapter 22.

How to Uninstall OS/2

OS/2 Warp offers an incredible amount of control over a computer. It offers more than fifty different settings for customizing how the mouse works, for example.

And that's part of its problem. Power-hungry computer users love OS/2 because it offers such an exceptional degree of control and fine-tuning of details. Others look at all of OS/2's settings and see too many decisions — as well as too many settings that can accidentally be set the wrong way.

If you've decided that OS/2's vast array of options and settings brings more confusion than control, here's how to remove OS/2 from your hard drive:

1. **Using the Dual Boot command, boot up the computer with DOS.**

2. **Type the following command at the root directory of each of your drives:**

```
C:\> ATTRIB EA*.* -r -s -h
```

3. **Type the following command at the root directory of each of your hard drives:**

```
C:\> DEL EA*.*
```

3. **Type the following five commands on your C drive.:**

```
C:\> C:\
C:\> ATTRIB WP*.* -r -s -h
C:\> DEL WP*.*
C:\> ATTRIB OS2*.* -r -s -h
C:\> DEL OS2*
```

4. **Delete these directories and all the files in them:**

C:\DESKTOP

C:\OS2

C:\SPOOL

C:\PSFONTS

C:\MAINTENA

C:\NOWHERE

C:\DELETE

C:\MMOS2

5. **Type this command on each of your hard drives:**

```
C:\> CHKDSK /F
```

If you're still running into problems with OS/2 remnants, your best bet might be to reformat your hard drive. It destroys all the data on the hard drive, but it's the best way of totally wiping it clean.

Chapter 21

Almost Ten Cool Ways to Arrange Your Desktop

*J*ust look at any magazine rack, and you see dozens of *Home* magazines. They all have big pictures of rich people's houses, with their barn-size kitchens, fine wood paneling, and mantels big enough for me to drive my Volkswagen through.

This chapter is a *Home* magazine for desktops. Here you can find pictures of several OS/2 desktops, each customized for individual needs. By grabbing ideas from the next couple of pages, you can create your own desktop without paying a decorator's fee.

The Author's Desktop

(Blush.) I used the desktop shown in Figure 21-1 while writing this book; here are a few key features:

Figure 21-1:
I designed
this desktop
for my work
on OS/2 For
Dummies.

✔ First, notice the Nikon object at the bottom. By double-clicking it, this OS/2 program captured 90 percent of the screen shots in this book.

✔ All my Windows, DOS, and OS/2 programs get their own folders, and those three folders live in the Apps folder. Apps is a work area folder, so when I open that folder, it automatically opens the Windows, DOS, and OS/2 folders. After I grab the program I want, I close the Apps folder, and it takes the Windows, DOS, and OS/2 folders down with it. Quick and easy. (Work areas are described in Chapter 9.)

✔ I customized the Launch Pad, shown in the upper left corner of Figure 21-1. I set it up to be vertical, with smaller icons. (The Launch Pad is described in Chapter 4.)

✔ OS/2 comes set up with a shadow of the Drive A object on the Launch Pad, but I added shadows of the Drive C and Drive D objects to the Launch Pad as well. The mouse arrow is pointing to the shadow of the CD-ROM drive in Figure 21-1. Using the Launch Pad is quicker than rooting through the other folders.

✔ You also can see shadows of the programs I access most frequently, all added to the Launch Pad: System Editor for jotting down notes, the Clipboard Viewer to see what's stored in my clipboard, and the Template folder. They're on the Launch Pad's topmost "ladder."

✔ Finally, I dump my stuff in the Trash folder rather than in the Shredder so that I have a chance of getting it back if I goof. (If you want a Trash folder too, see Chapter 22.)

The Commanding Command Line

Most OS/2 users head straight for the folders and begin playing. Others, however, prefer to stick with the command line they've been using for more than a decade.

- OS/2 can run dozens of command lines; the layout shown in Figure 21-2 has two DOS prompts and two OS/2 prompts, all running in their own windows.

- How do you get more than one DOS command line? By clicking the DOS Windows object with the right mouse button. (The DOS Windows object resides in the Command Prompts folder, which hangs out in the OS/2 System folder). Click Settings, click the Window tab, and click the Create new window option. That tells OS/2 to create a *new* DOS command line in a new window each time you double-click the DOS Windows object.

- If you're a real die-hard command line user, put a shadow of the OS/2 Full Screen object in the Startup folder. The desktop pops up for a brief moment but then disappears, leaving you a blank screen and a little [C:\] to type commands next to.

- If you press E at the command line, the desktop pops back up with the System Editor, ready for you to type stuff. When you close the System Editor, the desktop disappears as well, returning you to the command prompt.

- Or, if you type **Exit**, the command prompt disappears, leaving you back at the desktop.

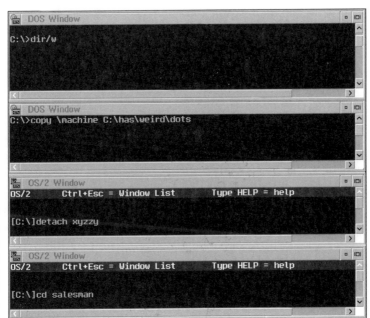

Figure 21-2:
This desktop features four command lines.

The Windows Look

Don't care for OS/2's funky folders and objects? Then stick with Windows, or, actually, with WIN-OS/2.

- ✔ The "full" version of OS/2 Warp (version 3.0) comes with Windows Version 3.1. Called WIN-OS/2, this version does everything that Microsoft's version of Windows can do. (Don't confuse WIN-OS/2 with Microsoft's Windows 95, however — that's a whole different ball of wax.).

- ✔ If you want to boot up WIN-OS/2 rather than OS/2's desktop, put a shadow of the WIN-OS/2 Full Screen object in the Startup folder. Then OS/2 boots up with a full-screen Windows session, as shown in Figure 21-3, rather than with the desktop.

- ✔ See the Desktop object in the bottom-left corner? Give it a double-click to head back to the desktop for OS/2 tasks. Use the Window List to hop on back to the Windows session.

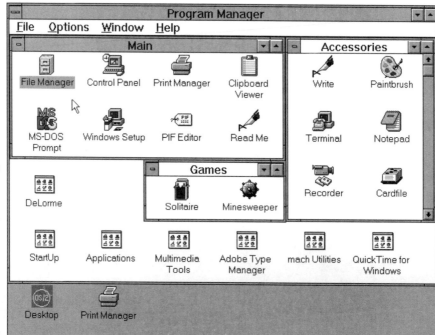

Figure 21-3: This WIN-OS/2 desktop works well for people whose hearts are still with Windows.

If You Build a Desktop, the Objects Will Come

When you drag an object to a new spot on the desktop and leave it there, OS/2 simply lets it lie. You can tell OS/2 to keep all the objects organized in neat and orderly rows, however, as in the desktop shown in Figure 21-4.

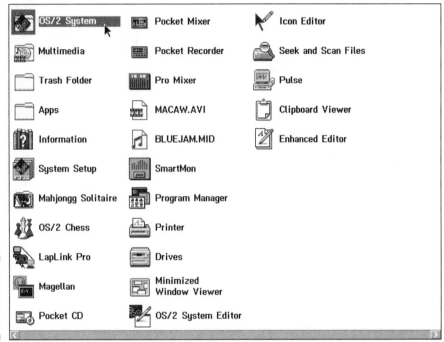

Figure 21-4:
This desktop is neat and orderly.

✔ When OS/2 automatically lines up the objects, none of them can get lost. They can't get covered up by a folder or by any other object. Everything is easier to find.

✔ To change a desktop to this neat and orderly layout, click the desktop with the right mouse button and click the little arrow next to <u>O</u>pen. Choose <u>S</u>ettings from the next menu and choose Flowed from the Format box.

✔ Whenever you move an object, OS/2 shifts the other objects around to take its place. The desktop always looks like a neatly plowed field of objects.

✔ If you prefer one long, steady string of objects flowing down the right side of the desktop, choose Non-flowed rather than Flowed. You have to keep hitting PgDn.

High-Resolution Yowzas!

Don't let anybody tell you that you can't play games under OS/2. Broderbund's Stunts, Britannica's Archipelagos, and Microplay's funky Weird Dreams are all running on the screen shown in Figure 21-5.

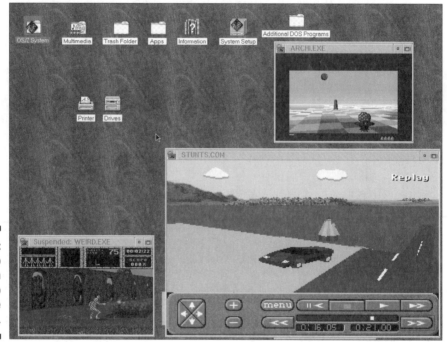

Figure 21-5:
This desktop has been organized to maximize productivity.

✔ How do you fit three DOS programs on the screen at one time? The secret is to use a high-resolution video card. For the screen shown in Figure 21-6, OS/2 is installed in 1024 × 768 resolution using ATI's "Mach32" Graphics Ultra Pro card.

✔ Using higher resolutions comes with a catch, however. You can pack more stuff on the screen, but it's much smaller, as you can tell by comparing the screen's icons with the icons on the desktops on the previous pages. The difference may not be very noticeable on the screen.

✔ Also, OS/2 sometimes runs a little more slowly in higher resolutions. It has more stuff to move around on the screen, so it takes more time to open and close windows.

✔ Some games have problems running in Windows. For example, Weird Dreams runs only in full-screen mode — that's why the word *Suspended* appears along the top of the window. For tips on setting up DOS games under OS/2, head for Chapter 14.

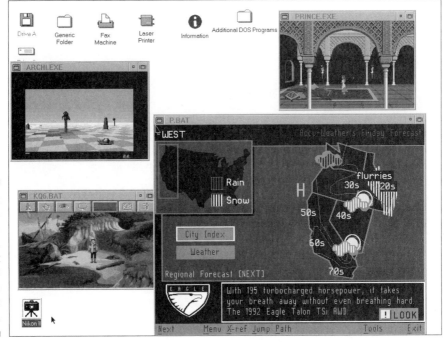

Figure 21-6: With a high-resolution video card, you can fit several DOS programs on the screen at one time.

Chapter 22
Ten Cool OS/2 Tips

Here's the ubiquitous list of Doughs and Dough-nuts, straight from the fryer. Enjoy.

Make a Trash Folder

The Shredder is a pretty dangerous piece of machinery.

If you drop something important into a normal wastebasket, you can pull it back out, and depending on how sticky your lunch wrapping was, it'll probably be fine.

But if you drop something into the Shredder, it's dead meat. To avoid having to rely on the Undelete stuff described in Chapter 6, try this technique. Drag a new folder out of the Templates folder and stick it next to the Shredder. Then change the folder's name to Trash. Figure 22-1 shows the Shredder and the new Trash folder.

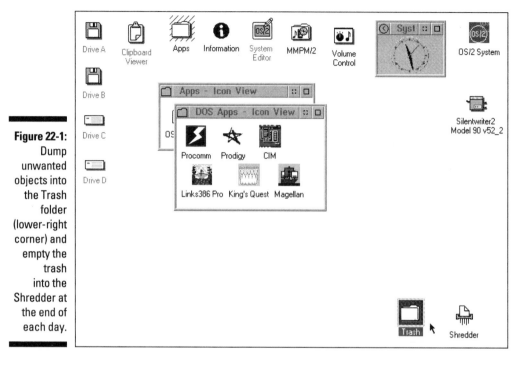

Figure 22-1:
Dump
unwanted
objects into
the Trash
folder
(lower-right
corner) and
empty the
trash
into the
Shredder at
the end of
each day.

Rather than drag unwanted objects to the Shredder, drag them to the Trash folder. Then, at the end of the day, after you've had a chance to think about whether you want to destroy them, drag the objects from the Trash folder to the Shredder.

- ✔ If you throw away something by mistake, you can just drag it back out of the Trash folder.

- ✔ If you're trashing a lot of stuff, empty the Trash folder a few times a day.

Use Work Areas to Switch among Dozens of Desktops

Work areas sound almost as boring as objects, but *au contraire* — they glisten with effulgence. Actually, work areas are just an easy way to make OS/2 take over much of your work.

When you work in OS/2, you spend most of your time opening folders and moving windows around on the screen. If you set up a work area folder for each of your projects, you can switch to differently organized desktops at the touch of a button.

Here's what you have to do:

Make a folder for each one of your projects. In each folder, put shadows of key objects as well as shadows of important files. Then open the folder's Settings notebook, click the File tab, and click the Work area button.

Next, open all the stuff that's in a project folder and organize it on the desktop the way you like it. Then close the folder, leaving its contents still lined up on the screen. When the folder *folds up,* it takes everything down with it, effectively cleaning off the desktop. And when you open the work area folder back up, it tosses everything back on the desktop exactly as you left it.

Opening and closing different work area folders is similar to having a bunch of different desktops to choose from. You can find more work area wisdom laid out in Chapter 9.

Start Programs Automatically with the Startup Folder

After you use OS/2 for a while, you get pickier about how to arrange your desktop. You want a clock in the corner, for example. Or perhaps you want Pulse pumping away near the bottom, showing you how hard your computer is working.

To make a program start automatically whenever you start OS/2, put a shadow of its object in the Startup Folder, which is found in the OS/2 System folder.

Every time you load OS/2, it glances in the Startup folder and loads up any programs that are sitting there. It's a quick way to get things rolling in the morning.

✔ You may want to put a shadow of your most used work area folder in the Startup folder. OS/2 then automatically spreads your work out over the desktop so that you can jump into the project with both feet.

✔ Or, if you use OS/2 mainly for Windows programs, you can put a shadow of the WIN-OS/2 Full-Screen object in there. OS/2 then starts up with a *Windows face.*

Spend Some Time Organizing Your Desktop

You never see two desktops that are the same in one office. And you shouldn't expect to see the same OS/2 desktop on other computers, either.

OS/2 can be set up in zillions of different ways. Check out Chapter 21 for some ideas, and start changing OS/2 around to suit the way *you* want to work.

The more time you spend customizing OS/2, the better OS/2 can suit your needs. If you leave OS/2's desktop set up the way it was when you first installed it, you won't be getting as much out of OS/2 as you can.

Don't Run These DOS Programs

Although OS/2 runs the great majority of DOS programs on the market, it chokes on these guys:

> **DOS programs that do funny things to the 386 chip in a weird *VCPI mode,* whatever that is.** (Not only are these programs few and far between, but they don't run under Windows, either.)

> **Programs that do funny things to the hard drive.** This category includes most of the DOS *Undelete* programs that come bundled with programs such as Norton Utilities. (OS/2 comes with its own Undelete program, so this restriction doesn't cause much of a loss.)

> **Some fax boards and fax programs.** Because of timing problems, OS/2 can't handle some brands of fax cards and software. If you're having problems, switch over to FaxWorks for OS/2, the fax program that's included with OS/2 Warp's BonusPak.

If you try to run some of these forbidden programs, you usually just get an OS/2 message telling you to knock it off, so no harm is done. If you try some of the fax boards using your DOS or Windows programs, though, you may lose some pages as your faxes fly through the phone lines.

Don't Install This Hardware

OS/2 is pickier about its chips than any computer nerd I've ever known. Just as some computer nerds love Pringles and others can't stand them, so too does OS/2 have its favorite.

In the chip area, OS/2's finickiness demands that the computer's memory chips — its RAM — all be the same type and speed. If the computer is new, you have little to worry about because the chips buried inside the case of a new computer are almost always the same.

But if you've added memory to your computer or paid somebody to add it for you, make sure that the new chips are the same type and size as the old ones.

- ✔ If the old chips say *70ns* on them, make sure that the new ones say *70ns* as well.

- ✔ Chips come in three types: *3s, 9s,* and big handfuls. Make sure that your *computer* chips are either all *3s* or all *9s.* Sure, this sounds weird, but the teenager at the RAM chips store will know what you're talking about.

Don't Forget to Shut Down OS/2

If you've used DOS or Windows before, you know that you're not supposed to turn off the computer when it's in the middle of a program. Turning it off midprogram can disrupt the data on the hard drive.

Conscientious computer user that you are, you always return to a C : \ thing before you flip the computer off.

Not under OS/2, though. You must use OS/2's Shut <u>d</u>own command or else you can wreak serious havoc. When you want to turn off the computer, follow these steps:

1. **Save any of your work — letters, reports, spreadsheets, or whatever — to disk.**

2. **Click OS/2's desktop with the right mouse button.**

3. **Click the Shut <u>d</u>own command from the menu that pops up.**

4. **Wait until OS/2 says that it's OK to turn off or reset the computer before you reach for the power switch.**

- ✔ If you don't follow these steps, OS/2 starts acting weird after a while, and you have to fix it with the Official CHKDSK Procedure, described in Chapter 23.

- ✔ If OS/2 *doesn't* shut down after you tell it to, tell it *again.* If it still doesn't shut down, wait until you don't hear any more hard disk noises. When all is quiet, turn off the computer and tiptoe away from it. (Sometimes OS/2 shuts down but forgets to tell you about it.)

Chapter 23

Ten Common Tweaks That Make OS/2 Work

Chapter 19 covered the stuff you need to know when something weird happens. But most of the stuff in Chapter 19 is *supposed* to be weird. Much of OS/2 is pretty strange, and you have to get used to it.

But when OS/2 acts funky and it's *not* supposed to, this chapter is the one you need. It lists the most common tweaks for yanking OS/2 out of the clouds and bringing it back to earth.

Running That CHKDSK Stuff

When OS/2 suddenly dies, whether it's because the dog pulled out the computer's power cord or because you pushed the Reset button, the hard drive sometimes gets confused.

OS/2 grabs lots of information from the hard drive, intending to put the information back when it's done. But if it's interrupted, it just tosses everything into the air. Then, when OS/2 starts up again and finds its information lying in bits on the ground, it starts acting weird. Objects may disappear from the desktop, duplicate themselves, or simply go on strike.

Luckily, the weird-sounding CHKDSK program can sift through all the data debris, dump the bad stuff, and put the good stuff back where it should be.

So if OS/2 starts acting freaky, CHKDSK is the first thing you should try. Grab the installation disks and begin at Step 1.

1. **Put the OS/2 Installation Diskette in drive A and press the computer's Reset button.**

2. **After a few minutes, OS/2 asks for Diskette 1; replace the Installation Diskette with Diskette 1 and press Enter.**

3. **After many more minutes, OS/2 finally puts its welcome message on the screen. Press F3.**

4. **The screen clears, and OS/2 leaves you at a funny-looking [A:\] thing. Remove Diskette 1 and insert Diskette 2.**

5. **Start the CHKDSK program by typing the following line, exactly as shown:**

```
A:\ CHKDSK C: /F
```

Or if you're using OS/2's High Performance File System (HPFS), type this line instead:

```
A:\ CHKDSK C: /F:3
```

6. **If the CHKDSK program finds some weirdness, it asks whether you want to recover *lost chains or clusters* or something. Press N because those things are just worthless remnants.**

CHKDSK finishes up and leaves you back at the [A:\] thing.

7. **Remove the disk and press the Reset button again to see whether you've fixed everything.**

✔ These steps can cure a large percentage of the problems you find in OS/2.

✔ If CHKDSK doesn't cure all the problems, try it again. Then a third time. If OS/2 *still* acts funny, try some of the other tweaks described in this chapter.

✔ If CHKDSK says that it found errors, it's not *that* big of a deal. The hard
drive is still OK.

✔ Although OS/2 puts a CHKDSK program on the hard drive, you can't use it.
Relying on it is similar to asking a loony psychiatrist to diagnose himself.
(If the hard drive is acting flaky, the CHKDSK on the hard drive may be
acting flaky, too.) Stick with the floppy disk version.

Make My Desktop Look the Way It Did When I Installed It!

Sometimes the desktop may be beyond repair. Folders suddenly stop opening,
for example, or files disappear without a trace, and the CHKDSK stuff described
in the preceding section may not seem to help.

Either way, OS/2 enables you to return to a working desktop by following these
steps:

1. **Close down OS/2 with the Shut down command; or, if the computer is
   frozen up, press Ctrl+Alt+Delete (or press the computer's Reset button as
   a last resort).**

2. **When a little white square appears in the upper-left corner of the
   screen, press Alt+F1.**

3. **When the RECOVERY CHOICES menu appears, as shown in Figure 23-1,
   press 1. If the menu doesn't list any numbered choices, press X.**

```
                          RECOVERY CHOICES

Select the system configuration file to be used, or enter the option
corresponding to the archive desired.

ESC - Continue the boot process using \CONFIG.SYS without changes
C   - Go to command line, (no files replaced, use original CONFIG.SYS)
V   - Reset primary video display to VGA and reboot
M   - Restart the system from the Maintenance Desktop (Selective Install)

Choosing an archive from the list below replaces your current CONFIG.SYS,
Desktop directory, and INI files with older versions. These older versions
might be different from your current files.  Your current files are saved in
\OS2\ARCHIVES\CURRENT.

1) Archive created 11-18-94 8:28:34PM
2) Archive created 11-17-94 7:12:21AM
3) Archive created 11-16-94 4:23:01AM
X) Original archive from INSTALL created 11-11-94  2:47:42AM
```

Figure 23-1:
The
RECOVERY
CHOICES
menu.

Pressing 1 tells OS/2 to re-create the last desktop that worked on your system — the desktop you used when you last started OS/2. It offers that option, however, only if you've told it to make backups of itself (a safety measure described in Chapter 16).

If OS/2 hasn't been keeping backup archives of its desktops, you're stuck with these choices:

Pressing Esc tells OS/2 to continue booting. This option usually doesn't work because it doesn't change anything. Don't bother with it.

Pressing C goes to the command line. It's for nerds who know what they're doing. Again, don't bother with this one, unless you're on the phone with an IBM tech-support geek who's walking you through a complicated fix.

Pressing V tells OS/2 to switch to regular VGA mode. It's a good option if you're having video problems with illegible screens or windows that don't look right.

Pressing M brings up the Selective Install. It's a good option if you're still trying to install OS/2; it lets you try different settings for multimedia gadgets and video cards.

Finally, pressing X brings back the desktop you had when you first installed OS/2. It's a good choice for people whose desktop is beyond repair.

✔ When OS/2 first installs itself, it stashes away a copy of its special setup files in case it needs to reuse them some day. Pressing X after using the Alt+F1 trick tells OS/2 that the time has come to grab those copies out of safekeeping and put 'em back to work.

✔ All but the first two options listed in the Alt+F1 trick restore your desktop, but they also wipe out any customization you may have done. You probably have to migrate your programs again, as described in Chapter 16.

✔ OS/2 renames the current versions of CONFIG.SYS, OS2.INI, and OS2SYS.INI with .001 extensions. Then it copies the earlier versions of those files into their places. Pretty boring, huh? It also saves the old desktop in a different directory.

After OS/2 Crashes, It Reloads the Same Program and Crashes Again!

In its fervent desire to be helpful, OS/2 always tries to re-create the desktop the same way you last left it. If the folders and documents were in an orderly fashion when you used the Shut <u>d</u>own command, OS/2 brings back that same orderly desktop the next time you start it up.

But sometimes a cranky program makes OS/2 crash or freeze up on the screen. When you press Ctrl+Alt+Delete to reboot the computer, the screen clears and OS/2 reloads itself. But nine times out of ten, OS/2 also *reloads the same program* that made it crash.

Talk about weird. You're caught in a dreadful, never-ending loop of reboot, crash, and reboot. You can tell OS/2 to wise up, however.

While the computer is rebooting, keep watching the screen until the cursor — the little clock thing — appears on the screen. Then keep holding down Ctrl+Shift+F1 simultaneously until OS/2's screen stops moving.

✔ Holding down Ctrl+Shift+F1 tells OS/2 to forget about restarting any programs that may have been running the last time it was alive. (Oh, you have to use the Ctrl and Shift keys on the *left* side of the keyboard. Picky, picky.)

✔ If you don't appreciate OS/2's efforts to restart any previously running programs, type the following line somewhere in OS/2's CONFIG.SYS file:

```
SET RESTARTOBJECTS=STARTUPFOLDERSONLY
```

That bit of *runtogetherstuff* tells OS/2 not to bother starting up any programs that aren't in the Startup folder.

Put Objects, Not Programs, on Your Desktop

When you see a folder on the desktop, your natural urge is to start filling it up with programs. Don't do it!

Folders are for program *objects,* not for the program's actual files.

You see, some DOS or Windows programs do not work under OS/2 until OS/2 knows how to treat them. You have to turn the program into an object so that OS/2 can look at the object's settings and say, "Ah, so this program likes its french fries *soggy!*"

Then, when OS/2 runs the DOS program, it lets the french fries sit for a while before it serves them. But if the program doesn't have an object, it doesn't get what it needs to run, and nobody is happy.

> ✔ Although *making an object* sounds dreadful, it isn't hard at all. In fact, OS/2 even makes an object for you if you *migrate* the program, as described in Chapter 16.

> ✔ For more DOS program details, head for Chapter 14.

Killing Objects That Simply Won't Die

Nobody knows why, but sometimes an object just won't die. You can drag it to the Shredder, but the Shredder refuses to touch it.

The Death to Obstinate Objects Committee recommends these techniques:

1. **Click the stubborn object with the right mouse button, click the arrow next to Open, and choose Settings. Click the General tab and look to see whether the Template box has a check mark in it. If so, click in the box to remove the check mark. Close the notebook and try dragging the object to the Shredder.**

2. **Drag a new folder from the Templates folder onto the desktop. Drag the invincible object into it and drag the folder to the Shredder.**

3. **Insert a blank disk in drive A and drag the overly sturdy object to the Drive A object. Then click the Drive A object with the right mouse button and choose Format disk from the menu. (Formatting the disk obliterates anything that is on the disk.)**

4. **Try heading for the OS/2 command line, heading for the object's directory, and deleting the object with the DEL command.**

With any luck, one of these tricks should purge the desktop of the unwanted object.

✔ You can also try the CHKDSK trick described at the beginning of this chapter. The problem may be related to something that CHKDSK can solve.

✔ Or if the CHKDSK trick fails also, try the Alt+F1 trick that's described after the CHKDSK trick.

Nothing Prints

We're getting into some weird territory here. The computer uses something called *interrupts* when it talks to the expensive stuff you attach to it.

It usually needs a different *interrupt* for each gizmo you fasten to it. So what? Well, the computer may not have as many *interrupts* as you have gizmos.

If you have a scanner, a sound card, or another such gizmo connected to the computer, the gizmo may interfere with OS/2's printing capability. Try turning off the computer and pulling out the gizmo's card. Then fire up OS/2 and see whether the printer works.

To get into this serious computer geek stuff, you're best off befriending a computer guru for some help. (Make sure that the guru doesn't drip any Hostess Fruit Pie filling into your computer's innards; gurus are usually careful to drip that stuff down the front of their shirts, anyway.)

OS/2 uses something called *Interrupt 7*, or *IRQ7*, to print stuff. Sound Blaster comes set up to use IRQ7 as well. If you connect Sound Blaster to the computer, you have an immediate problem right there. You have to set Sound Blaster's *jumpers* to use IRQ5, and then everything will be fine. (Unless you have two printers plugged into the computer, which brings up even more problems.)

Mistakes Everybody Makes with HPFS

OS/2's *High Performance File System (HPFS)* sounds way cool, and it is. It enables users of IBM-compatible computers to do what Macintosh users have done for years — use an identifiable name for a file. You can name a file something such as SUMMER SQUASH HARVEST rather than the traditional SMSQHVST.TXT.

But with the new technology comes new problems. HPFS has to remain compatible with the older way of storing files, too. As a result, when you're working with HPFS, you have to keep a few things in mind:

- OS/2 relishes HPFS filenames and directory names. But DOS programs can't read them. So if you keep your important stuff in an HPFS directory named ALL MY IMPORTANT STUFF, DOS programs don't know that the directory is there; even if a DOS program finds the directory, the directory is listed under a vastly shortened name. How can you get around this problem?

- Don't use HPFS if you're going to use mostly WIN-OS/2, Windows, or DOS programs.

- Don't use names longer than eight letters when you are creating folders.

My Screen Froze Up!

Under DOS or Windows, a *frozen* screen means that the computer has crashed and that you need to poke the computer's Reset button.

Not under OS/2, however. OS/2 keeps bubbling in the background. If a program (even a Windows or an OS/2 program) freezes, press Ctrl+Esc and wait.

Don't press any other keys and don't move the mouse. Just sit there, twiddle your thumbs, and wait. (You may find this a good time to spray Windex on a rag and wipe the thick layer of dust off the monitor.)

Sometimes you have to wait only 30 seconds; other times you have to wait a full minute. But OS/2 often breaks the silence with an error message or the Window List. If the Window List pops up, stop wiping off the monitor. Click the offending program's name on the Window List with the right mouse button and click Close from the menu.

Clicking Close may close down the malcontent program and make everything work OK again. Sometimes, though, you can leave OS/2 alone all night and return in the morning to find that it's still frozen. Just be as patient as you can before you poke that Reset button.

Chapter 24
More Than Ten Weird Abbreviations

*T*here are only 17,576 possible three-letter acronyms, as computer guru Paul Boutin observed in 1989. As a result, some four- and five-letter acronyms are starting to pop up. OS/2, an acronym itself (created by yet another acronym), is leading the way in using up all the available three-letter acronyms.

You'll probably run into all the acronyms in this chapter during your OS/2 experience.

ASCII

American Standard Code for Information Interchange. Basically, an ASCII ("ASK-ee") file contains plain old text — letters and numbers that humanoids can read. OS/2's System Editor reads and writes ASCII files.

ATM

Adobe Type Manager. ATM is a method of storing and using fonts — different styles of letters. IBM tosses ATM in with OS/2 Warp Version 3.0 so that users can install PostScript fonts in WIN-OS/2 sessions. The latest version of OS/2 can use the sexier Windows TrueType technology, but IBM still tosses ATM in with the package to give you the best of both font worlds.

DBCS

Double-byte character set. Some foreign languages use more characters and symbols than ASCII has room for. You need special DBCS software or hardware to type, display, or print these characters.

DLL

Dynamic Link Library. You can find plenty of DLL files on the hard drive. These files, ending in DLL, are basically nuggets of information that programs share among themselves. If a program can't find its DLL, it sends you an error message crying about it.

EMS

Expanded Memory Specification. EMS is one of several ways a computer can trick DOS into using extra memory. OS/2 can dish out EMS memory to DOS programs that ask for it. See *XMS*.

FAT

File Allocation Table. This one refers to the way DOS — and OS/2 — keeps track of files on disks. See *HPFS*.

HPFS

High Performance File System. HPFS is OS/2's fancy alternative to the aging FAT system in DOS. HPFS requires a computer with at least 6MB of memory, and it isn't as easy to set up on a Dual Boot system. See *FAT*.

IBM

The International Business Machines Corporation. IBM began creating OS/2 with Microsoft but took over by itself when Microsoft bailed to push its own Windows software.

IRQ

Interrupt Request. *Interrupts* are the attention-getting signals that run between the computer's hardware and its software. If two parts of a computer try to use the same interrupt, OS/2 freaks out. DOS is more tolerant about letting computer parts share the same interrupts.

LMB

Left mouse button. Some nerds say "LMB" rather than devote the energy required to say "left mouse button." See *RMB*.

OS/2 Warp

Operating System/2 Warp. It's the thing you're reading about.

PCX

PCX doesn't really stand for anything; a young programmer picked those letters to stand for his particular method of saving graphics in a file. Today most graphics programs can store files in PCX format. OS/2 can't read the PCX format, but Windows Paintbrush can read and write files in that format.

PIF

Program Information File/Picture Interchange Format file. In Windows, a PIF is a *Program Information File* — a file with instructions about how Windows should run a DOS program. OS/2's Picture Viewer program, however, says that PIF means *Picture Interchange Format* file. Be cautious when you're trying to decide which is which.

RAM

Random Access Memory. Computers store stuff on little memory chips, so the more RAM you have, the more your computer can do. Also, anything stored in RAM disappears when the computer is turned off or rebooted. See *ROM*.

REXX

Restructured Extended Executor. A programming language included with OS/2 for nerds to play with. It's like a turbocharged version of DOS's batch files.

RMB

Right mouse button. Some nerds refer to "RMB" rather than devote the energy required to say "right mouse button." See *LMB*.

ROM

Read Only Memory. Computers come with some instructions permanently stored in ROM. Unlike RAM chips, ROM chips don't lose their contents when the power dies. Also, a computer can't write information to a ROM chip.

TMP

Temporary file. OS/2 and Windows create temporary files to store notes in while they're working on something. If OS/2 and Windows get distracted, they often don't erase the temporary file when they're through. For example, OS/2's Icon Editor sometimes leaves files such as ICED10.TMP lying around. They can be safely deleted.

UAE

Unrecoverable Application Error. This is what Windows says when it crashes. (It also says "GPF" — General Protection Fault, but both terms mean the same thing: The ship is going down quickly.)

VDM

Virtual DOS machine. A confusing term to describe how OS/2 runs a DOS program: It tricks the program into thinking that it has the whole computer to itself.

VMB

Virtual Machine Boot. This means that OS/2 can boot up a *real* version of DOS by booting from a DOS system floppy.

WPS

Workplace Shell. All of OS/2's desktop stuff — the little folders, objects, and dangling menus — are considered the Workplace Shell.

XMS

Extended Memory Specification. XMS is one of several ways that programs can trick DOS into using extra memory.

Glossary

· ·

*O*S/2 comes with its own Glossary program. Just double-click the Glossary object in the Information folder and begin flipping through the electronic pages. But if IBM's official language gets a little obtuse, here's a less complicated version.

32-bit

Computers run their information through pipes; the more pipes a PC can use, the faster it can toss information around. The first IBM PC used eight pipes. The next version, the 286, used 16 pipes. A 386 computer can use 32 pipes, but most programs just shoot their stuff through 16 pipes. For extra speed and power, OS/2 uses all 32 pipes at the same time.

8514/A

One of the more expensive (and esoteric) video cards released by IBM and now copied by a few other companies. (It uses 1024×768 resolution with 256 colors, if you happen to have one.)

active window/object

The last window or object you've clicked — the one that's currently highlighted — is considered active. Any keys you type affect that window or object.

applet

OS/2 and Windows both come bundled with little programs called applets. Applets are real programs, but they generally aren't very powerful. A word-processing applet, for example, doesn't have a spell checker. OS/2's fax applet can fax only a single page.

AUTOEXEC.BAT

A file that an MS-DOS computer reads when it's first turned on. The file contains instructions that affect any DOS programs that run subsequently. OS/2 doesn't use an AUTOEXEC.BAT file, but it enables you to hand one to each DOS program that needs one.

BAT

A DOS program ending in *BAT* is a batch file. Batch files are usually collections of DOS commands created by nerds who want their computer to do a bunch of stuff unattended. See *REXX* in Chapter 24,.

bitmap

A graphic consisting of bunches of little dots on the screen. The dots are saved as *bitmap files,* which end with the letters *BMP.*

border

The edges of a window that can be moved in or out to change the window's size.

case-sensitive

A program that knows the difference between uppercase and lowercase letters. For example, a case-sensitive program considers *Pickle* and *pickle* to be two different things.

clipboard

A program that keeps track of information you've cut or copied from a program. It stores the information so that you can paste it into other programs.

command prompt

The little symbol that looks like C:\>, or [C:\], or A:\>, or something similar. It's a place where you can type verbal instructions *(commands)* for OS/2 or DOS to carry out.

CONFIG.SYS

A file that the computer reads every time you turn on or reset the computer. It contains information about how the computer has been set up and what it has been attached to. OS/2, DOS, and Windows programs all rely on information contained in the CONFIG.SYS file.

data file object

An object that stands for a file containing *information:* words, pictures, numbers, sounds, or other handy things. Like all objects, a data file object has a picture on it — an icon — for easy identification. If you delete a data file object by dragging it to the Shredder, you delete the file it represents.

default

Choosing the default option enables you to avoid having to make a decision. The *default option* is the one the computer chooses for you when you give up and just press Enter.

desktop

The thing on your screen where you move folders and objects around. Actually, the desktop is a big folder itself.

device object

An object on the desktop that represents something physical: a printer, for example, or a Shredder that can physically destroy files.

drag

A four-step mouse process that moves an object across the desktop. First, point at the object. Second, hold down the right mouse button. Third, point at where you want to move the object. Fourth, let go of the right mouse button. The object is *dragged* to its new location.

drop

Step four of the *drag* stuff, described in the preceding entry. It's merely letting go of the mouse button and letting the object fall onto something else, whether it's a folder, the Shredder, or a Zip-Lock baggy.

DRV

Short for *driver.* A file ending in *DRV* usually contains a *translator,* which enables OS/2 to talk to computer gizmos, such as video cards, sound cards, CD-ROM drives, and other stuff.

extended attributes

Extra information OS/2 stores about a file. DOS and Windows programs can't handle extended attributes. They don't even know that extended attributes exist. (Hip, young programmers also call extended attributes "EAs.")

folder object

A container for storing things on the desktop. It can be opened and closed, just like a real folder. A folder is an *object.*

formatting

The process of preparing a disk to have files written on it. The disk has to have little *electronic shelves* tacked on it so that DOS or OS/2 can store information on them. Formatting a disk wipes it clean of any past information.

highlighting

The different colors appearing over an object or file to show that it has been *selected*.

icon

The little picture that sits on an object, making it easier to figure out what that object's function is in life.

INI

Short for *initialization*, INI usually hangs on the end of files that contain special system settings. OS/2 stores most of its settings in two INI files, OS2.INI and OS2SYS.INI.

maximize

The act of making a window fill the entire screen. You can maximize a window by double-clicking its title bar — the long strip across its top. Or you can click its Maximize button — the button in the window's upper-right corner.

migrate

The process of creating an object for a program and placing that object in a folder for easy access. OS/2's Add Programs application handles this chore, scouting out newly installed DOS, Windows, or OS/2 programs and placing buttons for them on your desktop.

minimize

The act of shrinking a window to a tiny icon to temporarily get it out of the way. To minimize a window, click the Minimize button — the small square next to the large square in a window's upper-right corner.

Minimized Window Viewer

A folder in which OS/2 places icons for minimized windows.

multitasking

Running several different programs simultaneously.

multithreading

The best OS/2 programs are multithreaded, which means that they're composed of little *threads* of program chores. A program runs a few threads and then checks to see whether any other, more important, threads are waiting to run. If not, it runs some more of its threads.

notebook

A graphic that looks like a notebook. It's used for filling out information about an object — changing its settings, giving it a new icon, or making similar adjustments.

object

Something you play with on the desktop in order to do something useful. To delete a file, for example, you drag its object to the Shredder object. See *data file object, device object, folder object,* and *program object.*

operating system

Software that controls how a computer does its most basic stuff — stores files, talks to printers, and performs other gut-level operations.

partition

A smaller portion of a large hard drive that has been designated as its own *hard drive.* For example, a single hard drive can simply be drive C. Or you can divvy up the hard drive into two more partitions, effectively creating a drive C, a drive D, and a drive E. You don't have to worry about partitions unless you're *installing* OS/2 and want to use Boot Manager — one of the Advanced Installation options.

path

A sentence of *computerese* that tells the computer the precise name and location of a file.

Presentation Manager

A term for the overall concept behind OS/2's object stuff. The Workplace Shell is part of the Presentation Manager, which is abbreviated *PM.* In fact, you can find the initials *PM* tacked on to several OS/2 programs.

program object

An object representing a program on the hard drive (or on the floppy drive, for that matter). The object contains all the settings required to make the program work well under OS/2.

seamless window

Microsoft Windows programs normally run on top of the Windows program, with wallpaper and a copy of Windows Program Manager running in the background. OS/2 enables a Windows program to run "seamlessly" on its own desktop. A seamless window describes a Windows program that's running in its own window on OS/2's desktop — not within Windows itself.

settings

Tidbits of information that enable OS/2 to know how to treat a program or object. For example, a DOS program's settings tell OS/2 whether that program should take up the entire screen, how much memory it needs, and other pertinent information.

shadow

An object providing a *push-button link* to an object stored in some other folder. When you change the shadow, you also change the *real* object it's linked to, and vice versa.

shut down

The process of telling OS/2 that you're about to turn off or reset the computer. The computer then puts away all its toys in preparation for the big event.

template

An object you can use as a handy model to create additional objects. When you drag a program template onto your desktop, for example, it's similar to plucking a form letter off a stack. You then *fill out* that program template with information about the program that you want the object to represent.

virtual

A trendy word to describe real-life experiences simulated on a computer. It is commonly used to describe things that *look* real but that aren't really there. For example, OS/2 comes with a *virtual desktop.*

Window List

A pop-up box that lists all the programs that are running. To see it, press Ctrl+Esc or click both mouse buttons on the desktop simultaneously.

work area

A special folder that, when opened and closed, automatically opens or closes all the objects stored inside it.

Index

• E •

(continued)

• G •

• H •

(continued)

• S •

• T •

(continued)

• *X* •

Files I Should Never Delete

Filename	In English

Files I Should Never Delete

Filename	In English

Files I Should Never Delete

Filename	In English

Computer Guru	Phone #	Favorite Snack Bribe

Computer Guru	Phone #	Favorite Snack Bribe

Stupid Computer Mistakes I've Made
(And Should Never Make Again!)

Stupid Computer Mistakes I've Made
(And Should Never Make Again!)

Stupid Computer Mistakes I've Made
(And Should Never Make Again!)

Computer Toys I Would Like to Own Someday

Important Stuff I Learned in This Book

Important Stuff I Learned in This Book

Important Stuff I Learned in This Book

Important Stuff I Learned in This Book

Notes

Notes

Notes

Title	Author	ISBN	Price
			11/11/94
INTERNET / COMMUNICATIONS / NETWORKING			
CompuServe For Dummies™	by Wallace Wang	1-56884-181-7	$19.95 USA/$26.95 Canada
Modems For Dummies™, 2nd Edition	by Tina Rathbone	1-56884-223-6	$19.99 USA/$26.95 Canada
Modems For Dummies™	by Tina Rathbone	1-56884-001-2	$19.95 USA/$26.95 Canada
MORE Internet For Dummies™	by John R. Levine & Margaret Levine Young	1-56884-164-7	$19.95 USA/$26.95 Canada
NetWare For Dummies™	by Ed Tittel & Deni Connor	1-56884-003-9	$19.95 USA/$26.95 Canada
Networking For Dummies™	by Doug Lowe	1-56884-079-9	$19.95 USA/$26.95 Canada
ProComm Plus 2 For Windows For Dummies™	by Wallace Wang	1-56884-219-8	$19.99 USA/$26.99 Canada
The Internet For Dummies™, 2nd Edition	by John R. Levine & Carol Baroudi	1-56884-222-8	$19.99 USA/$26.99 Canada
The Internet For Macs For Dummies™	by Charles Seiter	1-56884-184-1	$19.95 USA/$26.95 Canada
MACINTOSH			
Macs For Dummies®	by David Pogue	1-56884-173-6	$19.95 USA/$26.95 Canada
Macintosh System 7.5 For Dummies™	by Bob LeVitus	1-56884-197-3	$19.95 USA/$26.95 Canada
MORE Macs For Dummies™	by David Pogue	1-56884-087-X	$19.95 USA/$26.95 Canada
PageMaker 5 For Macs For Dummies™	by Galen Gruman	1-56884-178-7	$19.95 USA/$26.95 Canada
QuarkXPress 3.3 For Dummies™	by Galen Gruman & Barbara Assadi	1-56884-217-1	$19.99 USA/$26.99 Canada
Upgrading and Fixing Macs For Dummies™	by Kearney Rietmann & Frank Higgins	1-56884-189-2	$19.95 USA/$26.95 Canada
MULTIMEDIA			
Multimedia & CD-ROMs For Dummies™, Interactive Multimedia Value Pack	by Andy Rathbone	1-56884-225-2	$29.95 USA/$39.95 Canada
Multimedia & CD-ROMs For Dummies™	by Andy Rathbone	1-56884-089-6	$19.95 USA/$26.95 Canada
OPERATING SYSTEMS / DOS			
MORE DOS For Dummies™	by Dan Gookin	1-56884-046-2	$19.95 USA/$26.95 Canada
S.O.S. For DOS™	by Katherine Murray	1-56884-043-8	$12.95 USA/$16.95 Canada
OS/2 For Dummies™	by Andy Rathbone	1-878058-76-2	$19.95 USA/$26.95 Canada
UNIX			
UNIX For Dummies™	by John R. Levine & Margaret Levine Young	1-878058-58-4	$19.95 USA/$26.95 Canada
WINDOWS			
S.O.S. For Windows™	by Katherine Murray	1-56884-045-4	$12.95 USA/$16.95 Canada
MORE Windows 3.1 For Dummies™, 3rd Edition	by Andy Rathbone	1-56884-240-6	$19.99 USA/$26.99 Canada
PCs / HARDWARE			
Illustrated Computer Dictionary For Dummies™	by Dan Gookin, Wally Wang, & Chris Van Buren	1-56884-004-7	$12.95 USA/$16.95 Canada
Upgrading and Fixing PCs For Dummies™	by Andy Rathbone	1-56884-002-0	$19.95 USA/$26.95 Canada
PRESENTATION / AUTOCAD			
AutoCAD For Dummies™	by Bud Smith	1-56884-191-4	$19.95 USA/$26.95 Canada
PowerPoint 4 For Windows For Dummies™	by Doug Lowe	1-56884-161-2	$16.95 USA/$22.95 Canada
PROGRAMMING			
Borland C++ For Dummies™	by Michael Hyman	1-56884-162-0	$19.95 USA/$26.95 Canada
"Borland's New Language Product" For Dummies™	by Neil Rubenking	1-56884-200-7	$19.95 USA/$26.95 Canada
C For Dummies™	by Dan Gookin	1-878058-78-9	$19.95 USA/$26.95 Canada
C++ For Dummies™	by Stephen R. Davis	1-56884-163-9	$19.95 USA/$26.95 Canada
Mac Programming For Dummies™	by Dan Parks Sydow	1-56884-173-6	$19.95 USA/$26.95 Canada
QBasic Programming For Dummies™	by Douglas Hergert	1-56884-093-4	$19.95 USA/$26.95 Canada
Visual Basic "X" For Dummies™, 2nd Edition	by Wallace Wang	1-56884-230-9	$19.99 USA/$26.99 Canada
Visual Basic 3 For Dummies™	by Wallace Wang	1-56884-076-4	$19.95 USA/$26.95 Canada
SPREADSHEET			
1-2-3 For Dummies™	by Greg Harvey	1-878058-60-6	$16.95 USA/$21.95 Canada
1-2-3 For Windows 5 For Dummies™, 2nd Edition	by John Walkenbach	1-56884-216-3	$16.95 USA/$21.95 Canada
1-2-3 For Windows For Dummies™	by John Walkenbach	1-56884-052-7	$16.95 USA/$21.95 Canada
Excel 5 For Macs For Dummies™	by Greg Harvey	1-56884-186-8	$19.95 USA/$26.95 Canada
Excel For Dummies™, 2nd Edition	by Greg Harvey	1-56884-050-0	$16.95 USA/$21.95 Canada
MORE Excel 5 For Windows For Dummies™	by Greg Harvey	1-56884-207-4	$19.95 USA/$26.95 Canada
Quattro Pro 6 For Windows For Dummies™	by John Walkenbach	1-56884-174-4	$19.95 USA/$26.95 Canada
Quattro Pro For DOS For Dummies™	by John Walkenbach	1-56884-023-3	$16.95 USA/$21.95 Canada
UTILITIES / VCRs & CAMCORDERS			
Norton Utilities 8 For Dummies™	by Beth Slick	1-56884-166-3	$19.95 USA/$26.95 Canada
VCRs & Camcorders For Dummies™	by Andy Rathbone & Gordon McComb	1-56884-229-5	$14.99 USA/$20.99 Canada
WORD PROCESSING			
Ami Pro For Dummies™	by Jim Meade	1-56884-049-7	$19.95 USA/$26.95 Canada
MORE Word For Windows 6 For Dummies™	by Doug Lowe	1-56884-165-5	$19.95 USA/$26.95 Canada
MORE WordPerfect 6 For Windows For Dummies™	by Margaret Levine Young & David C. Kay	1-56884-206-6	$19.95 USA/$26.95 Canada
MORE WordPerfect 6 For DOS For Dummies™	by Wallace Wang, edited by Dan Gookin	1-56884-047-0	$19.95 USA/$26.95 Canada
S.O.S. For WordPerfect™	by Katherine Murray	1-56884-053-5	$12.95 USA/$16.95 Canada
Word 6 For Macs For Dummies™	by Dan Gookin	1-56884-190-6	$19.95 USA/$26.95 Canada
Word For Windows 6 For Dummies™	by Dan Gookin	1-56884-075-6	$16.95 USA/$21.95 Canada
Word For Windows For Dummies™	by Dan Gookin	1-878058-86-X	$16.95 USA/$21.95 Canada
WordPerfect 6 For Dummies™	by Dan Gookin	1-878058-77-0	$16.95 USA/$21.95 Canada
WordPerfect For Dummies™	by Dan Gookin	1-878058-52-5	$16.95 USA/$21.95 Canada
WordPerfect For Windows For Dummies™	by Margaret Levine Young & David C. Kay	1-56884-032-2	$16.95 USA/$21.95 Canada

Fun, Fast, & Cheap!

11/11/94

CorelDRAW! 5 For Dummies™ Quick Reference
by Raymond E. Werner

ISBN: 1-56884-952-4
$9.99 USA/$12.99 Canada

Windows "X" For Dummies™ Quick Reference, 3rd Edition
by Greg Harvey

ISBN: 1-56884-964-8
$9.99 USA/$12.99 Canada

Word For Windows 6 For Dummies™ Quick Reference
by George Lynch

ISBN: 1-56884-095-0
$8.95 USA/$12.95 Canada

WordPerfect For DOS For Dummies™ Quick Reference
by Greg Harvey

ISBN: 1-56884-009-8
$8.95 USA/$11.95 Canada

Title	Author	ISBN	Price
DATABASE			
Access 2 For Dummies™ Quick Reference	by Stuart A. Stuple	1-56884-167-1	$8.95 USA/$11.95 Canada
dBASE 5 For DOS For Dummies™ Quick Reference	by Barry Sosinsky	1-56884-954-0	$9.99 USA/$12.99 Canada
dBASE 5 For Windows For Dummies™ Quick Reference	by Stuart J. Stuple	1-56884-953-2	$9.99 USA/$12.99 Canada
Paradox 5 For Windows For Dummies™ Quick Reference	by Scott Palmer	1-56884-960-5	$9.99 USA/$12.99 Canada
DESKTOP PUBLISHING / ILLUSTRATION/GRAPHICS			
Harvard Graphics 3 For Windows For Dummies™ Quick Reference	by Raymond E. Werner	1-56884-962-1	$9.99 USA/$12.99 Canada
FINANCE / PERSONAL FINANCE			
Quicken 4 For Windows For Dummies™ Quick Reference	by Stephen L. Nelson	1-56884-950-8	$9.95 USA/$12.95 Canada
GROUPWARE / INTEGRATED			
Microsoft Office 4 For Windows For Dummies™ Quick Reference	by Doug Lowe	1-56884-958-3	$9.99 USA/$12.99 Canada
Microsoft Works For Windows 3 For Dummies™ Quick Reference	by Michael Partington	1-56884-959-1	$9.99 USA/$12.99 Canada
INTERNET / COMMUNICATIONS / NETWORKING			
The Internet For Dummies™ Quick Reference	by John R. Levine	1-56884-168-X	$8.95 USA/$11.95 Canada
MACINTOSH			
Macintosh System 7.5 For Dummies™ Quick Reference	by Stuart J. Stuple	1-56884-956-7	$9.99 USA/$12.99 Canada
OPERATING SYSTEMS / DOS			
DOS For Dummies® Quick Reference	by Greg Harvey	1-56884-007-1	$8.95 USA/$11.95 Canada
UNIX			
UNIX For Dummies™ Quick Reference	by Margaret Levine Young & John R. Levine	1-56884-094-2	$8.95 USA/$11.95 Canada
WINDOWS			
Windows 3.1 For Dummies™ Quick Reference, 2nd Edition	by Greg Harvey	1-56884-951-6	$8.95 USA/$11.95 Canada
PRESENTATION / AUTOCAD			
AutoCAD For Dummies™ Quick Reference	by Bud Smith	1-56884-198-1	$9.95 USA/$12.95 Canada
SPREADSHEET			
1-2-3 For Dummies™ Quick Reference	by John Walkenbach	1-56884-027-6	$8.95 USA/$11.95 Canada
1-2-3 For Windows 5 For Dummies™ Quick Reference	by John Walkenbach	1-56884-957-5	$9.95 USA/$12.95 Canada
Excel For Windows For Dummies™ Quick Reference, 2nd Edition	by John Walkenbach	1-56884-096-9	$8.95 USA/$11.95 Canada
Quattro Pro 6 For Windows For Dummies™ Quick Reference	by Stuart A. Stuple	1-56884-172-8	$9.95 USA/$12.95 Canada
WORD PROCESSING			
Word For Windows 6 For Dummies™ Quick Reference	by George Lynch	1-56884-095-0	$8.95 USA/$11.95 Canada
WordPerfect For Windows For Dummies™ Quick Reference	by Greg Harvey	1-56884-039-X	$8.95 USA/$11.95 Canada

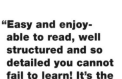

"Macworld Complete Mac Handbook Plus CD covered everything I could think of and more!"

Peter Tsakiris, New York, NY

"Thanks for the best computer book I've ever read — Photoshop 2.5 Bible. Best $30 I ever spent. I love the detailed index...Yours blows them all out of the water. This is a great book. We must enlighten the masses!"

Kevin Lisankie, Chicago, Illinois

"Macworld Guide to ClarisWorks 2 is the easiest computer book to read that I have ever found!"

Steven Hanson, Lutz, FL

Macworld QuarkXPress 3.2/3.3 Bible

by Barbara Assadi & Galen Gruman

ISBN: 1-878058-85-1
$39.95 USA/$52.95 Canada

Includes disk with QuarkXPress XTensions and scripts.

Macworld PageMaker 5 Bible

by Craig Danuloff

ISBN: 1-878058-84-3
$39.95 USA/$52.95 Canada

Includes 2 disks with Pagemaker utilities, clip art, and more.

Macworld FileMaker Pro 2.0/2.1 Bible

by Steven A. Schwartz

ISBN: 1-56884-201-5
$34.95 USA/$46.95 Canada

Includes disk with ready-to-run databases.

Macworld Word 6 Companion, 2nd Edition

by Jim Heid

ISBN: 1-56884-082-9
$24.95 USA/$34.95 Canada

Macworld Guide To Microsoft Word 5/5.1

by Jim Heid

ISBN: 1-878058-39-8
$22.95 USA/$29.95 Canada

Macworld ClarisWorks 2.0/2.1 Companion, 2nd Edition

by Steven A. Schwartz

ISBN: 1-56884-180-9
$24.95 USA/$34.95 Canada

Macworld Guide To Microsoft Works 3

by Barrie Sosinsky

ISBN: 1-878058-42-8
$22.95 USA/$29.95 Canada

Macworld Excel 5 Companion, 2nd Edition

by Chris Van Buren & David Maguiness

ISBN: 1-56884-081-0
$24.95 USA/$34.95 Canada

Macworld Guide To Microsoft Excel 4

by David Maguiness

ISBN: 1-878058-40-1
$22.95 USA/$29.95 Canada

FOR MORE INFORMATION OR TO ORDER, PLEASE CALL ▶ **800 762 2974**

For volume discounts & special orders please call
Tony Real, Special Sales, at 415. 312. 0650

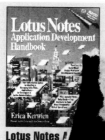

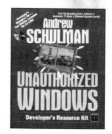

Order Center: **(800) 762-2974** *(8 a.m.–6 p.m., EST, weekdays)*

11/11/94

Quantity	ISBN	Title	Price	Total

Shipping & Handling Charges

	Description	First book	Each additional book
Domestic	Normal		$1.50
	Two Day Air		$2
	Overnight		$3
International	Surface		
	Airmail		
	DHL Air		

*For large quantities call for shipping & handling charges.
**Prices are subject to change without notice.

Ship to:

Name _____

Company _____

Address _____

City/State/Zip _____

Daytime Phone _____

Payment: ☐ Check to IDG Books (US Funds Only)

☐ VISA ☐ MasterCard ☐ American Express

Card # _____ Expires _____

Signature _____

Subtotal _____

CA residents add
applicable sales tax _____

IN, MA, and MD
residents add
5% sales tax _____

IL residents add
6.25% sales tax _____

RI residents add
7% sales tax _____

TX residents add
8.25% sales tax _____

Shipping _____

Total _____

Please send this order form to:

IDG Books Worldwide
7260 Shadeland Station, Suite 100
Indianapolis, IN 46256

Allow up to 3 weeks for delivery.
Thank you!